PROPAGANDA PRISONS

BREAKING THE BARS

TOM RIZZI

COVER PAGE GRAPHICS BY
ANDREW DUNN

ISBN 978-1-63814-348-2 (Paperback)
ISBN 978-1-63814-349-9 (Digital)

Covenant Books, Inc.
11661 Hwy 707
Murrells Inlet, SC 29576
www.covenantbooks.com

To Walter Cronkite (1916–2009), the most trusted
man in America—authentic, factual, accurate. Thank
you for having been my greatest inspiration.

Woe unto them that call evil good, and good evil;
that put darkness for light, and light for darkness;
that put bitter for sweet, and sweet for bitter!

—Isaiah 5:20

Contents

Introduction

This book discusses the existence and spread of propaganda through technology, as well as its role in most other aspects of daily life.

The material limits itself to the discussion of four major topics: uncovering propaganda; enhancing ability to identify propaganda; its use in technology, media, and other sectors of life; and the use of fact checking, empathy, and perspective taking as a defense against propaganda messaging.

Other than the label, fake news is nothing new. It has been a constant companion of information for centuries. What is relatively new is its latest means of communication—the Internet and media platforms. Quite often, they are abused to spread lies and misinformation.

Our country is under immense pressure with respect to democracy and social change. The overall situation that has emerged is deeply concerning. The exploitation of information coupled with personal vulnerabilities is manipulated in such a way so as to limit thought processes, different perspectives, and deductive conclusions. The influence threats being used have to be examined and understood and must be answered with counterstrategies that can minimalize the efforts of the propagandist. Unless we act now, we will continue to place ourselves in danger of transforming our nation through a deception of acceptance.

There is a stark reduction in public trust, an increased lack of respect for authority, an uptick in anti-American rhetoric and anti-democratic philosophy. Young adults display lower levels of attachment to our country's history, traditions, and religious affiliations. It is my belief that both cultural and religious factors have a prominent impact on our ability to live in harmony. These interactive basics of unity are sometimes being denied altogether. If left unchecked, the political and cultural turmoil we are currently experiencing will destroy the aspirations we hold for a better future. It is my hope that this book helps the reader to better understand the uncertainty we face, and the effect of propaganda on our lives, beliefs, norms, and values.

A Narrowly Focused View

This book is not only about propaganda but also shares certain aspects as well. It was written with a biased belief that we have to change the way we accept information. There is a point being made in the book, as well as an argument to support that point. This is not an interpretive piece. It leads you down a specific path with a definitive conclusion. It has as its mission to clarify. The reader, upon finishing this book, should have a clear perspective on how the presentation of information, not only the information itself, affects our thinking.

In simple terms, the idea behind all propaganda is to make you believe something based on bias or deceit. Quite a bit of everyday life becomes involved with its use. It always has a goal or purpose. To understand the outcome is secondary to understanding the mechanisms used. The purpose can either result in a positive or negative outcome. But the main focus should remain on the methods utilized. Whether it is used for the common good or as a tool to promote a false construct is not the main topic. What should be emphasized is that all propaganda, both negative and positive, has both an origin and reason behind it and that requires our utmost attention. In today's media, we are overwhelmed with information, especially of a biased or misleading nature, that is used to promote a particular political cause or point of view. The propaganda promoter uses ideas, catchphrases, or words with the intention of achieving a specific goal. For example, in the realm of advertising, we have propaganda that is used to promote products or ideas that are generally acceptable and noncontroversial. We all become subject to the promotion of the latest technology or must-have fashion. The reason propaganda has fostered a more negative than positive connotation is that it is deceitful and boils down to a subversive effort to promote. It never uses a wide-angle lens. The real purpose, quite simply, is to imprison the mind using a narrow frame of information.

The propaganda process, as stated, does not always promote a negative influence. It can be used by governments, medical, business establishments, and other groups to promote a positive message and lifestyle. It plays a very big role in many of the decisions made by those individuals that comprise its audience. Propaganda can have an influence on the choices we make and the attitudes we form with respect to contentious issues and problems both cultural and political. It has helped transform our society in a way that makes it harder for people to reach an unbiased conclusion. It exerts influence and control over what people believe, how people analyze, what they buy, and how they live their lives. It becomes a prison without visible bars.

People rely on information to determine what they want to purchase. Commercials about cars, phones, or medications stress the positive aspects of the product. If the advertiser has to embellish or, for that matter, convince the public into making a purchase, they do so. What is not stressed in many commercials is the possible negative or unsatisfactory outcome of a purchase or product. We are treated to generic labeling that covers that possibility: "Individual results may vary" is a great one, as well as "may be harmful to your health" or "may cause serious injury." But these "may" labels fail to convey sufficient detail. As with all information, it is up to the consumer to do the research, homework, and investigate reviews.

As one example, bicycles offer enjoyment, exercise, or transportation. But you may never hear a bicycle- or bike-sharing business inform you about the increased risk of possible facial and head injuries. In 2018, 857 bicyclists were killed in traffic accidents, and there were over forty-nine thousand injuries. Bikes do not come with a warning label, like "can be a leading cause of preventable accidents." The argument can be made that practically anything you do can be dangerous. How many people are killed or injured simply crossing the street? But there is a difference in levels of control and occurrence. The suggestion for bicyclists to wear a helmet helps narrow the focus, ease concerns, mitigates anxiety, as well as being a method of controlling risk. In addition, bicycle infrastructure, in many cases, leaves a lot to be desired, as well as drivers who are not cautious or disobey traffic laws; and both are usually not mentioned. I am not saying avoid biking. I am saying be aware of all factors involved. Analysis and investigation are the only venues to ascertain all the components involved in this sport as well as others.

This same method of constricting focus is used to influence opinions and ideas as well. The propaganda of omission can impact both our objectivity and response. Social media is undeniably a major source of disinformation, which has become a steady part of our media diet. The First Amendment and Freedom of Speech limit most controlling factors. Even scientific truth can be used as a tool for propaganda when it becomes extrapolated from real fact and presented as a causal factor for a media belief. As with consumerism and sports, the information supplied through media and print requires both research and analysis.

Empathy and Perspective Taking

Emotional insight is truly needed to grasp both subtle and complicated feelings. It is through emotional perception or empathy that you experience the feelings of another human being. A very special mode of understanding is involved. Particularly for therapy, the capacity for empathy is an essential prerequisite. This point is well-known in psychoanalysis, and more emphasis should be placed on this subject. It is also an important tool in unmasking the propaganda and disinformation found in social media. There is another important yet distinct social competency—perspective taking (the cognitive capacity to consider the world from another individual's viewpoint).

Living a life without either empathy or compassion is living a life without a soul. The ability to identify with what someone else is feeling and thinking exists in all of us but in varying degrees and levels. Some people find it very difficult to understand the emotions of others. The expression of kindness or sympathy seems to be less pronounced in our society. The power of a touch, a smile, a kind word, a listening ear, an honest compliment, or the smallest act of caring is being largely replaced by communication through technology which is limiting personal interaction. Although empathy is crucial for social interaction, it can sometimes be unpleasant. If that neuro circuit is hit too frequently through the excessive sharing of others' negative experiences, it can result in emotional exhaustion. While we are generally pretty cognizant of our own feelings and emotions, placing yourself in someone else's position can be difficult indeed. The reason for this appears that we all have in common a neurological lever that is activated upon experiencing the distress of another. Research shows this same circuit is self-activated when we see others suffer pain or emotional distress. So, through empathy, seeing the suffering of others causes us to suffer as well. We literally "feel" for the person in distress. This may be a reason some friends and relatives seem to abandon us when we most need emotional support. A display of emotional distress can become an invitation to close yourself off to the other person. It can result in a lack of empathy and compassion in communication.

Behavioral and cognitive studies and experiments indicate that individuals come to understand the emotional and affective states expressed by others with the help of the neural brain functions that produce similar emotional feelings in themselves. Such a mechanism gives rise to shared feelings, which constitutes one important aspect of empathy, although not the only one. Other components, including people's ability to monitor and regulate their emotional thought processes to prevent misunderstandings and perceptions in dialogue, are equal and necessary parts of a functional model of empathy.

In 2012, scientists at the Chinese Academy of Sciences found that the brain chemicals of people who habitually used the Internet (to the point of being an addiction) had abnormal connections between the nerve fibers in their brain. These changes are similar to other sorts of addicts, including alcoholics. This can impact communication, relationships, and our day-to-day interactions with others. Is this constantly connected world permanently affecting the way we interact with other humans?

The connected world's larger behavioral impact is dependent on how we interact with each other on a daily basis. Studies show the effects that phones have when people talk face-to-face. As an example, in one study, one hundred friendly couples were placed in a situation having a ten-minute conversation while their phone was present. Researchers noticed that the individuals still continued to fiddle with their phones. When those same couples conversed without a phone present, their conversations resulted in greater empathy.

Even when they are not in active use or buzzing, beeping, ringing, or flashing, digital devices are representative of people's wider social network and a portal to an immense compendium of information. With cell phones present, people have the constant urge to seek out information, check for communication, and direct their thoughts to other people and worlds. Their mere presence in a socio-physical milieu has the potential to divide consciousness between the proximate and immediate setting and the physically distant and invisible context.

We are awash in technology. It's estimated that 93 percent of Americans now use cell phones or wireless devices. And one-third of those people are using so-called smartphones, which means the users can browse the Web and check e-mail on their phones. Most of us spend our days walking around with our noses buried in our cell phones, and we tune out the people who are actually in the same room as us. We seem to have long ago crossed the line as to where doing this stuff has become appropriate and accepted; people take calls while they're out to dinner, text or check their e-mail while on a date, you name it—all at the cost of empathy.

Prejudice plays an important role in interpersonal sensitivity. In scientific studies, prejudice predicts a reduced mental assimilation of others feelings. We understand the thoughts and feelings of others by using our own mind as a model, and it is an essential aspect of empathy. Research bears this out. Important predictors of empathy are both nonreligious spiritual cognitions and religious spiritual experiences. Both cognitions magnify introspection as part of the process and, therefore, enforce thought based on emotional and spiritual self-awareness.

Empathy is an essential tool in many aspects of social life. Its close relative, compassion, is a feeling of concern for the problems of others. Compassion seldom involves the emotional distress that empathy can foster but rather can elicit a response to help another and at the same time develop a sense of peace and inner satisfaction from easing the suffering of others. However, keep in mind that the two related yet distinct social competencies—perspective taking (the cognitive capacity to consider the world from another individual's viewpoint) and empathy (the ability to connect emotionally with another individual) are important antecedents to develop emotional understanding. Empathy does not prove nearly as advantageous and at times is detrimental to discovering a possible solution to a disagreement. However, it is my contention that it is a strong precursor for the development of high-level perspective-taking skills. If you think that your emotional finesse could use a little work, maybe it's time to put your phone away and really listen to the people around you.

When you are empathetic, you emotionally understand what another person is experiencing. Essentially, you are putting yourself in someone else's position and feeling what they must be feeling.

You are able to see yourself in the other person's place and feel an emotional connection for what they are going through. The empathy I am referring to is not saying you are praying for the president and later tearing up his State of the Union address.

The ability to feel empathy allows you to experience and understand another's emotional frame of mind. Appropriate responses flow from those who truly understand and care about how others are feeling and thinking. It helps us with the regulation of our own emotions and promotes helpful behavior toward others. We all have the ability to improve our empathy, but that requires us to acknowledge our biases and move beyond our own emotional vulnerabilities.

To understand the implications caused by the lack of empathy and the inability to view a situation from another's perspective, we must examine the genesis in the shift away from the capacity for both emotional constructs. We are at a point where we find it very hard to accept the feelings, thoughts, and ideas of someone whose world perceptions may not fit into the construct trench we have formulated in our minds. It is my opinion that 9/11 not only changed the world we live in—it has also changed humanity.

With 9/11, many people have slowly been developing what I call a moral distancing. Moral distancing is further being enhanced with the evolution of technology which reinforces a climate of impersonal, rather than interpersonal, communication. It is a symptom of the illness our nation is now experiencing. In Proverbs, there is the following verse: "All the ways of a man are right in his own eyes." This very phrase is the antithesis of empathy. And it is what humanity is currently experiencing. The ideas of universal "moral order and moral right" are no longer in the forefront of human reasoning. It's our individual construct of order and right that motivates actions and thoughts. As a nation, we are moving away from a universal definition to an individual definition that feeds into the narrative that defines the way we perceive our world.

When George Washington was inaugurated president at Federal Hall, some of his first words summarized the thought process at that time. "The propitious smiles of heaven can never be expected on a nation that disregards the eternal rules of order and right which heaven itself hath ordained." We now have a society where both order and right are being ordained by the media. This is leading our nation to an erosion of not only values but an erosion of hope and ultimately an erosion of faith. It is not my intent to say that everyone needs to put God back into their lives, but it is my intent to say that we have to recognize the power of the moral construct that guided our founding fathers, a moral construct based on God and which is consistently being chipped away. So one might ask, "Can we turn this thing around?" And my answer is that we have the ability to do so. Although the moral distance that separates us from God is infinite, the moral distance that separates us from order and right is finite, is measurable, and has the capacity to be changed by us. At the end of this book, some suggestions will be presented that perhaps can, indeed, help return us to a higher realm of order and right, of empathy and acceptance of those with conflicting mind-sets from our own, as well as methods of truly analyzing the information we receive.

People of all ages are trying to learn and understand by tuning into social media. It is a fast-growing platform in our society whose main agenda is to tell everyone the right way to behave and more importantly how to think. New things go viral every day, and the trending lists on the various social media platforms perpetuate them. Some of the stories are promoting positive change, while others are attacking either people on a personal level or companies and countries on a national level. The big question is how our ability to empathize is affected by social media. While I believe that media can do amazing things in fighting a common cause or connecting us with people around the world, it can also be a major cause of the death of both empathy and perspective taking.

It is easily understandable, given the current direction of social media, why people are so unable or unwilling to empathize with others on the Internet. Media is a dominant cause of empathy fatigue, which is what occurs when people are constantly bombarded with conflicting stories and eventually get emotionally worn out. We also experience varying levels of compassion fatigue with wars overseas, tragedies at home, and other awful things that occur in the world around us. We see the same thing over and over and eventually lose the ability to empathize. Over time, we become numb to the tragedy around us. Our emotional feelings dissipate quickly. We have to distance ourselves from the tragedies for self-preservation, to not allow the stories to compromise our own emotional well-being.

Another cause of the lack of empathy created by social media is information bias. This occurs when individuals only expose themselves to information that reinforces their own thoughts repeated in the media echo chambers of either increasingly radical or exclusionary thought. In other words, we are able to understand and empathize with the information that we agree with, but when it comes to disagreeable facts, we find ourselves unable to empathize or understand the perspective from which they form, and we become easily capable of demonizing them.

As a personal example, I have a friend whom I interact with weekly on a personal basis. When we are together, both of us try to avoid any discussion of politics. The few times we interacted on that subject, the conversation was uncomfortable for both of us. His mind-set on politics was the antithesis of how I felt about the subject. More importantly, no matter how often I told him I understood his point of view, he could not accept any of the opposing points of view I held and often ridiculed my mind-set. Basically, we were both pointing out facts that supported our views, but to him, his facts were the only ones that mattered. We experienced a situation that oftentimes resulted in a demonization process—two fairly intelligent people resorting to this kind of behavior. The situation was somewhat improved by our mutual acknowledgment that we can maintain our friendship by agreeing that we both share a right to disagree which I never questioned in the first place. However, this "truce" has led to the almost total avoidance of the subject altogether—what I term a lose-lose situation. We will go on being friends, but neither of us will be able to ever share perspective or understanding when it involves certain subjects. Neither one of us will be able to share our thought processes when it comes to those topics. Now multiply this situation by millions and millions of others experiencing the same dilemma. With certain topics, we have agreed to maintain a state of cognitive paralysis.

In the media, there are three levels of news. Starting with the lowest level, we have what has been termed "fake" news. When you move to a level above, you reach an area of "official" news. The next level, which is the rarest, is "the real" news or news that is unadulterately factual, unencumbered by human emotion or motivated truths. As an example, in the area of UFO phenomena, we deal on levels of fake news or official news but almost never reach the third level.

Media personalities, as well as politicians and students, should be required to take a course in empathy and perspective taking. Those in positions of power and privilege are most times the least empathetic and unable to accept an alternate perspective. To view a concern or problem from someone else's perspective is, indeed, becoming a rare attribute. There appears to be what I call a "discerning" empathy in place. It is easier to empathize with people who are similar to you and harder to empathize with those who are different from you. It is no longer our problem to fully understand a situation that requires our cooperation. What comes to mind, as an example, is the callous behavior of students on spring break during the beginning of the COVID-19 virus epidemic. They pretty much ignored health requests to isolate themselves, thus forcing spring break states to close their beaches. Empathy and perspective taking are not natural inclinations on the part of humans. The new rule for empathy seems to be that it should be reserved just for those who are most like us.

Empathy through Questioning

Empathy is a broad concept that refers to both the cognitive and emotional reactions of an individual to the feelings, thoughts, and experiences of another. Having empathy increases the likelihood of helping others by showing compassion and understanding. It always helps when we can put ourselves in someone else's mind-set in looking at an observable situation. That does not necessarily mean that you have to agree with the other person; but empathy helps us understand the perspectives, needs, and intentions of others. It plays a crucial role in human, social, and psychological interaction during all stages of life. It helps us to communicate our ideas in a way that makes sense to others and helps us understand others when they communicate with us. Many people believe turning off one's feelings and creating an emotional distance will help them remain objective and equip them to "change" the thought process of another individual. In doing so, those you communicate with become distrustful, disgruntled, and less cooperative. And it makes for lonelier, less effective, and more burned-out relationships moving forward.

Empathy and the lack of empathy were crucial ingredients in the 2016 election results. The outcome was shocking to most people in our country on both sides of the aisle. We have also seen this play out on the world stage in England. A lack of empathy in the Brexit election recently produced a similar outcome. Pollsters and political party leaders didn't understand voters. Politicians spent more time criticizing than listening to each other. Citizens have taken sides and set up simplified caricatures of others without fully seeking to understand them. There is a drastic need for more empathy in the political realm, but we also need more empathy in all aspects of life.

Empathy and perspective taking are the most underused and underdeveloped skills for communicating, building trust, influencing, and resolving conflicts. It is a fundamental and powerful tool in the understanding of a problem. If success in life and work is about building effective relationships, then success in relationships is about building empathy.

Put yourself in another person's shoes. Identify and understand the thoughts, feelings, and experiences of someone else. It doesn't mean you completely understand, and it doesn't mean you agree. But in showing empathy, your intention is to understand and seek to help another person feel understood. In media, this happens all too infrequently.

To foster empathy and perspective taking in politics, it is important to address how we communicate our feeling to others. Sometimes, the best way to engage in conversation is through questioning and listening.

The ability to listen to someone else and asking questions to clarify are important communication skills. Many times, the best way to develop collaborative constructive conversations is to offer a little less analysis and ask a few more questions.

Asking effective questions is a key skill to fully understand a problem. At the same time, make your opinion known through the process but not your viewpoint. A viewpoint is the broader particular way you perceive the world. An opinion is the narrower concept encompassing your view about a particular subject. Keep the emphasis on the issue. This means taking the focus away from your viewpoint and place it on the problem or disagreement. Offer your opinion but not your ideology.

To fully understand a concern requires that you move out of your defensive zone and really pay attention to what the other person is saying. If you ask a question, be ready to listen to an answer. Conversation involves both an informational and emotional transaction of viewpoints and opinions. Questioning solicits clarification and support for the feedback you are listening to. To understand and appreciate what someone else is saying does not mean you agree with them. It only means you recognize their opinion or point of view.

The right questions will foster a better dialogue and perhaps lead to productive communication. The questioning should not be aimed at "rocking the vote" or changing someone else's mind. That will very rarely, if ever, spontaneously occur. You do not want to remain that person who becomes critical of someone else's perspective but rather try to view a concern from the other person's opinions.

When you shift from confrontation and assertions to asking questions, you might at first feel a little anxious. But if you think about it, asking questions can be a great way to practice thoughtful communication. It is a way to move the conversation from a contest of who is right and who is wrong to establishing a clearer understanding of both a problem's complexity and the experiences of the other person involved. Asking questions is a form of thoughtful communication—being able to listen to answers rather than interjecting and expressing your own thoughts.

Perhaps the most positive aspect of all is that when you know what questions to ask and how to ask them, you can run through such a conversation in a shorter amount of time and with greater results and understanding. With a clear objective, misunderstandings and misconceptions in dialogue are minimized. Not only is it important to structure your questions positively, but also as important is to ask the type of question that will elicit a more effective dialogue.

In order to shape the conversation, keep in mind key questions and the ways in which to ask them. The trick to asking questions well is dependent on knowing where your questioning will lead and less with knowing your audience This strategy is similar to that of chess. Always keep several moves and a game plan in mind.

A good opening question will begin the conversation quickly and effectively. The question should elicit a response that can be built upon. The response you are looking for should be issue oriented rather than ideology oriented. The first answer someone gives may not completely express their opinion. Continue with a line of questioning that will give the other person a chance to generate more ideas and possibilities to enhance clarity.

Asking questions may help in prioritizing the concerns of the other person or group. None of the above is met with either a combative response or a constructive response. The point is to identify a real conversation while being empathetic to the concerns of the other person through neutral positioning. The idea is for both parties to walk away feeling that the conversation was constructive. Just the approach of asking questions shows your curiosity, care, and empathy for the person you communicate with. You leave the conversation without feeling you were in a boxing ring. It also forces a constructive discussion of the issues and may help in clarifying possible solutions as the conversation continues.

Now here is a question for all the readers: Do you experience this kind of questioning approach when watching the media outlets? Their process is to lead you down a specific path rather than a true concern about the feelings of their audience. What you think is secondary. What they think is of utmost importance. Is what they think an example of journalism or opinion? Many outlets are downright honest about their coverage being opinion, but that fact is often lost as their programming continues. It is an attempt to make their point of view your point of view. Simply put, media coverage borders on brainwashing and appears to be having a negative effect on our country. Is this empathetic dialogue or a form of propaganda plain and simple? And the question is, Why is this "we are right and you are wrong" dialogue allowed to continue? One reason is ratings. Another reason is money. And, to be sure, there are other reasons that will be discussed in later chapters. Empathy in the media is almost nonexistent. The outcome that media desires is for you to walk away with what is their truth. And, yes, that is my opinion.

It is true that the foundations of empathy and perspective taking are implanted through social and personal experiences. But the media is very lacking when it comes to creating opportunities for empathetic experiences. There is a need to understand and feel what we have in common with others rather than blatantly exploit differences. Empathy and perspective taking are qualities that can truly change the world.

There is a profound need to strengthen the ties that bind us together rather than a rationale that can only lead to division. Both empathy and perspective taking have the capacity to foster positive social interaction. It can go a long way in reducing misinterpreted rhetoric and increasing and maintaining understanding and cooperation. I believe there is one thing that most of us can agree on, which is that expressions of our political and social differences have become markedly less cordial and is being fueled by media platforms which make it harder and harder to find common ground and solve common problems.

Some people believe that there is no place for empathy in politics, that it would only add difficulty to the process of decision making. My feeling is that better understanding and empathy may help to find better solutions to a conflict. To try to understand your opponent may lead to resolution insight. But I can also imagine certain situations where empathy and perspective taking would not serve as a benefit. There are times where rigidness and an uncompromising stance would be the right course of action and flexibility of feeling would be inappropriate, unconstructive, and a sign of weakness. There are situations that require control, leverage, and authority in order to bring about a positive outcome; but leadership that demonstrates these qualities along with empathy may be needed now more than ever.

Ideology, Deception, and Moral Persuasion

We cannot discuss the ongoing pollutive quality of communication without addressing purposeful deception. If propaganda had a soul, it would be control. For the purpose of propaganda is to influence. When a situation is discussed in the media, most often we are treated to a number of sound bites rather than the whole picture. Likewise, whenever a new drug is discussed in a media commercial, much more time and energy are utilized to explain the efficacy of the drug than the side effects which are basically glossed over. In my view, both examples present a deception with the "soul" purpose of manipulating and controlling the viewer's mind.

How often do we hear the sensationalism of a news story, only to see it altered moving forward—all in the name of opinion rather than unbiased, factual, unopinionated news presentation? It is not my purpose here to fill these pages with example upon example to intensify a point but rather to stress that propaganda, either covert or overt, is a functional aspect of most media coverage of current events. Yes, there are exceptions to the rule, but they are just that—exceptions. There is a relationship between specific media sources and personal moral philosophy and judgments that reinforce the effectiveness of materials designed by media groups to sway public opinion about the subject at hand. When watching media, I sometimes feel I am in a court of law. All evidence furnished is thoroughly explained for us prior to being presented. God forbid, you should come to your own conclusion of the facts. We are now at the point where the job of media is to look for sound bites that reinforce their agenda and point of view. If this occurred in *Star Trek*, Dr. Spock would be unable to exist in this environment. He would be on the first starship heading out of town.

With propaganda, we are dealing with a method whose "soul" purpose is either the manipulation or reinforcement of attitudes. Attitude and interpretation in media are not only manifested verbally. Sometimes, facial and body gestures are more powerful than the spoken word. The tone of a voice, the snicker, the raised eyebrow, the clenched fist, and other gestures speak volumes when it comes to meaning. We basically become Pavlovian dogs responding to the influence of media stimulation. We are being conditioned, and the cost is our intellectual curiosity.

A certain amount of propaganda exists within the educational environment. Most educators are not part of this activity designed to promote ideologies. However, that is not to say that college campus cannot be a breeding place for beliefs based more on the personal feelings of the professor than the substantive facts of the whole picture. When the discussion centers around politics, social equality, climate change, and so on, you are sometimes presented with a healthy serving of the professor's point of view rather than just plain fact.

It is likely but not at all certain that some students already share his feelings. But, in a way, those students who happen not to share them are the main target of the professor's persuasive aims. Moreover, even in the case of students who do share them, their hostile feelings on the subject are reinforced by being provided with new biased input. The persuasive use of presuppositions is manifest in college discourse, when a professor addresses the students directly rather than from the information and material at hand in order to gain their approval.

Another use of presuppositions, which I take to be aimed at persuasion, consists of conveying accusations or criticisms without spelling them out explicitly. In many cases, vagueness becomes a learning tool to profligate propaganda. Provide the student with pieces of information he or she is unlikely to have and create the impression that there is an ongoing story which began some time ago and which reinforces the professor's ideology.

Ideology and the reinforcement of personal viewpoints have become somewhat inevitable in today's universities and colleges. It is not a question whether or not schools of higher education engage in propaganda but rather a question of how and how much. A percentage of educators do engage in ideology training. Professors and teachers are perfectly positioned to be agents of propaganda and ideology. They are at the helm of a willing and captive ship of participants. Propaganda has become so problematic partially because of the blurred lines between the information, persuasion, and the entertainment value of the teacher's discourse. To be successful, the requirement includes taking a well-planned and sophisticated approach on the part of the instructor, and the implications for ethics are striking. Some educators have developed a troubling symbiotic relationship with media solely to continuously pollute communication with biased input. Students are consumers of information, and educators have a responsibility to do the right thing. When educators misuse information, when they blur the lines between facts, value judgments, and inferences, they do a moral disservice not only to the student but also to society as a whole. The moral purpose of education is relegated to a less lofty position. Morality can be described as humanly generated, objectively constrained, and contingent on the source from which it is derived. Universities are some of the most powerful political institutions in the nation.

The world is filled with tools of propaganda. Our educational system is one such conduit to disperse it. The ability is there to indoctrinate a personal philosophy on the minds of students which in turn spills out to the rest of the world. Educational institutions should provide the pedagogical conditions for critical and engaged citizenship. Crucial to such a challenge is the role that higher education can play in reclaiming the links between education and democracy, knowledge and public service, learning and democratic social change.

Ideology in education should refer to the values that give direction to education in the area of curriculum. Economics, politics, morality, religiosity, aesthetics, and artistic viewpoints are also part of the educational environment. Currently, there is an ideological power play on the part of some educators to underestimate curriculum and overestimate the role of political and economic power and involvement. Educational development not only concerns itself with curriculum but also places tremendous emphasis on the various political and economic concerns of society. Ideology matters in education on more than just one level. Oftentimes, political and social concerns are presented in a one-sided manner, sometimes being able to be placed in the category of biased thinking bordering on propaganda.

Both education and propaganda communicate knowledge. But the knowledge communicated through education aims at knowing the truth, making independent judgment. It encourages free thinking and critical analysis in all aspects of learning, while propaganda discourages free thinking. Most students are unaware that they are falling prey to it. It seeps into their lives not only through education but all forms of entertainment, media, and technology as well.

Some researchers claim that education is perhaps the greatest tool of propaganda. Almost every person is susceptible to manipulation no matter how intelligent that individual may be. The purpose of propaganda is control—to control not only the future but the past as well. If the propagandist says that an event never happened, some view it as the gospel truth. It just never happened. This behavior is not enough to sway entire national viewpoints, but people merely accepting these "truths" helps convince them that they are their own. When the propagandist begins to tie their interest with that of their students, a terrifying unity occurs, the likes of which can be seen in almost every dictatorship throughout history. Slogans and themes are repeated over and over again in order to beat them into the minds of the people. Slogans, through media, develop a life of their own; and the educational environment sometimes acts as a life support system for those catch lines: "Hands Up," "Don't Shoot," "Trump Is a Racist," "End White Privilege," "End Gun Violence by Banning Guns," "End Corporate Climate Change."

More importantly, anything contrary to the end goal must be squashed immediately. Anyone speaking out against them must also be destroyed in the name of national well-being. A skillful propagandist has the ability to actually mold the minds of their audience in any direction they so choose, and even the most intelligent and independent of people may not entirely escape their influence. The important thing is to ensure they are isolated from all other sources of information. Education, specifically that which is received at schools in controlled and regimented settings, can be a tool of propaganda. It has the ability to modify human behavior, influence thought patterns, and shape the entire worldview of students impacting, among other things, their responses to social order. Pressure is sometimes put to bear on individuals to foster this goal. That goal being to control thought processes.

The real purpose of education is to equip our young people with the knowledge, skills, and attitude to become a positive and viable part of society. It develops and reinforces critical thinking, interpersonal professionalism, and creative thinking skills to influence success in our personal life, work, and the search for our own truth. When a student learns to believe and value himself, the true understanding of why and how to learn begins. Life is an environment of lifelong learning; and the future, more than any other time, may require flexibility in the learning of new skills. Education's role is similar to that of the family and organized religion. Some may label this purpose as a method of indoctrination. And it may very well be. But to what purpose? To support a system that provides an individual with the social, economic, and spiritual values to become an effective and positive contributor to both oneself and to the society they will have to function within.

Reporting News or an Agenda

Another venue, besides education, where audiences are swayed and come under attack is the various news programs purporting to be balanced and without bias. News propaganda is covertly packaged as credible news but overtly come across lacking sufficient transparency concerning the source of the news item, as well as the motivation behind it as being considered newsworthy. News propaganda is also associated with crises events as a method to either secure calmness especially in times of war or domestic upheaval or to motivate action on the part of the audience. What is extremely disturbing is news reporting with the targeted purpose of promoting bias and self-interest. When reading or watching a program about a cause or an issue, the audience needs to recognize whether they are taking in actual news or opinion and propaganda.

When you watch cable news programs on CNN, FOX, or MSNBC, they often switch between straight news reporting and personal commentary. Are the news reporters journalists or political pundits? Can you tell which person on screen is a journalist and which is a pundit? The ability to distinguish news from opinion is an important news literacy skill, and it's an essential one for everyone engaged and concerned about a specific social, economic, or cultural problem. And if that isn't enough, one must also learn to know the difference between opinion and on-the-lower-rung-of-the-ladder propaganda.

Quality journalism aspires to ethical standards. These standards are taught, with some variations, by journalism schools, professional journalism associations, and individual news organizations. These standards include the following:

- Truthfulness or accuracy: Using multiple original sources (both various individuals and independent documentation) wherever possible and verifying all details that can be possibly checked.
- Independence: The interests of the public come first. Self-interest or special interest plays no role in quality journalism.
- Balance: Give a voice to multiple perspectives.
- Fairness or avoidance of bias: Facts and details are presented in appropriate context, using neutral language.
- Accountability: When errors are made, acknowledge them quickly, and correct them promptly.

Quality news articles can be objectively identified using such standards.

The American people are very aware of the input of both propaganda and biased news reporting in what they read and watch. Surveys show that between 44 and 64 percent of audiences are aware of the slant and inaccuracy of news on social media and elsewhere. The same survey registers 80 percent of audiences as being unhappy with receiving inaccurate or biased information. There are those who are convinced that there are no unbiased American news sources, and more troubling is that this conviction is applied to international news sources as well.

My feeling is that the truth lies somewhere near the center. It is a serious mistake to overemphasize propaganda in the discussions of news and an erroneous assumption to think as some people do that everything on media and news platforms is propaganda, that all media content is deceitful or otherwise improperly motivated. This is ridiculous, but having said this, media platforms can be used for propaganda, disinformation, or misinformation. They can be used for both negative propaganda as well as positive propaganda. And they can be utilized to dispense information that is not propaganda at all. A democratic nation knows that freedom of expression and opinion, unencumbered by government restrictions, is fundamental to the intelligent participation of citizens.

The journalist of today has a responsibility to report facts as accurately and objectively as possible. An honest, self-disciplined, well-trained journalist will seek to be a proponent for nothing but the truth.

However, quite often, propaganda does come into play. Sometimes, it is presented in unvetted impartial fact, but quite often, the journalist is a conscious propagandist. And sometimes, it is so obvious in a news story that is of importance to the audience that the media platform presenting it knows that the audience will easily recognize it for what it is and evaluate it for themselves. This is the best of all worlds, when news is vetted by the audience.

All this imposes a responsibility upon the audience, because it is with them that the power of evaluation ultimately should and does lie. A good journalist does their best to confirm the news and to remove propaganda that isn't news. Having done that, they leave it up to the audience for evaluation and criticism. Unfortunately, quite often, with today's media, that is not always the case.

It is important to determine the purpose of what you're reading, watching, or hearing. Opinion presents a specific perspective on a topic or issue. They (opinions) are often described by news outlets as either commentary or editorials/op-eds. Emotional appeals are often utilized to persuade readers, listeners, or viewers to consider the position being argued for or against. The message includes verifiable facts and evidence. This evidence may be open to some interpretation, but it is still presented as clear and reinforced by reasoning. Other perspectives and positions may also be presented for balance and contrast. The best opinion pieces use facts coupled with coherent arguments to explain why we should be in support of the position discussed.

Negative propaganda has a wide variety of definitions, but the elements needed to consider what is viewed as propaganda are that it reinforces fear and insecurity. Facts and information are distorted and manipulated. It often includes falsehoods, and it's almost always one-sided. Negative propaganda most commonly uses illogical distortions in its efforts to persuade—especially attacks on issues or persons that conjure strong emotional appeal. It often uses misinformation or disinformation. As previously mentioned, they are not synonymous. If the person who is sharing the information does not know it to be true or not, that is misinformation. If the person who is sharing the information knows it is not true but is sharing it, anyway, that is disinformation.

The ability to distinguish among news, opinion, and propaganda becomes particularly important when the viewers become engaged in a social, economic, moral, or political cause. As they learn more about an issue, they will need to be able to distinguish reliable and factual sources and to ignore misinformation and disinformation.

With this skill, the audience can move from passively consuming information to actively engaging the veracity of what is being presented. When people become more sophisticated in the ability to dissect the information presented, they become empowered to express their own beliefs and add their voices to discussions of issues and policy.

Distinguishing fact from opinion is a skill that needs to be addressed in order to foster responsibility when it comes to reacting on what is viewed by an audience.

Facts are verifiable, hence the term "fact check." Facts can be agreed to by experts on the topic in question. On the other hand, an opinion might be able to be supported by facts, and thus it becomes an argument. People can draw opposite conclusions about someone's opinion even if they agree on the fact presented. Opinion moves beyond the facts presented into the realm of interpretation, and this is where we all have to determine if the facts, indeed, reinforce and justify the opinion being offered.

The ability to distinguish between fact and opinion helps the audience develop critical and analytical skills. Most often, we are presented with fact and opinion in the same dialogue. It is, therefore, crucial that the audience is able to decipher the ingredients that comprise truth from ingredients that are simply opinions or beliefs. For the audience to successfully distinguish fact from opinion, a closer examination of the wording used may be helpful. Examples of wording that support fact are *confirms, according to, demonstrates, uncovered, discovered,* etc. Wording such as *argues,* suspects, *claims, views,* etc. are all indicators of opinion.

Viewing and hearing media information should always incorporate the question of separating what's true from what journalists and commentators think is true. How do you know whether you are being given solid information or whether the presenter is trying to persuade you to embrace a point of view? Facts are supported by evidence that everyone can agree on. However, opinions are based on personal beliefs and judgments. There is also a distinction to be made between an informed opinion and an uninformed one, and this is where agenda bias can blur the line between reality and fiction.

The verification of facts and the forming of opinion are two separate and distinct entities. An opinion is not a fact by any stretch. A fact is a product of research and homework. A fact is more powerful than the best opinions out there. A fact can contradict an opinion. But with media, day in and day out, we are supplied with a healthy dose of "someone else's opinion." Someone once asked me, "What is this obsession you have with the truth?" Truth is like Superman, able to leap tall buildings in a single bound, whereas opinions and assumptions may be faster than a speeding bullet but almost always miss their mark.

Free Speech and Propaganda

The line between free speech and propaganda is very fine, indeed, and has the ability to cause all sorts of mayhem. Digital media, newspapers, and magazines disseminate information with careless disregard for that fine line. The difference between the two becomes clouded. These outlets have the responsibility to present information that the public can depend on as "factual." The audience has a responsibility to recognize the difference between free speech and propaganda because at some point a future action on the part of the viewer will be taken and what is seen or heard becomes a part of that action. We must remember the old cliché that knowledge is power and that ultimately the audience is the entity that has right and responsibility to exercise this power.

A complication for the audience in distinguishing fact, free speech, and propaganda is the use of syndicated journalism with stories written by less-than-neutral sources like the *Washington Post* and the *New York Times*. Most often, these syndicates have an agenda or motivation that has little in common with unbiased reporting. These agendas are slipped into newspapers, magazine articles, and digital media sometimes in either a covert or overt manner. When these types of deceptions are used, they always prove pernicious and destructive to the public trust and hopefully will be identified as such in the name of journalistic ethics. Check an article or newspaper source as to who the writer is and their reputation to determine for yourself if it can be believed.

It is difficult for the information audience to know everything, but everyone involved has a responsibility to "fact-check" articles and stories. In order to make informed decisions moving forward, it is a requirement. If the truth becomes a casualty in the "information war" (and make no mistake, it is a war), then we all lose. We, as the information audience, must become a part of the solution in the name of factual clarity and the promulgation of an informed society.

Information transgressions of this type have touched on such topics as global warming, so-called white privilege, conservatism, and liberalism. Fabrications that have no basis in fact are being reinforced in the media and have made their way to the printed page and digital media. Responsible journalists are the first line of defense against falsehoods being disseminated to the public. But it is the information audience who is ultimately responsible for searching out the truth. Quite a difficult task, with little opposing view and a nearly constant barrage of misinformation. The average person is at a distinct disadvantage without the input of good and responsible journalism. It is basically unlearning what is considered normal.

The question of how free speech impacts propaganda is important. Is there a free speech breaking point, a line in the sand, at which hateful, harmful, or controversial reporting should require censorship? When should media platform content lose its constitutional protection under the First Amendment? The American people carry a strong support for free speech in general, but that number decreases when the focus is on current forms of controversial rhetoric.

Movements such as Me Too, Antifa, and Black Lives Matter have raised an awareness and national dialogue centering around racism, ideology, sexual harassment, and more. With raised awareness comes an increased call for laws punishing dialogue that is racially harmful or at best offensive and controversial.

At the present time, hate speech is not prohibited or punished. Speech that threatens or incites lawlessness or acts as a motivator for civil disobedience may, in some case, be punished as a hate crime but not as offensive speech. Offensive speech that creates a hostile environment or becomes a disruptive influence may be prohibited. But apart from these exceptions, the Supreme Court has strongly defended the belief in the public exchange of ideas and open debate that the reasonable response to offensive speech is to speak back in response.

A very visible controversy is the role and credibility of the news media. A steady barrage of accusations about "fake news" and the "fake news media" has placed it front and center in the public eye. Media critics view the current rhetoric as unfair, unbalanced, and unobjective. The First Amendment protects the ability of the news media to operate free of government interference. However, their job should be to provide the essential facts that can support public discourse and serve as a protector to hold government accountable for its actions.

A question may soon have to be answered. Should there be a point where propaganda, disinformation, or hate speech should lose its protection under the First Amendment? A consciousness has been raised as to the fake news we are all subjected to, and that dialogue may very well lead to the question posed above.

Because something may be very "believable" does not mean that it is true. Perhaps just the opposite. Perhaps what is easiest to believe is the easiest for someone to view as the truth. This is an appeal to the inherent laziness of most people in actively searching for the truth. What comes to mind is the Orson Welles broadcast *War of the Worlds*, where he went on the air to say that Martians had invaded New Jersey. Welles and a troupe of radio actors interrupted the Columbia Broadcasting System's programming to announce that our planet had been invaded. Since then, it's been an accepted fact that that the news media can convince people of almost anything. Many of those listening actually panicked, thinking the story was real. Some frantically began to flee the area of the invasion. To be sure, the broadcast seemed real and believable, and many had no inkling that it was a hoax.

Propaganda can have a similar effect as the hoax just described. Throughout history, it has been used to start wars. In early civilization, most wars began with a consultation with the priests (closest to God) or otherwise the assurance that God willed the war, and those who opposed his will were infidels. As an example, the Crusades. The examples are more than numerous where propaganda was used to justify war—"weapons of mass destruction" being one of the most recent claims to legitimize. And as with Mr. Welles's broadcast, many in the audience were eager to believe. Propaganda has been used to rationalize one atrocity after another. And to this day, I don't think this fact bothers enough people. Propaganda is truly a contradiction of reality. In our current society, it is a rhetorical device used to spin information in order to claim importance to any piece of trash. And the most essential part is to foster the beliefs, attitudes, and emotions associated with its spread. It is clear that propaganda preys on fear and ignorance. The cure for it is a questioning mind, one that defends itself through an ability for cognitive analysis, the rational ability to dissect information. Of utmost importance is that you trust yourself.

A very common label to describe news stories is "fake news." Let's start with a definition to ensure clarity. Fake news is simply a story that is circulated and is known by the circulator to be false. They are filled with made-up facts or outward lies about a particular topic or at best, a biased analysis. Sometimes, they describe events that just didn't happen—or take place the way the story describes. It is a fictional account or explanation of a real news event. You find fake news stories in social media feeds and on news websites. These sites intermingle actual news events with fake news articles. The stories posted then get shared via social media, which is why you see them posted by your friends in your Facebook and Twitter news feeds. The intent of these sites is to mislead people into thinking they're really viewing or hearing real news. They are not accidental mistakes by any means. The writers purposefully craft believable-sounding but totally fraudulent information, typically for their own philosophical gain. Because of the influence of fake news sites, most importantly during the 2016 presidential election, many people viewed this sort of news as a threat to democracy. If enough people believe fake news stories, not only are viewers misled but also genuine news is delegitimized. It is a news-reputation killer. It becomes more and more difficult for people to determine real news reporting from the fake variety.

Not all of the untruths spread online come from news media sites. Some of what you read on Facebook and other social media are just plain lies or a deliberate false analysis of a news story. You know, when someone deliberately explains something to fit their narrative but that they know just isn't true.

Some people actually have trouble calling a lie a lie. In mainstream media circles, you're likely to hear that someone misspoke or didn't mean what they actually said or their words were taken out of context. No one is going to say, "I was lying." Sometimes, a person is confronted with "distorting the facts." And now we have a new reference popping up called "alternative" facts. But whatever you label it, a lie is still a lie. And, yes, if someone lies, they are a liar. And if a person doesn't tell the original lie but just passes it around via a social media platform, isn't that just as dangerous to real truth?

In any case, many people are sharing lies on Facebook and other social media. Just because someone says something on media doesn't make it true. Fake news no matter how it is disseminated is just as false.

Conspiracy theories have been around as long as anyone can remember. Some people want to believe that certain events are much more complex than we are led to believe. There are those who believe that UFO investigations, as well as the assassination investigation of JFK, are nefarious plots to hide the real story. Even the moon landing is considered fake by some reports. And Elvis is alive and well (but much older). Despite facts proving the opposite, conspiracy theories continue to persist and generate a life of their own.

Conspiracy theorists have become more prominent in recent years, thanks to theory sharing via the Internet. Social media makes it easier for the passing of theories back and forth, which leads to an additional exposure to theory.

Social media has also helped spread newer conspiracy theories, often immediately after some tragic event in the news. Hot button topics such as climate change, the 9/11 attack, and vaccines as a cause of autism remain controversial; but many people accept opinion on issues such as these to be the truth, encouraging their reiteration and providing an expanded audience, especially in social media. It's a belief that there has to be more to the story. The creation of a conspiracy theory is more interesting than the acknowledgment that events sometimes just happen as reported.

Some of what people call fake news is actually propaganda—disinformation used to mislead or promote a particular point of view. It is particularly popular in politics, where one side spouts selective facts in an effort to promote its cause or disparage the opposite side.

We're all targets of propaganda from both political parties, from our own government and even from foreign governments. You hear it every day on the news repeated over and over to enforce its belief.

Conservatives in our country see certain news media as spreading left-wing propaganda—just as some liberals view other news media as spreading conservative propaganda. There is enough going around on both sides. It has always been used to influence the masses and will undoubtedly continue to do so. What's changed is they're now doing it via social media.

You're bound to hear that this or that specific news outlet is espousing fake news. Although this can be the case, in most instances the person talking about the news story simply doesn't like the viewpoint of that news outlet. That doesn't make the news from that outlet fake, but it could certainly be biased. We live, now more than ever before, in a politically polarized society. One side doesn't trust the other, and working together for the common good is very rare indeed. This polarization of philosophy has spread to news outlets big and small, each claiming that media with a different viewpoint are biased and not to be believed.

It is true that some news media strike a liberal or conservative slant in their presentation. Propaganda does not establish itself as the sole ownership of one side or another in the political arena. It is a tool that may be used by both sides. Assigning the propaganda label to the opposite camp can in itself be labeled as propaganda. FOX News is somewhat biased in a conservative direction, and MSNBC and CNN hold somewhat of a liberal viewpoint. This is evidenced by the stories they choose to cover, the people they interview, and the analysis they offer with their coverage. That simply means their coverage comes with a certain viewpoint. Take that into account when you watch it. Some people feel it is not a bad idea to get a variety of viewpoints. But when events are construed with a specific polarization in mind, your unbiased analysis (if there is such a thing) should be used as a deciphering tool. The reporting of news in an impartial manner has become a very rare bird. That kind of reporting just does not fly today. Some reporters argue that impartial reporting can also be labeled as a bias. It is seen as a bias toward not wanting to take a stand—a bias toward neutrality, if you will. The positive aspect of neutrality in reporting is that it allows the viewer to develop their own self-reflecting viewpoint.

The antidote for propaganda is the process of finding factual truth through inquiry and research. We all currently live in very uncertain times where truth is often obscured by controversy and opinion. The world is changing faster than it ever has before. The attack on the World Trade Center feels like it happened ages ago. And recently, a disease unknown a few years ago is now claiming the lives of many and has changed our world again. Communication and information which was once difficult to find has now become almost effortless. If there is only one truth we can have certainty of, it is the fact that our world will continue to constantly change.

I believe that with this ongoing change, we have a power that was unavailable a few decades ago. It is the capacity to access more information, and that affords us more control. Not only is information more available and accessible, but also research has accelerated so rapidly that new tools for discovery are being created as we speak. Use the digital tools at your disposal to review the source of information to determine its reliability. Check for accuracy as a measure of information quality. Ask yourself, What were the resources for the information being presented, as well as the purpose? Always keep in mind that anyone can put information online and for any number of reasons. Investigate the claims made, the quotes given, the source, media, and original context from which the information originated. Information evaluation is a job but much needed in a post-truth world.

Propaganda and Emotion

Propaganda involves emotions and feelings which can be either positive or negative. The propagandist appeals to our fears as well as to our personal philosophy. It can rally courage in us, as well as hatred and even love. Therefore, our emotional well-being can actually be manipulated either positively or destructively. A propagandist processes information by the means of distorting or altogether ignoring the facts. He knows how to sell a product, and in this case, it is his ideology.

Most people look for information that supports their own personal belief system or as I call it—a "fact bubble." The propagandist's appeal to emotion is, therefore, bound to find a more ready reception when it is in agreement with that preexisting belief system. When emotional reactions agree with a personal belief or fact bubble, it can overtake intellectual analysis and fact-based reasoning. The propagandist draws his power in large part from an audience that is not aware propaganda is being used. Propaganda is, to put it simply, a con. A mind that is not trained to detect and neutralize propaganda is vulnerable to its targeted effect. The audience must learn to be analytical.

There are several ways the propagandist achieves their goal as evidenced in the current media. The use of name-calling is used to label an opposing point of view nefarious. Diminishing an opponent's standing or intimidating them enforces the propagandist viewpoint and can also have a detrimental effect on reputation and credibility.

Another way to promote propaganda is the use of *catchphrases*. For example, "Hope and Change. Make America Great Again." The point here is to get the audience to buy into a feeling that they believe is of particular importance. It eases our minds and makes us more susceptible when the speaker begins telling us about a philosophical catchphrase that encompasses a plan of action the United States must undertake in order to preserve democracy and accomplish nation-wide progress.

Another tool of propaganda is *transfer*. The propagandist reaches out to an esteemed group or entity (a church or national organization) to approve a campaign on behalf of a specific belief. They, thereby, transfer their belief through the authority, sanction, and prestige of that group. Thus, we may be more willing to accept the entire campaign because of that specific belief.

Another ploy is the use of *testimonials* to forward a viewpoint. The propagandist uses a variety of techniques to get their false message accepted by their audience. For example, the use of a well-respected personality to enforce an acceptance of the message or idea is common. Then there is the plain folks' strategy. The propagandist goes to extremes to appear just like us. An ordinary person is used to convince listeners that a prominent person and their ideas be accepted by the audience in question. The combination of both can be applied to many areas—reverse mortgages, homeowners' flood insurance, and so on to either calm people's fears or, just the opposite, to magnify a fear. However, a message can just simply be illogical. An illogical message is not necessarily propagandistic. It can simply be a message with a flaw in its logic. But if logic is "manipulated deliberately" to promote a cause, it is propaganda. As an example, to make huge predictions about the future on the basis of a few small facts. The effect of this sort of personal narrative is easier to comprehend and carries much more emotional weight.

Then there is what I call the *camouflage* strategy. For example, the propagandist creates a smoke screen by raising a new issue when they want an embarrassing matter forgotten. They divert attention away from the matter they do not want revealed. They use the technique of underemphasis in the area they are trying to avoid and overemphasis in another area to dodge issues and evade facts. They resort to distortion and omit facts.

And, finally, there is the *bandwagon* approach. Our identity and strength are derived from our affiliations with organized groups. Humans have a strong desire to belong and are terrified of social rejection and isolation. We are conformist by design and strongly susceptible to peer pressure. For examples, simply turn on your TV, and watch some of the major news networks. Our emotions in all the above examples trigger an unconscious response to information that is presented to a mostly unsuspecting audience.

Because propaganda uses a variety of communication techniques to create an emotional appeal, to adopt a certain behavior or to perform a particular action or to accept a particular belief or opinion, it is important to recognize it for what it really is—a dishonest message. There is a difference between persuasive communication (advertising, etc.) and propaganda, but there are instances in which the propaganda label can be applied to advertising promotions as well. Everyone should have a working knowledge concerning the different types of propaganda techniques to help decipher hype and emotional appeal from unbiased fact. We are in the midst of psychological warfare when it comes to propaganda. Psychological warfare is a broad term with the general meaning that it is the use of actions intended to reduce an opponent's morale or mental well-being. The goal is to intentionally use propaganda to manipulate another and break down their will without using physical force. It uses fear to break down the psychological health of an opponent. The news is a large information source that we all tap into. It has the ability to spread whichever information it chooses. Propaganda has taken on psychological associations as well as moral and partisan attributes. When it infiltrates the news, a population could be tainted by volatile information. The ethical and political standards of social and political groups are reinforced by the propaganda they allow themselves to be subjected to. In itself, it steers clear of arousing any reflective thought.

So to be truly liberated and safe, we must be educated about the process of propaganda. It's very likely that with the expansion of social media, the audience is becoming more and more irrational. Although we have access to more information and participate in more public debates about issues that affect us as individuals and as a society, that doesn't mean we're doing so more rationally or based on arguments that are purely factual. We can conclude that presidential campaigns, moving forward, will feature unprecedented amounts of disinformation. With the constant barrage of propaganda, we may see more isolation between political groups, less individualism, and less social cohesion, which do not bode well for the survival of democracy.

The Internet has clouded our understanding of what communication should be, who furnishes it, how, and to what effect. It has always been and will always be an evolving complexity of technology coupled with the changing dynamic of social norms, rules, and patterns of use. The shape and direction of digital communications are constantly in flux—and the browser is no longer the primary method utilized by people to interact with an information infrastructure. The bulk of digital communications is no longer between people but has shifted to communication between devices. Political strategists make use of technological proxies in the form of proprietary algorithms and semiautomated political bots in a subtle attempt to manipulate public opinion. These tools are now the foundation to achieve a level of human control and thought manipulation.

Algorithms are simply instructions for solving a problem or completing a task. They are similar to math equations. Computer code is algorithmic. The Internet runs on algorithms, and all online searching is directed through their use. E-mail knows where to go, thanks to algorithms. Smartphone apps are nothing but algorithms. Artificial intelligence (AI) is based on algorithms. Computer and video games are simply algorithmic storytelling programs. Everything from product research, online dating, vacation websites, and information research would not function without algorithms. GPS mapping systems utilize algorithms to get people from one place to another. The material people see on social media is brought to them through the courtesy of your friendly media algorithms. Pretty much, most of what people see and do on the Internet is a product of algorithms. Every time someone uses excel to sort a column in a spreadsheet, algorithms are at work, and most financial business today is conducted through algorithms. They help Siri and Alexis respond to voice commands, recognize faces, sort your photo collections, and will soon be driving your car. Hacking, phishing, and other cyberattacks exploit code-breaking algorithms. Self-learning and self-programming algorithms are now being created, which will make it possible in the near future for algorithms to write their own algorithms.

They are incredibly useful tools in accomplishing tasks. However, sometimes the application of algorithms created with a good intention can lead to unexpected consequences. Quite often, manipulative narratives are spread by algorithms, bots, and humans, and are commonly utilized in many areas of the information ecosystem. It is the people who manage the algorithms, on behalf of strategists, that control and populate the feeds of more than two billion users.

Essentially, propaganda is information with an agenda. Algorithms serve as the orchestra conductors of information leading to an end result. Sometimes, direction of information is not objective, but also it is not completely false. In fact, to be most effective, propaganda is often hinged to a partial truth. But regardless of whether it's true or false, the aim is to influence the audience to feel a certain way or to form a certain opinion about the topic being discussed. It is often associated with political parties, media companies, and activist groups. The virality engines that direct our attention are being used both to inform as well as to influence. They range from manifesting national concerns to sharing moments of joy and humor. But when information manipulation is used to forward a false maligning narrative, there are serious implications for all of us. With the broadening of the artificial intelligence revolution, it will continue to steadily infiltrate decision-making processes to help determine choices for you.

Shadow Government,
Disinformation, Misinformation

Propaganda has been used as a political tool of manipulation since the time of the ancient Greeks and Romans. The term itself comes from the Vatican, the administrative governing body of the Catholic Church that was dedicated to extending and introducing the Catholic faith in non-Catholic countries. Kings, as well as religious leaders, used it; and even the Founding Fathers of our Constitution used it to shape opinions and influence thought. Some believe that propaganda was an essential aspect in the formation of our democracy.

The manipulation of audience opinion is an important element in both democratic and totalitarian societies. There exists a strong belief that those who manipulate are in reality an invisible government unto itself and are considered by many to be the true ruling power of our country. Its existence has been reinforced by those who believe it exists as a contingency plan should a country be successful in attacking Washington and our ongoing government. Some believe it has been instrumental in developing attitudes, giving life to new ideas, and developing political direction primarily by men who remain in the shadows. This theory is partially a result of the way in which our democratic society is organized.

The term "shadow government" has been loosely bantered about in the media for several years. It is based on the notion that real and actual political power resides not with officials elected to office and in charge of enacting laws, national security, defense, and foreign and domestic expenditures but with private individuals who are exercising control in much the same manner as a puppeteer behind the scenes and beyond any scrutiny. According to this theory or belief, the officially elected government is subservient to the shadow government, which is the true executive power and puppeteer behind the curtain.

It has been the subject of numerous books and movies. What is not theory is the existence of manipulation within our democratic society. Opinions and predispositions of all Americans are to some extent being influenced and controlled, but the question of whether it is being accomplished through the influence of an inconspicuous power base remains a theory. No matter the origin, minds are being manipulated, and ideas are being formulated via manipulation and oftentimes on a subconscious level. We have all become vulnerable and susceptible.

Questions and theories abound concerning shadow government, its decisions and who carries them out. Where is their center of operation? Who are members of the shadow government? A lot of questions about an entity the existence of which has yet to be proven and which some believe not to exist at all. Some, who find it credible, think it is comprised of a few major financial institutions. Others believe its central structure can be found in the intelligence apparatus within our country. Still others theorize that it has no permanent center of operation with the membership conferring through various means of communication. Decisions are made through consensus agreement. The real power lies with those who belong to a secret society of both influence and unbounded wealth.

The definition of "shadow government" describes a country that is not governed through democratic principles but rather a government in which actual political power resides not with publicly elected officials but with private individuals who exercise power behind the scenes, beyond the control of a democratic nation. According to this theory, the official elected government rules in deference to the shadow government, which holds true executive power.

My concern is not the existence of this entity but rather the feeling of distrust that shadow government represents. It is very difficult to maintain leadership in a divided country in which a spirit of trust and unity has been compromised. It is the very antithesis of a democracy and a concept that has been accepted by a large part of the population. This term is used in the media to define the actions of those whose agenda is to bring down a legitimized government.

Attempts to debunk conspiracy theories only succeed in giving them more life. These theories are a tool for stifling free thought. It is almost as if the end game is not to make the audience believe lies but to make information irrelevant altogether.

Again, the feeling behind the concept is one of mistrust, manipulation, and control. We are not the authors of our own destiny. The very idea of democracy under this belief is a fairy tale. Under this theory, the concept that voters steer the government through the election process is a fallacy. Elected officials are basically just figureheads without any substantial control over our country's decisions. And most importantly, the hardworking public-spirited voters who act in good faith and conscience at election time are going through the motions of a meaningless activity. It basically is a rationale for the helplessness many people feel when it comes to government. This belief in shadow government is more a symptom of a disease that is infecting our society—mistrust.

For large numbers of individuals to cooperate, some form of directive process must be in place if they are to live together in a functioning society. That directive process begins with informing and at the same time actively directing, persuading, and ultimately integrating people into larger and larger groups. With the emergence of a small number of social platforms that serve billions of us, some consequences stemming from the design of these platforms are having a manipulative effect on choice and democracy. Some effects are for the common good, such as social distancing and the stay-at-home directive during the COVID-19 epidemic.

But these platforms sometimes distribute misleading information over their networks. If you watch news today on social platforms in the United States, the United Kingdom, or the rest of Europe, you will probably be hearing and watching a healthy diet of disinformation. Misinformation and disinformation are both, at their core, misleading. As previously mentioned, the difference between the two is intent. Misinformation is the sharing of false information unintended to mislead people and genuinely believed by the disseminator. Disinformation, in contrast, is the deliberate creation and sharing of information known to be false. The explicit aim of disinformation is to cause confusion and to ultimately lead the audience to believe what is not true. Computational propaganda is a tool embraced by media platforms as a tactic used in disinformation campaigns that takes place online. These include the use of automated social media accounts to spread messages and the use of algorithms on social media platforms to disseminate it. These tools facilitate the disinformation campaign whose ultimate goal is to manipulate a narrative or simply push false information into mass awareness.

Disinformation is not a new phenomenon. Especially during the World Wars and the Cold War, it was widely used to sow distrust and cause confusion. But with today's technology in place, disinformation is computationally driven and is actually an effective method used for information warfare. It is implemented in everything from elections to dividing society even further. Unbiased news is altered, and the altered version appears on an active site or blog or as a message board post. It has its birth outside of the more carefully scrutinized news and is then presented in a mass social ecosystem using deliberate, coordinated algorithmic tactics designed to forward the altered version as unbiased reality. The manipulators strive to ensure that content will jump from one social platform to the next. Eventually, the goal is that it will be picked up on mainstream media, blanketing that media as much as possible and impacting a mostly receptive audience. Telling a lie over and over reinforces its acceptance. You actually turn it into something considered the gospel truth by the audience.

The Internet has certainly expanded the limits on what communication can be, as well as the effectiveness of what is being communicated. Digital communications are no longer between people but between devices. We live in a world where information is disseminated through the use of technological substitutes in the form of proprietary algorithms and semiautomated social contacts (bots) in subtle attempts to manipulate both information and public opinion.

Political deception through the use of disguised propaganda in digital media present challenges to those who wish to out this behavior and counter it. To do so will require the cooperation of social media companies who should not only be held accountable but also can supply the necessary support to diminish the problem. As more and more data becomes available from social platforms, their pervasiveness in the everyday life of millions of Internet users will increase. These communication platforms provide the environment as well as a great deal of incentives for deceptive actors.

Misinformation can be the most difficult communication to discern since its inaccuracy stems from not being properly vetted. It becomes a natural response in a crisis situation where there is uncertainty about the event itself. Take in any new information with a little bit of skepticism. Does the subject of the information involve a complicated issue? Is it something that is effecting an emotional response? If possible, compare the information through various sources. Expect proof with a conclusion. Because it is the act of unwittingly sharing erroneous or incorrect information, it is in direct contrast to disinformation, which is an act of purposeful deception. Disinformation intentionally attempts to mislead, whereas misinformation does not. It is mostly poorly researched data that results in misinformation.

What is the difference between disinformation and propaganda? To some extent, the meaning of both terms overlap. However, a distinction can possibly be forwarded with respect to intensity and intent. Disinformation does not always use untruths or fabricated stories. The intent is narrower than that with propaganda. It can be considered a distorter of truth used as a method to dismiss the actual facts within a single story line. Propaganda, on the other hand, can be viewed as having a wider objective which is to alter viewpoints on both ideology and social issues. But without question, disinformation can be considered a close relative in the propaganda family.

Advertising

The early creators of the Internet valued open participation and the free flow of information. Anyone could create a site in which they could develop and share a point of view with their audience. The platform for the expression of ideas was open but decidedly unorganized. Everyone could have a voice. Eventually, this open platform was generally termed as the fifth estate. In this environment, it was difficult to find information, let alone reach large audiences or make the content trend to outside media. But with the creation of social networks (Facebook, Twitter, etc.) in the early 2000s, online audiences and activity gradually gravitated to a handful of media platforms.

The social web is a big success, drawing millions and millions of willing participants. It is a fun way to communicate with friends and family, and there is the ability to easily discover new contacts who share the same ideas and interests. What started out as a decentralized Web has become very much centralized. Facebook began as a place for college students to interact with their classmates. Over time, it has become a platform for over two billion people to connect with friends and family.

It evolved into a news source, a place to find groups with similar interest as yours and a place to share photos, live videos, and events. It also developed as a market for online sales. It further expanded after the acquisition of platforms such as Instagram and WhatsApp. Google is also developing and expanding at the same time. It is now the web's dominant search engine, a social network, and a major e-mail platform. With the acquisition of YouTube, it became one of the world's largest video-sharing platforms. Reddit and Twitter also emerged as a venue to discuss and disseminate news.

Advertising became a centerpiece of media platforms, powering its success. It is most effective when it targets a specific and intended audience. Users have become addicted and spend inordinate amounts of time on these platforms. Information is gathered and utilized on what audience members are following and are interested in, what they click on, what they like, and how long and often they remain on a site.

The platforms process your actions into a systematic profile, thereby using your behavior to gather an information portrait. Then they use that data to inform companies about perspective customers. This model came to be called surveillance capitalism by its many critics, and the sophistication in gathering information about the audience is now at the level of being a science.

Keeping people engaged is critical because there are now several platforms competing for their users' time and attention. Based on an algorithm that ran correlations between people with overlapping interests and proclivities, audiences were identified. Advertisers no longer had a need to create their own target-based demographic. The ads are indistinguishable from the rest of the content on the platforms, and the tracking has become increasingly more refined.

The targeting of massive numbers of people consolidated on a handful of social platforms was not just a boon for advertisers; it was also a boon for the propagandist. Marketing has become another stronghold for propaganda. In the marketing of a message, communication utilizing falsehoods, untruths, or exaggerated messaging is not at all uncommon. The name of the game has become persuasion. Truth-in-advertising and consumer-protection regulations go a long way in deterring businesses from including deceptive or misleading statements common to propaganda. But that has not resulted in the extinction of manipulative practices. A small percentage of advertising remains deceptive.

Commercial advertising and product information can be misleading. Disinformation has led in the past to the sale of defective products and inferior services. Product recall lists are a testimonial to the problem, as well as consumer service complaints. More is promised than is received. Through the use of deception, consumers sometimes choose both products and services that result in substandard satisfaction. Disinformation comes in various forms including hidden costs, product direction disinformation, sale items with purposeful limited availability, and questionable customer agreements.

Sometimes, purchases are made that result in the addition of hidden fees you were not made aware of. Whenever you see a price followed by an asterisk—caveat emptor. Anyone who has purchased put together furniture may have experienced the following. Beware of the words "easy to assemble." Sometimes, it winds up being sort of uneasy to assemble and more time-consuming than the estimate given.

You do your research, and now you are in the market to purchase an item. You find it advertised but are told it is not available, and you are offered a different product that is praised to the high heavens, but unfortunately, it comes with a less-than-heavenly price tag. Purposefully limiting the quantity of a lower price item in stock and offering a higher-cost item as a substitute is just another economic strategy. Baiting and switching are actually illegal, but it is the consumer who makes the choice to settle on another product.

Technology has created new bait and switch nightmares, for example the fine print in technology-oriented customer agreements that makes it difficult to benefit from a product discount, as well as disclaimers and user agreements that come with electronic devices. The Federal Trade Commission enforces law against underhanded practices, but it is the consumer who has to initiate a complaint.

Advertising is used to influence consumer attitudes toward a product. The purpose is to direct public attention to products, services, and ideas. Business advertising is the way the bills are paid by media platforms. However, the advertising stressed here is the kind that is done by certain groups who have an agenda in mind. Noncommercial advertising spends money on publicity in the hope to raising awareness for a cause or to promote a specific point of view. These include public interest groups, political parties, governments, and religious organizations.

Some commercial organizations have as their intention the spreading of a particular message with the purpose of convincing the viewer to heed their message or philosophy. Nike, and their sneaker controversy, comes to mind where not only a sneaker is being sold but a point of view as well. They are not only selling a product but also more importantly an idea or opinion.

Some experts say companies can promote their businesses, attract customers, and increase sales by taking a public stance on a controversial issue. It could also increase interest in buying the company's products. Research has shown that millennials are significantly more likely to buy products from companies that take public stands on controversial issues.

More than half of consumers say they would buy or boycott brands based on the brand's stance on a social or political issue. Companies feel increasing pressure to take social or political action. And more than two-thirds of issue-motivated buyers say they will not purchase products from a company that remains silent on an issue they believe requires a stance. But besides being a company that decides to "talk the talk," they have to have a reputation of "walking the walk." Consumers can evaluate the authenticity of a company position. A company should never take a stand when their values and business model point in an opposite direction.

Sometimes, a political or social stance by a company can either hurt or elevate it in the eyes of the audience. If incorrectly handled, it could jeopardize a company's reputation. On the other hand, it can also be a venue to express leadership with regards to an issue. It can either create a feeling of good will toward the company or incite a call for a boycott depending on the issue. But in most cases, doing so ends in zero gain for the company.

When a brand develops a social voice, it becomes a company that many consumers feel they can trust, and at the same time, it becomes a trigger for negative crossing of swords. Taking a position on social or political issues poses substantial risks. When taking a side, companies may alienate a portion of their potential customers. When a political stand is made, the brand may gain little long-term benefit.

Despite growing pressure from activist consumers, companies should think carefully before doing this. A political stance may do little to improve either sales or its stock value, and it can alienate a large part of their consumer base.

And there are marketers who feel a company's political stand can increase sales by strengthening loyalty among consumers. On the other hand, loyalty may not increase a brand's sales, since loyal customers already are consumers of its products. Instead, sales grow by gaining new customers. Although public relations and marketing departments may believe they understand how their audience will react, the prediction of how large numbers of people will actually react to sensitive issues is extremely difficult to assess. Brands should be extremely cautious and do their research before utilizing this market strategy.

The larger companies have a better handle on the social and political outlooks of the consumers of their products. They develop a good fundamental idea of how their customers would react to their potential stand. The acceptance by customers toward companies taking a hard stand on social issues varies greatly among consumers.

Sometimes, companies rely on audience dissemination and national notoriety to move a company outlook. In order for ideas to spread, you have to not only get people to believe in them, but you need a majority of people to believe in them. Viral ideas are the holy grail of marketing. Why spend money on huge advertising campaigns when you can get people to spread your ideas for free? Unfortunately, it is very hard to get things to go viral and nearly impossible to do so with any predictability or consistency.

Algorithms and Memes

To keep users engaged, platforms developed built-in prompts to increase participation and, thereby, increase information gathering. They created friendly dialogue fields that simply asked about what's happening in your life or what are you concerned about. Barriers to participation, over time, decreased through the numbing of the process, and every user became a self-information source. People have become very comfortable talking about their feelings on climate change, politics, flight delays, culture changes, and religion. The content and scope of information became enormous and impossibly difficult to manage because of the informational volume, hence the development of such features as the Retweet button and hashtags that cluster tweets into topics, as well as the Share and Like buttons. Messages spread across various platforms and reach very large audiences.

Computational propaganda is both a media networking tool and a disinformation weapon. It is a tool used to push a malignant narrative that can go viral and spread far and fast on social media. It is extremely difficult to refute it after the fact. The narrative often continues to be algorithmically amplified by the platforms themselves. To aid in solving the problem of having massive amounts of information deluge the platform, media policy has developed a curator plan of action. The curator functions are abundantly found across the Web in forms such as recommendation engines and trending features and searches. A very comfortable environment for motivated propagandists.

Searching seems like a straightforward process. An individual can search for a keyword or ask a question, and the platform returns the most relevant content that answers the inquiry. But search has become a method by which a specific agenda can be forwarded. The signals used by Google and other platforms to rank content can be manipulated, based on techniques broadly associated with the terminology "search engine optimization" (SEO). It is practiced by legitimate companies trying to be one of the first businesses listed in response to a keyword search relevant to their company. It is also employed by groups who want to push a particular agenda. Sometimes, the only content that will turn up in search is manipulated to be the content produced by that group. It ensures that someone curious about a particular issue or concern will first see the message the propagandist wishes to promote. This can have a serious implication when the keyword is related to an area where conspiracy type of misinformation and disinformation exists.

Search algorithms exist to help users to find answers. An algorithm that shows users what large groups of people are talking about or discussing is called a trending algorithm. These algorithms draw signals from URLs or keywords and hashtags. These signals point to information about something important or interesting that is currently in the media forefront. Trending targets user curiosity and is a draw for users who want to engage with others about a topic that is currently being discussed or in the limelight. It is also a haven for propagandists to manipulate the algorithm for their own agenda. They can deluge an active hashtag with self-benefitting propaganda, or they can push or shift an agenda to derail the conversation altogether. Derailment is accomplished by creating a new trending topic through coordinated manipulation using bots, which are fictional accounts that pretend to be real users. This is done to spread and trend an illusory message creating the false appearance that large numbers of people feel a certain way about a topic. It is sometimes described as a manufactured consensus. Trending is a powerful tool that can be used for manipulating media users. Mainstream reporters who use Twitter and notice a trend and then decide to forward it on their larger platform without any verification of legitimacy are guilty of a disservice to their audience. Even if the reporters refute the trend or ignore it, the propagandist can still push their disinformation on conspiracy-type platforms claiming that the mainstream media refuses to proclaim the truth.

Recommendation engines are another type of algorithm that is used to spread computational propaganda and disinformation. Content is suggested that is a draw for users and presents disinformation in a compelling manner. In simple terms, this is accomplished by content filtering. The users are shown content from a site or related to a topic that they already engaged with and like. Another version is based on collaborative filtering. It is a type of algorithm filtering that informs the user of what people similar to a given user like. For example, pinning investment advice to banking corporations because investors are often interested in dealing with reputable companies.

Conspiracy theories thrive on social platforms via recommendation engines because the best predictor of belief in one conspiracy theory is belief in another conspiracy theory. Researchers share a troubling concern that recommendation engines on social networks may be suggesting increasingly extreme content to users who are most prone to be accepting and socially affected.

Algorithms are designed to process simple social signals. They do not assess factual accuracy. There is no ethical drive to recognize the negative consequences of extreme propaganda. In summary, curatorial algorithms can be manipulated to lean toward producing a specific result. The use of human editing can also lend itself to bias. This was the case when Facebook eliminated human editors from an oversight role on its trending topics list after allegations that the humans were biased against conservative media.

The original belief that the web would act in a procedurally neutral manner in establishing access to world information and thus give everyone a voice seems lost in today's reality. By design, incentive technology has developed a manipulative system that is being heavily utilized by propagandists. It applauds political sentiment over factual accuracy. Accurate content is no longer a goal. Social algorithms are now in place to manipulate how people view what is being talked about. Topics are numerous, with most propaganda focusing on social issues that have high emotional appeal: LGBTQ rights, political affiliation and beliefs, religion, and Second Amendment rights among others. When the propaganda is very shareable, the user participation is very high.

Social media can have a huge impact on social communication and political discourse. We increasingly find political and social discourse that employs the use of digital media and automated scripts for social control. Computational propaganda via algorithms has become one of the most concerning impacts of technology innovation. Both social and issue-focused groups are particularly susceptible to disinformation campaigns and are being targeted with computational propaganda. The targeting of these groups will continue and potentially worsen. The purpose of computational propaganda is to make unpopular opinions appear to be more popular in social media conversation, as well as stifle and erase the influence of underrepresented groups essential to the functioning of democracy. Regardless of whether propaganda is foreign or domestic, motivated by ideology, politics, or profit, citizens must be prepared and educated in order to deal with the challenges of this concern every single day.

If we are not vigilant and educated with respect to this problem, the idea of an information ecosystem controlled by a central authority that dictates what the information audience sees and hears may in fact become a reality. In the twenty-first century, it is truly a job to distinguish truth and opinion. *Every* media outlet is guilty of distracting their audience, to some degree, through computational manipulation. Algorithms are inadvertently becoming an invisible controlling entity that influences audiences in the millions.

The digital age has ushered in a new form of artistic expression: the meme. It is impossible to discuss current-day propaganda on the social web without the mention of memes. The term was coined in 1976 by Richard Dawkins in *The Selfish Gene*. He wrote, "We need a name for the new replicator, a noun that conveys the idea of a unit of cultural transmission, or a unit of imitation."

Memes are cultural magnets. They adhere to and become part of the body of a society and rapidly transmit from person to person while undergoing adaptive mutations. Memes can be icons, catchphrases, pictures, lyrics, or anything that individuals can immediately recognize and that the audience can apply to other scenarios. For example, memes involving "Winter is coming"—a phrase from the *Game of Thrones* series—are used by thousands of people to describe any situation of impending upheaval among other things. "Make America Great Again" has led to the creation of a multitude of memes. It has become an extremely fast and mobile meme generator.

Digital visuals, such as memes, are easily produced, mass-disseminated, and effectively used as a cultural stimulant, with the potential to alter personal outlooks of American politics and society. They are intended to alter the way an audience feels about an issue or a person. They can reach a mass audience with images and digital art to advance a political cause.

On the surface, memes may seem harmless, but they pose a psychological impact on audience outlook. No one is immune to propaganda. It spreads quickly with the tap of a finger and becomes viral through the power of mass dissemination. It is too early to tell if memes will become a permanent fixture in our culture, but for now, we are still experiencing the effects.

Memes seem harmless, but they stand for information which can have an impact on people. They are popular, and people enjoy using and sharing them. They feel comfortable to use, and their message is without question understandable. Researchers believe that they can change individual and group behavior, attitudes, and values. They easily mold into our information discussions and convey specific meaning, a limited descriptive message capable of being understood thoroughly with minimal effort.

Person-to-person transmission and social virality tools enable them to spread easily and jump from group to group, evolving and changing as they do. They can solidify cultural ideas and attitudes and are ideologically identifiable as to meaning. They turn ideas into emotional epithets. They have staying power and are readily viral. They quickly become part of our cultural language at digital speed. Memes are a propaganda of the digital age.

They are such a powerful tool that highly authoritarian governments ban memes. Their use to make fun of a politician does not exist in this kind of government structure. Ridicule is one of the most successful methods used to break a powerful brand or cut down a symbol of authority. Meme culture is extraordinarily adept at ridicule. Meme warfare takes control of and exemplifies the feelings used in dialogue, narrative, and Internet social media.

It could be said that trolling is the social media equivalent of psychological warfare, and memes are one of the weapons of choice. A *troll* is someone who starts arguments and quarrels among audience members on the Internet to upset the viewer and initiate discord by posting inflammatory messages to an online audience. Trolling campaigns are also used to silence opposing voices. Campaigns appear to be spontaneous and sporadic, but they are nothing of the sort. They harness hate to persecute, terrorize, and discredit. Aggressive trolls deliver false information capable of targeting individuals to initiate confrontational behavior. They build on a feeling of fear and apprehension that is already, to some extent, present in their audience. The intent is to provoke readers into an action through the elicitation of emotional responses which are part of the troll's agenda and purpose and sometimes reinforced through the use of memes.

Generally speaking, one of the key problems in the information game is trying to decipher fact from fiction. Computational propaganda, trolls, memes, and influence agendas are inexpensive to utilize, but they appear to be an effective method to get a "compromised" truth to an audience. The infrastructure itself has a very difficult time trying to stop them after developing a life of their own. Therefore, we have terrorist networks, politicians, various ideologues, conspiracy theorists, and individual Internet users able to create and distribute propaganda; and it is very difficult to remedy this online manipulation. If democracy depends on an informed nation, then the increase in confrontational-oriented behaviors is a definitive problem.

Who's at the Helm?

When it comes to verifying truth and authenticity, there appears to be very few people at the helm. There is an epidemic of propaganda on social media, and we must be knowledgeable about the effects and social ramifications of the biases that propagandists spew out. Tensions have been created and are being fostered. One just needs to tune into media to see how invasive compromised truth and biased fact reporting have become.

There are also human biases that are compounding the problem. I believe that if the situation is left unaddressed, propaganda will become a news reporting norm in itself. We are deluged with information. The content is enormous; therefore, platforms decide what we will see in the time we allot to them. To be fully informed with the true facts of an issue, we need to allocate sufficient attention to the subject at hand and utilize our analytical skills. How does the description of an issue conform to the worldview of the platform as well as our own worldview? People have an emotional response to certain content, and the simple and yet successful algorithms of the curatorial administrators serve up content that meet with the acceptance of a targeted audience.

Computational propaganda is fueled by the enthusiasm of the audience who are receptive in receiving it. This welcoming audience spreads the message on digital platforms such as Facebook and Twitter. No need to meet in a public square or street. Digital facts are becoming irrelevant. False news reaches more people than the truth. In addition, it is disseminated faster than the truth. Power lies in the speed of dissemination. If you control the algorithms that decide on dissemination, you control the messages people get. Message control lies in the hands of a small number of persons who understand the mental processing and social bend of the audience. They are essentially guiding the world, and the audience is allowing it to happen. The viewers are essentially being exploited when it comes to social issues and, yes, to voting as well.

The owners of the platforms that created the algorithms are struggling to define their responsibilities. They grapple with the subtle distinctions between propaganda, disinformation, and misinformation; and they wish to be seen as having a neutral agenda and espouse their desire to maintain a commitment to free speech. The question of whether and how to present content is complex. There are, of course, First Amendment issues and protections. However, the platforms try to maintain that they are not information influencers. This is partially out of a commitment to the ideal of free speech, but also and more importantly, there is the desire to avoid the controversy of censorship allegations and bias that inevitably are brought to the forefront.

The platforms that power the information dissemination of a free and democratic society are much less vulnerable to censorship than the platforms that operate in an authoritarian regime. Commitment to free speech has made the platform managers hesitant in taking down disinformation and propaganda until they are concretely identified as such beyond any reasonable doubt. That hesitation gives the disinformation an opportunity to take root and gives propagandists an opportunity to infect their audience in the manner intended.

Conversations about fake news and the effects of computational propaganda are taking place in earnest now. Some people are taking the approach of stressing more media literacy and trying to educate people about how to avoid falling victim to disinformation. Organizations and activist groups are lobbying the platforms to take responsibility for reducing the supply of disinformation. Conversations with the engineers and decision makers who work at the companies are supposedly taking place to try to limit both disinformation and propaganda; and legislators are getting actively involved, considering legislation on a variety of issues from breaking up the platforms on antitrust grounds to improving privacy by restricting the gathering of personal data, as well as requiring the disclosure of automated accounts and bots to improve information transparency.

The primary problem with finding a solution is that the platforms themselves are individually controlled and the information managers only have the power to make changes in their own fiefdom. Some platforms are in a better position to make changes than others. This is because, although the problem is "systems" wide, each platform has a view of primarily its own data and very little concern of what is happening elsewhere. No central organization oversees the health of the information system in which two billion people get their news and information throughout the world.

Trust in the media is at an all-time low. Trust in authority figures is also at a low ebb. As the vulnerabilities in the media platform systems have become more obvious, we are seeing not only an erosion of trust in the tech platforms but also a rising suspicion of fellow audience members. People are accusing one another of being disingenuous simply because they disagree.

There has always been propaganda. But it has never been previously fostered by the use of an algorithmically designed science which deliberately targets an audience with precision. It is easy to produce and fairly inexpensive to disseminate. Polarized partisan politicians and extremists are pushing self-serving propaganda that is an assault on the very idea of objectivity. It is now necessary for our polarized politicians to present their alternative reality to information being presented.

The infiltration of propaganda in media is a distortion engine that colors the truth and facts to fit a personal narrative rather than enhance actual information that adds to analysis and clarity when a topic is discussed. Add to this a personal emotional equation, and we have all the ingredients to further distort the truth beyond the original audience. Technologies will continue to evolve, and the disinformation programs will continue as well. It is being enhanced by audio-and-video backup. After all, how can audio and videoed information be altered? The answer is it can and does happen. Video can be presented in such a way as to make us distrust what we see with our own eyes.

Facebook has a manipulated media policy in place that prohibits content that has been covertly edited in ways that would be unapparent to the average person. For example, videos that would lead viewers to believe someone in the video said words which in reality they did not say. It also prohibits videos that merge, replace, or superimpose content into a video in such a way that makes it appear to be authentic. This is a positive stance, but it raises the question of not only where to draw a line between acceptable and nonacceptable but also who will make that decision.

Over the past two years, YouTube has also become an increasingly viable pathway for spreading disinformation, most often through short videos that alter clips and photos from news outlets in order to present misleading narratives about major news events. These videos and the channels that post them are developed in a sole attempt to cause fear or animosity. YouTube has to develop tools to scrutinize content with the utilization of fact-checking sources. A method has to be created to inspect and label this kind of propaganda as to what it is—a cancer of hate and fear. They take advantage of the adage that a picture is worth a thousand words. In this case, it is videos that send a clearly intentional misleading message. We are left with the realization that words are an important aspect of communication, but a visual presentation can either enhance or bend the truth right before your objective eyes.

Election Impact

Social media plays a large role in elections, and the manipulation of social media can both affect a voter's perception of a candidate and compromise the voter's decision-making abilities. We all have an idea of right and wrong that helps us decide what and what not to believe. But that idea is influenced by the media we are exposed to. Today's news audiences get their basic information from media platforms that have separated themselves from reporting only basic facts and have now become immersed in news content and analysis. Political advocates may try to support their cause through active manipulation techniques.

Altering or manipulating polling numbers can affect a viewer's conclusion about candidate popularity. The use of biased sampling can produce a skewed result. Election polls that are slanted can serve two purposes: to alter the enthusiasm and confidence of a voter base and to affect the confidence of the political partners, fellow politicians, and political party of the targeted candidate. Viewers are first overwhelmed with biased information by the media outlet conducting the poll; and then a so-called opinion poll is conducted which, more times than not, reflect the biased reporting which took place previous to the poll.

A term used to describe platform manipulation is Google bombing, which is a type of Web spam that has had an impact on past elections. The impact is less effective now that search engines, including Google, have adjusted their ranking methods to defend against this kind of attack. However, Twitter bombing which creates a large number of Twitter accounts and sends a large amount of unsolicited tweets to unsuspecting users within a short period of time can potentially confuse voters, especially if it is done shortly before the elections.

Twitter bombing and astroturfing, which is a term used to describe a fake grassroots movement, have become common. This activity surges in the last week before an election, when there will be little time to refute claims. Voters should be aware of how misinformation can influence our thinking, and they should be ready to use their common sense to decide whether they should trust what they are hearing. Critical thinking is as important a skill now as it ever has been, and it should be an important part of media analysis According to the presidential opinion polls a year before the election, the 2020 presidential campaign was over. At that time, Newsweek reported the latest FOX News poll concerning the future 2020 election, showing that President Donald Trump was losing to every Democratic front-runner including Joe Biden, Bernie Sanders, and Elizabeth Warren. The problem is that polls taken so far out from an election are seldom a good indicator of outcome. But that bit of information is never voluntarily offered to the audience.

The FOX News poll described above was not actually conducted by FOX but instead was the work of an outside research company, Beacon Research and Shaw and Company Research. Calling it a FOX News poll was part of the propaganda, meaning that if Trump's favorite news network thought his electoral prospects were in the dumpster, then it must be really impossible for Trump to be reelected.

The poll was based on about a thousand random registered voters. More than one hundred and twenty million plus people voted in the previous election. Another fact is that only about half of registered voters actually vote. Newsweek reported that Biden had a double-digit lead on Trump at the point where he was the most popular Democrat in the field. Bernie Sanders was at number two in beating Trump. Third-place Elizabeth Warren was polled to defeat Trump as well in the hypothetical matchups.

However, the survey used also asked, "Do you think Donald Trump will be reelected president in 2020, or not? By a 46-40 margin, those surveyed answered yes. Despite their preference for anyone but Trump, the plurality believed that Trump would be reelected. It is not surprising the survey didn't ask if respondents believed that Russia would hack the election again as they were purported to do in 2016 with Trump's blessing. Many Democrats actually refused to believe this story was untrue even after it was debunked two years later. Some news anchors still believe it happened with no substantiated evidence to support that belief.

Surveys are as good as their samples. It goes without question to say that if you asked who was the favorite candidate for president at a Trump rally, the results will be diametrically opposite of the above poll. A fair survey of American voters' political preferences should reflect the approximately equal split in political affiliation of voters between the two major parties as reflected in the last election. The so-called FOX poll did not select a representative sample. The political identification of participants was heavily weighted toward Democrats by 49–39 percent, a ten-point difference. That would make the poll's fourteen-point lead for Biden over Trump at the time dwindle down to four points and within what is described as the margin of error.

This poll is not the only example of the propaganda used at that time. A Quinnipiac poll came out with the announcement that every major 2020 Democrat would beat Trump by at least nine points. It's all over, folks. Trump might as well not run at all according to Representatives Adam Schiff and Jerry Nadler.

At the same moment in the time line, left-leaning Vanity Fair proclaimed that Trump was losing his mind over another bad FOX News poll. But I never saw a Trump interview where he seemed fazed at all. There were contrary polls out there as well. Rasmussen, the most accurate pollster in the 2016 election, in a daily presidential tracking poll taken near the same time, had Trump at a 52 percent total approval percentage, compared to only 46 percent for President Obama at the exact same point in his presidency. Some pollsters describe Rasmussen as having a pro-GOP bias. Perhaps this is because Rasmussen wasn't part of the onslaught of pollsters that predicted a Hillary Clinton landslide victory.

In a review of Gallop poll results in comparing Obama and Trump, we will find that President Obama began his administration with a much higher job approval rating compared to President Trump. But while Obama gave us his namesake takeover of health care and Trump gave us an economic boom with record low unemployment for three years, polls showed Trump with a 43 percent job approval rating compared to Obama at only 40 percent during the same point in their presidencies, thus confirming the Rasmussen poll. As we all know, the economic boom was shattered by COVID-19 in 2020.

Propaganda is information put out oftentimes by political media allies to push an agenda and influence people rather than to inform them. Much of mainstream journalism today falls into the category of propaganda, with the media presenting only part of a story or fabricating news entirely in order to further their political cause.

Recent examples include baseless accusations against Supreme Court Justice Brett Kavanaugh, accusing him of sexual assault, omitting the fact that the accuser had little factual knowledge of the events in question, or that presidential lawyer Rudy Giuliani covertly met with Ukrainian officials, omitting the fact that there was a controversy as to whether the US State Department had asked him to do so. Story lines can be just as misleading as the story itself if all the information surrounding the story is not brought out into the open and more importantly—verified.

In 2016, on the evening of Election Day, after most voting across the country was completed, one of the top news outlets, the New York Times, was still determined to push its disinformation agenda and perhaps keep a few western state Republicans from voting before their precincts closed. Ignoring reality, the New York Times stated without any hard facts or evidence that Hillary Clinton had an 85 percent chance of winning the election she had all but lost.

Federal government efforts to protect Americans from foreign propaganda have been hampered by a host of factors, including the fact that false information protected by free speech isn't inherently illegal in the US and US intelligence agencies haven't traditionally been tasked with directly countering foreign influence efforts. The

US Intelligence Community should not and does not serve as the content police for American consumers of social and or news media.

A lack of action at the federal level has prompted many states to develop their own programs designed to counter outside influences from foreign countries to undermine American democracy. It would be a much better idea to educate the next generation of voters starting in our schools. The message that must be instilled in our youth is not to trust the Internet without checking the sources of the information presented. The biggest issue facing the American people is trust in the election process.

The intention of all election material is to convince the voter to cast a ballot in one way. There is probably no easier area to expose propaganda than in politics. Campaign content is deliberately designed to influence the electorate to the outcome desired by the authors of the material. The material is formulated to induce a voter to choose a specific candidate for the office in question.

As a result, elections create a highly manipulative environment, whereby the widely unsuspecting public becomes increasingly prone to influence. Polling, propaganda, fear based on social concern, and fake news are all methods of manipulation, to which we are all vulnerable. Countercomplaints about political claims being false and misleading without truth or accuracy are less informational and educational and appeal rather to emotion. That is why it is important to be aware of the techniques so far discussed that are used in modern political campaigning to win your vote.

What you hear, see, or read can influence what you do in the voting booth. A good amount of what you see and hear in election coverage has become more and more infatuated with a concern for style rather than substance, with persona over substantive issue. Marketing consultants are becoming a dominant part and indispensable part of election campaigns. Together with the policy statements and campaign promises, today's political landscape is loaded with disinformation and deception that is intended to mislead the public. To be able to sort out the unspun fact-based information, as well as real news versus fake news, is truly a learned skill in this day and age.

As Thomas Jefferson once said, an informed citizenry is vital to a free society.

In summary, political campaigns utilize methods intended to persuade and influence the public. Every election utilizes both misdirection and spin to manipulate. Strategies such as rigidly scripted stump speeches and staged photo ops are designed to stir political feelings and garner support for the candidate the information supports. We are pretty good at seeing through promises and campaign antics to win votes, but, as mentioned earlier, today's candidates and other political players are utilizing new methods to influence the online electorate. Well-known newspapers run articles promoting certain candidates over others without disclosing their political agenda and connections to certain political action committees (PACs). And false quotes continue to circulate on social media. Many of these tactics are very simply propaganda: emotionally manipulative claims and disinformation designed to influence voters' thoughts and actions.

Try to discipline yourself to pay attention to substance and issues rather than personality and emotional rhetoric. The purpose of verifying news content is to prevent the spread of truth decay. Think twice about emotional attacks and issues that tug at the heart. Rather, concern yourself with issues that tug at the mind, issues involving the long-term future of our nation.

Self-regulation should not replace enforceable regulation but must be part of the equation as well. Special consideration should be applied to the ethical presentation of public service media and the improvement of fact-checking services and credibility controls.

Truth versus Alternative Truths

When I hear the term "alternative truth" or "alternative facts" being used, I find myself at a complete loss. Just what is meant by the term? I believe its current meaning is to refer to another way of explaining something or analyzing something that leads to the exact same endpoint. In that case, perhaps a better terminology could be "alternative method of explanation" or "alternative viewpoint." The alternative would be better labeled as a theory or supposition.

But using the term "alternative truth" means that more than one truth exists in reaching a definitive conclusion. I find that hard to comprehend and believe the term is a poor choice for the purpose it is currently used for. The biggest problem is the term "truth." A precise definition of *truth* infers that there is one analysis that leads to one conclusion. There can be other viewpoints, there can be other explanations or theories, but there can only be one truth. And one can also say that truth can be fluid. Truth can be refined or even dismissed due to the disclosure of new research or information. This is a far cry from the concept of alternative truth or fact. All beliefs in a singular truth or fact are based on current and ever-changing limited information. A truth can change overtime with the discovery of new facts, but this results in a new singular explanation for the same observation, not an "alternative truth," which continues to give credibility to the original analysis.

Disinformation is introduced into media by injecting so-called alternative truths into the mix. The world of alternative truths are not truths at all but a complex maze of claims and counterclaims, where untruths spread with frightening speed on social media and spark angry backlashes from people who take what they read at face value. Controversial, fringe views can become the focal point of conversations through the power of search engines.

It is an environment where the mainstream media is constantly and repeatedly accused of peddling fake news by proponents of an alternate view. The audience is misled by the very media they rely on for accuracy in reporting. Even scientific research, a reliable basis for decisions, is often dismissed as having little value.

Because of our inner "fact bubble," we depend on a biased set of cognitive processes to arrive at a given conclusion. Our fact bubbles produce a natural tendency to choose only the facts that fit with our existing beliefs. They are a pervasive part of our cognition map. It keeps us on a particular path no matter what we come across on that map. It influences emotion, intuition, and judgment. We have the ability to rationalize; but when thoughtful and rational analysis interferes with our fact bubble, our thoughts, interpretations, and conclusions are often likely to only accept something as true if it supports what we already believe. The term "alternate truth" was created to aid and foster the symbiotic relationship between our inner fact bubble and the information we gather. But in reality, there is no such entity as alternative truth.

I believe that the most direct path to outsmarting propaganda's manipulative messages lies both in our self-analysis or self-awareness and empowerment through education. As voters begin to navigate the seemingly never-ending onslaught of campaign media and related online information, there are red flags we can all look for to sort fact from propaganda or the nonsense of alternative truths.

Propaganda simplifies a situation. If the facts are one-sided and do not present any counterarguments or facts, a strong possibility of disinformation exists. It presents an explanation as perfect or nearly so. It also uses our emotions and fact bubble against us, exploiting our weaknesses and deepest opinions. It is most likely at play if the message content makes you feel afraid and then conveniently offers a cure for that fear.

In order to engage the public to be more aware and be better equipped against disinformation, public discourse must be improved.

There must be a focus on the negative effect of disinformation on digital platforms and the development of ways to counter it. Even though more attention is being given to the subject of foreign interference and digital disinformation before elections, it is critical to continue raising awareness as well to biased internal public discourse and encourage the further development of fact checking when it comes to our elections. If done in a coordinated manner as information hits the platforms, it will lead to a stronger understanding of how the information we are receiving impacts the democratic process and will offer a clearer understanding of the actual facts.

As mentioned, adding to the problem is the fact that Russia and other foreign countries, including China and Iran, conducted influence activities and messaging campaigns targeted at the United States. And our country has been accused of the same thing. The Obama regime directed similar interference activities at Israel prior to the election of Benjamin Netanyahu which serves to point out that when it comes to political influencing, there are no innocent parties. In order to solve a problem, you must identify the source as cause. And that is what we are trying to say. There is an ongoing steady diet of data on all sides that push an agenda of propaganda both on the national and world level. It is causing a distrust in democratic institutions and a lack of confidence in the communication of truth.

Elections are not the whole story. Modern information operations are less discrete about attacks and concentrate more on a steady information influx that pushes negative and conspiracy-type agendas with the main purpose of causing chaos in democratic institutions. Not only is disinformation effective as interference with the election process, but it is also an assault on American citizens, aimed at undermining both the trust and confidence they have in their democratically elected government. It affects their trust in media, as well.

Once formulated and disseminated, it is almost impossible to completely eliminate digital disinformation spread through the use of what has been termed alternative truth on an open information platform. It develops a life of its own, and it becomes extremely difficult to recognize whether an information piece is either factual, semifactual, or an outright fairy tale.

Ambiguous disinformation which is continuously spread digitally across social media cannot be automatically regulated by the social media platforms they appear on. Of added concern is the question of where the line is drawn between addressing and correcting disinformation and being accused of limiting freedom of expression, a predominant cornerstone of our democracy which must be protected at all costs.

Even without the existence of disinformation and propaganda, there would still exist a level of division in our democratic society. Advocacy groups exist for pretty much every cause under the sun. And this I view as healthy. There is a rising trend of democratic dissatisfaction by citizens across the Western world which is resulting in the ever-increasing supply of social movements in the US. The goal of a democratic society is to pay attention to the grievances of citizens. If citizen discontent is not addressed and recognized by the governing authorities as a moral concern, disinformation is likely to be more effective.

Political disagreements should be analyzed as opposing and different points of view, rather than personal attacks on a political rival or opposing party. The role of a true democracy in this context is central in connecting our political institutions and governments with citizens.

But it is propaganda that is deceitfully amplifying division. Therefore, democracies should emphasize the need to continuously improve public discourse, encourage fact-based debates, and not accept unconnected information as an acceptable starting point. When a topic is discussed, be clear about defining an understanding of the issue. In other words, clear any ambiguity of what your point will be. State your position, and present the facts. For example, if your discussion centers around whether or not there is clear proof that General Mike Flynn (Trump's National Security Advisor) collaborated with the Russians, there is no need to talk about lying to the FBI or Vice President Pence. This is a separate issue and should be discussed as such. The debate should be solely centered on establishing verifiable proof that Flynn and Kislyak were furthering a corrupt alignment. No evidence has been found to support this claim.

The lying issue should be relegated to a separate discussion, as well as all the ramifications involved.

In March 2012, a conversation was picked up via an open microphone, in which President Obama is overheard telling Russian president Dmitri Medvedev that he would have "more flexibility" to negotiate on the missile defense issue after his November election. Even though this may be considered troubling and disconcerting, not much more can be gleaned from this conversation. And yet we heard on the media, Flynn is collaborating with the Russians and Obama is selling out America. These are not facts, folks, just unsubstantiated opinions.

Fake news threatens the democratic process itself. Having a large segment of the population misinformed and unshakably clinging to their own set of fake news facts and so-called alternative truths is absolutely devastating and extremely difficult to undo. Made-up news stories are a cause of confusion about the basic facts of current issues and events. Deciding who to trust and who not to believe has been a facet of human life since the beginning of complex societies. Politics has always had its share of those who will mislead to get ahead. But the difference today is how we get our information. The Internet has made it possible for many alternative voices to be heard. There should be a great concern about how we control the dissemination of information that has been poorly labeled, among other things, as "alternative truths."

Another observation worth mentioning is that the actual bona fide truth can sometimes have very little impact on what we believe. I can envision many family get-togethers where a political discussion ensues and winds up with someone saying, "I will believe what I believe, and you can believe what you believe." I say this because I have experienced it quite often. How is that for a scientific explanation? Seriously, I feel it is this impasse that has helped cause the use of the term "alternate facts." If I can't dispute what you're saying, I will develop another reason for the outcome. The simple explanation is that many people hold on very tightly to their personal fact bubble beliefs, and it is very difficult to get them to divorce themselves from those beliefs.

Misinformation and Alternate Viewpoints

The use of disinformation in democratic systems is not a new phenomenon. The central strategy and goal to counter disinformation is to develop a robust public discourse that ultimately will lead to the exposure of fake, polarizing, misleading, and extreme content. The healthier that a public debate is, the more likely it is that citizens will not be manipulated into believing information that has been created or narrated to create distrust and spread propaganda. The challenge is to have relevant and evidence-based debates.

To help develop a better scrutiny of disinformation, we also need to improve deterrence, increase resistance, and develop a strong ethic barrier. International and domestic organizations should improve coordination mechanisms between different agencies of government in order to protect all citizens from false information about issue-based concerns and grievances. Educators who teach the youngest generation of future voters have a responsibility to be unbiased in their presentations, and the same goes for representatives of the private sector, particularly in social media platforms.

Improved coordination between all information media in democratic societies would help prevent the spread of disinformation and help ensure that new technologies cannot be used to undermine our democracy or regulate content. We must continuously raise awareness in a coordinated manner with governments sharing their information and experiences. It would be part of a long-term effort that goes beyond election periods and continuously focuses on disinformation activities. It includes enhanced media literacy and other skills necessary for life in a world of growing digital information.

Many commentators named the breakdown of trusted sources of information as one of the most pressing problems in the news world today. Without, at least, a shared starting point or facts that an audience with otherwise different viewpoints can agree on, it is difficult to discuss any of the concerns that the world faces. Misinformation is absolutely devastating and extremely difficult to cope with in finding consensus on an issue. Many leading researchers, tech companies, and fact-checkers have written about the threat posed by the spread of misinformation. Disinformation and propaganda are signs of deeper social and cultural problems in our society, and the media environment must do their part in presenting an unbiased account of facts.

Reputation must be considered as an important factor when it comes to figuring out whom to believe and what to believe. It has to play a more dominant role when looking at the reliability and veracity of information. Inaccurate information is a regular occurrence on many websites, and weeding out the real facts may come down to carefully checking the reputation of the materials source. My father used to say that if you lie to him, that's okay. But if you lied to him and you expected him to believe it, then you really are insulting his intelligence. This may be a good mind-set for all of us to have. Links to websites masquerading as reputable sources are appearing on social media sites like Facebook where information shared has had little or no background check as to its veracity. It seems that for every fact, there is a counterfact. There are times when counterfacts and the actual facts look almost identical with the main difference being in its analysis.

Those behind the made-up stories who share them widely on social media reap a financial benefit. They may receive a portion of the advertising revenue that comes from clicks as people follow the links to their webpages. Social media has made it easy to find others who share your worldview. In the past, it was harder for fringe opinions to get their views widely recognized. Personal debates were the norm prior to digital media. But such debates are occurring less frequently. In minutes, information is spread around the world with the potential to reach billions of people. It is certainly true that it can be rejected with a stroke on a keyboard. However, most of us choose to engage with information that reinforces our existing beliefs, and we zoom in on the material that corroborates those beliefs. It results in information being reiterated in an echo chamber of preexisting viewpoints. It simply comes down to this—if you agree with me, I believe you. If you don't agree with me, you are lying. On top of this, the public views what politicians and government tell them with increasing skepticism.

The challenge here is how to change this behavior, to get the audience to be open-minded and questioning. One approach that has been tried is to challenge facts and claims when they appear on social media. Organizations like Full Fact, for example, look at persistent claims made by politicians or in the media and try to correct them. This approach may not be the best solution where social media is involved. Those that spread misinformation far outnumber those who try to correct it. A correction does not spread as rapidly as the misinformation itself. There is also a lack of overlap in the audiences spreading misinformation and the audience trying to correct it, most especially when it comes to political issues.

Political entities can promulgate disinformation, pay for the advertising space, and put it in front of a huge media audience; and the viewer who sees this and is not part of their target audience remains unsuspecting. Social media is the most powerful advertising platform that has ever existed. There has never been a time when it has been so easy to advertise to an audience of millions and at the same time have others outside that audience take notice. Yes, there are strict rules on what can be advertised, particularly when it comes to political advertising. But misinformation and disinformation continue to impact via media platforms. There is a lack of transparency and media scrutiny.

Some media sites are already in the process of trying to remedy this situation. There is a concern about the spread of disinformation, misinformation, and polarizing effects on social media. The media platforms and tech giants are trying to reduce spam sites that profit off fake stories and add tools to make users more aware of fake stories. Google is working on ways to improve its algorithms, so they take accuracy into account when displaying search results.

Determining which pages on the Web best answer a request for information is a challenging problem. Some improvements to algorithms that help the user search for more high-quality, credible content on the Web is being undertaken. The creation of automated fact-checkers that will monitor claims made on media is another plus, the targeting of claims that have not already been fact-checked by humans and sending out automatic corrections if necessary.

Needless to say, there is a long way to go to remedy this problem. There is a need in media for higher moral standards. A number of different groups around the world are working on an automated fact-checking system. They include IBM, Indiana University, and other groups as well. As improvements in AI continue to progress, this corrective measure will become even more accurate and sophisticated. All in an attempt to help the Internet audience distinguish what is true from either misinformation or disinformation.

But in summary, an algorithm is only as good as the people instituting them. Search algorithms can be flawed or flawless depending on the people who develop them. For now, and for the most part, users will continue deciding what they believe without fact-checking and without seeing both sides of an issue. They will probably continue to be unopen about discussing issues and venturing outside their own isolated view parameters. It is crucial that constructive debates come to the forefront of any discussion. There is a need for agreement on commonly accepted facts that people can use as a starting point in debate.

More respect for alternative viewpoints is very much needed. The best way to accomplish this may be in small steps through perspective taking, moving audiences outside their comfort zone but by small info increments rather than an all-out alternate viewpoint. Steps needed when discussing viewpoints are better scrutiny to check veracity of information as accurate and then an analysis and self-awareness by the audience concerning the bubble of facts that each member surrounds themselves with; and only then will the audience be better equipped to come to a more open-minded and thoughtful conclusion in a discussion.

The fact remains that part of the problem rests with audience bias. This has never been more evident than in family circles. Families should be a center of cohesiveness. Yet some families experience quite a bit of anger when they discuss media information from the comfort of their fact bubble which many times are in direct conflict with the fact bubble of another or other family members. Nothing like the game show Family Feud but real outright and overt anger. Some families have a problem dealing with their own "public relations."

The communications revolution has brought about a massive, worldwide proliferation of debatable information. We are overwhelmed by more messages than the human mind can possibly pay attention to. Our minds are assaulted by a large array of information about politicians, political programs, doctrines, repeatedly advertised commercial products, morality viewpoints, ecological disasters, and military clashes. The audience is tuning out to much of this discourse, and the overload of information can be expected to reach even higher levels in coming generations.

In order to deal with this information onslaught, audiences have developed, either consciously or unconsciously, the formulation of defense mechanisms—selective attention and selective recollection—when it comes to what is viewed on media. Large portions of the messages that the viewer finds contrary to facts in their bubble are ignored. That is why there is such a push to determine audience preference in viewing. Media wants to know the makeup of the choir they want to preach to. The best audience is the one that likes you even before the show begins.

People as a rule gravitate to communication not because they want to learn something new or reconsider their own fact bubble viewpoint but because they seek psychological reaffirmation about their existing fact bubble beliefs. When the propagandist gets their attention by delivering a message the audience already believes, they find it that much easier to hold that attention. They must formulate the message so as not to stray very far from what the audience already believes. The fact is that the most skilled propagandists are the ones who start out with a very modest goal which is to deliver a message in such a way that much of it is familiar and reassuring to the intended audience. Propaganda that aims to generate ideas with a focus on large changes as a goal is certain to become an information battle.

The most effective media is the one that makes the audience feel secure in their beliefs. Anything that reinforces and protects their fact bubble makes the audience feel right at home with the media content they are viewing. In this case, the media content amplifies what the audience already believes. They are sure to receive a certain degree of positive emotional feedback and personal protection. The propagandist goal is to have this audience spread their message for him. By concentrating on a receptive audience, they increase their chances of reaching many more possible converts when that audience relays the message to others in their sphere of influence.

As with every audience, the participants cannot be conveniently placed in one apple cart. There are those who are predisposed to the message, but there are also some who can be categorized as indifferent and some who are opposed to the messaging. The extremes are a catalyst for furthering divisions in our country. As already discussed, propaganda is most likely to evoke the desired responses among those already in agreement with the propagandist's message. Those who are neutral to the message are minimally affected if at all. Those opposed to the message seek other assurances that reinforce their fact bubble.

The news is concentrating a lot of messaging on examples of civil disobedience lightly veiled as freedom of speech. The aim is to generate a climate of social pressure for change, but in reality, it is reinforcing divisions in culture and is reaching a very attentive audience through propaganda—either the extremes of those in agreement or those opposed to the messaging. Cultural divisions are reinforced by this approach. However, there are times when this type of action goes well beyond decency and has a backfiring effect which we see all too often.

Media is deluging the audiences with all kinds of disinformation or, at best, misinformation. As mentioned, there is an undeniable connection between the beliefs in one's fact bubble and the type of media information a person exposes himself to. Most people put a lock on their fact bubble door when it comes to allowing alternate viewpoints to enter. This is more or less "human nature." Propaganda reinforces a strong resistance to "perspective taking" (the cognitive capacity to consider the world from another individual's viewpoint). A resistance builds up through constant propaganda reinforcement that insinuates itself deep down into the audience's mind. Another way of putting it is that most people are "set in their ways." As a result, there is much to be learned by studying the "setness" of an audience. A research device developing a center stage for the propagandist is information gathering. The object is to obtain a great deal of data about your lifestyle, beliefs, value systems, media habits, opinions, and even heroes and role models. The propagandist hopes to use this knowledge in devising ways to better influence their audience. They are looking for the best way to either reinforce or alter your viewpoint.

The study of propaganda has somewhat been attempted through the scientific method, but cost factors and questionable experimental parameters among other things do not lend to this method as being the best means of measuring and studying the process. The best method of studying the effects of propaganda may be through extensive observation, guided by rational theory and conclusions. And this is the current strategy being imposed on all of us. Everything we do is subjected to enhanced scrutiny for one reason or another. A tremendous amount of data to influence the effectiveness of political propaganda can be obtained through checking voting results and voter parameters. Political inferences may be able to be made by audience member attitude toward other topics of importance such as health care or climate change. The propagandist can at least make reasonably dependable quantitative measurements of the reception of his propaganda or that of others. By quantifying data about their message, they can bring a high degree of precision into play using various messages aimed at the same results. They can also increase the probability of acceptability of information and opinions attributed to different sources.

The use of counterpropaganda as a tool to suppress propaganda is only effective when it has substance—facts that undermine the credibility of the propagandist. To see this in action, one only has to tune into some of the major media networks. Sometimes, it is reminiscent of the Hatfields and the McCoys. Those of you in my generation know what I'm pointing out. The generalities and name-calling that we as an audience are subjected to is either too unintellectual or too abstract to really have an effect on most individually held fact bubbles. The main result is that it acts as a catalyst to further divide our culture rather than change viewpoints. In any case, with propaganda and counterpropaganda, there are no winners, only losers as far as the audience goes. It's a battle in which both approaches are trying to estimate in advance their opponents' strategy and capability and working to develop countermeasures against their measures.

In an ideal world, there would be no need for propaganda. Dependable and relevant information would be presented in a non-biased manner by public-spirited and uncensored news organizations and educational platforms. But let's get back to reality and put utopian philosophy on the back burner. Let's deal with what we have. The assumption is that if propagandists are free to continuously and publicly ply their trade, eventually the best ideas for society will make their way to the forefront through investigative instinct and questioning. But to attain this result, certain requirements need to be in place. The majority of audiences in general would have to be reasonably well-educated, public-minded, analytical, and most importantly have an ability to look and investigate facts outside their own fact bubble. And this last requirement is where the problem creeps in. Instead, it seems we have audiences that are, at best, mostly either confused or alienated by the type of communication they are subjected to if it does not agree with their predetermined set of beliefs.

One way used to influence a viewpoint is through a more indirect third-party approach. A PAC is a popular term for a committee organized for the purpose of raising and spending money to elect and defeat candidates. Most PACs represent business, labor, financial, or ideological interests. In an effort to guard against hidden propaganda, PACs are required to declare and name their organization so as to somewhat uncover the motive behind the message. They are basically lobbyist groups. They are the cheerleading team at a football game. They serve a purpose which is to influence morale and support for the team they represent. But, in reality, they add no substance to the game and are only trying to influence your viewpoint for their financial or political gain. Their agenda is obvious and biased in one direction. The success of such PACs, however, depends on the message and the audience.

The same goes for political advertisements in newspapers. Who are the moneymen behind the ads? Political advertisements both in newspapers or on television are required to include the name of the person or group responsible for the ad, but that person or group may be a straw man for the actual individual or organization backing the advertisement or message. The same goes for foreign organizations who register with the government to engage in message dissemination. It is difficult to know whether the forms filed are truthful or correct or tell the whole story about the sponsoring group. When we are offered a stock, bond, or bank opportunity, the originator, by law, is clearly spelled out for us. We know who is disseminating the information and what organization it is coming from. This type of disclosure, sadly enough, is not often applied to PACs, media advertisements, or propaganda. True disclosure can be easily circumvented. Quite often, these activities are generated by the Lone Ranger, or someone who wears a mask. There are times, however, when we discover who is really behind that mask.

There is a need for unbiased consumer research organizations, either privately or publicly supported, to examine the claims fostered in the messaging we are subjected to. There are standards in place requiring equal time and space in political campaigns when it comes to answering oppositional accusations or statements. And that's a good thing. There should also be a mechanism in place to increase exposure for even the underfunded in the political arena.

It may also be constructive to limit all political advertisement for a short period prior to major elections to allow for unencumbered voter reflection. Your viewpoint is extremely important, and any change should come from an unbiased reflective process that is owned solely by you.

Culture, Propaganda, and Fact Bubbles

Propaganda most commonly uses nonlogical distortions in its efforts to persuade—especially attacks on issues or persons that conjure strong emotional appeal. It often includes falsehoods, and it's almost always one-sided. Facts and information are distorted and manipulated. It is something we are exposed to on a daily basis be it recognizable or not. It was and always has been a part of our culture.

Social platforms and media news platforms are marketing machines for ideas, philosophies, government, politics, products, and much more. Government decision making is preceded by a healthy dose of propaganda. The link between media platforms and governing body philosophies is without question. What would be the best way to go about investigating the impact of propaganda? The prime approach to examining how it works may be by tuning into the various news platforms for a day.

Propaganda follows a strategy of cause and effect with propaganda taking on the role of cause. A cause can serve as the catalyst for the effective use of a propaganda agenda. It filters through our media platforms and governmental institutions and, to an ever-increasing extent, through our social interactions as well. It is easier to approach a subject simply through exposure rather than a deep analysis. The fact remains that the media is preoccupied with propaganda.

We live in an ever-changing society where values are not at a high point in the realm of moral standards. Propaganda gets it fuel and energy from the pervasive uncertainty of values in our present-day culture. Our world order is becoming more and more complex, and propaganda is utilized as a panacea and a mechanism to clarify. The media is becoming a judgment tool by utilizing techniques with the main purpose of building a compliant audience in their struggle for social acceptance and power. All propaganda gets its validation through its rationale which is to achieve a democratic end. But the techniques utilized are truly irresponsible as they foster division rather than a democratic purpose. Unbiased truth is being replaced by the use of such techniques as defamation of character, so-called alternate truths, and negative extrapolation that goes well beyond universal fact. Taking a stand against propaganda will involve unlearning what has become considered as normal.

Social media plays a major role with respect to discussing issues of major public concern. The platforms not only map and prioritize the issues for us but are also kind enough to remove the job of analysis out of our hands. Along with both the analysis and processing of information, we can observe a high tolerance for presentations that are less than ethical. Quite often, through repetition, we are encouraged to buy into the ideology of an exploitive business model. When it comes to ethics and reporting news, the bar has been lowered both in media and print.

With ethical behavior, we all have our own personal placement for that bar. But the responsibility of media in setting a high standard of ethics cannot be overemphasized. We cannot raise or lower the bar as a reaction to the practices of another group or media source. Media platforms have a responsibility in choosing what is morally right over what is morally wrong. Their actions affect the way the audience thinks. They wield an enormous power, and with that comes an enormous responsibility. Propaganda has the ability to divide, to persuade otherwise reasonable people to accept facts, issues, and substance through the lens of a "purpose" agenda held by the social platform involved in the reporting. In the media world of politics, national media coverage has become almost issue-free. Most of what the public sees reported are the character flaws of the politicians involved in the report. It has become more important to report on who is ahead and who is behind in the polls. Facts, issues, and substance are all largely ignored.

Coverage focuses on name-calling of the worst kind, unsubstantiated rumors, sensationalized details, and nonsubstantive issues. During the 2016 election, both major presidential candidates consistently attacked each other for using slanted truths and outright propaganda. Both candidates were the victims of outrageous fake news that went viral. Search engines were awash with this kind of rhetoric.

The media did an inadequate job of curtailing propaganda in the 2016 political campaign and in informing the electorate with respect to substantive policy issues. As previously mentioned, the audience needs to educate themselves so that they can vote as informed individuals. We need to demand accountability from both media platforms and from the candidates themselves. This is not only essential for the continuance of our democracy; it is essential for the continuance of our civilized society.

Propaganda influences attitudes, beliefs, and behaviors. Ideas, information, or fake news are spread for one specific purpose—to legitimize the beliefs of those doing the spreading. It is evolving into a science capable of influencing much larger audiences utilizing a simpler method—through its constant reiteration on media platforms. In politics, candidates are using propaganda techniques to gain an advantage over the opposition. It involves the use of a multimedia approach to spread its message, including the Internet, press, radio, and television. The purpose or goal is to shape people's opinions. Those who control the media platforms have a front-row seat advantage when it comes to the potential control of public opinion.

To foster disparaging and negative messaging aimed at political candidates, the use of digital disinformation campaigns are playing a prominent role. Disinformation and hostile digital propaganda are causing chaos and polarization, and it is asymmetrical on both sides of the aisle. If the American people do not address this issue, it will continue unchecked. The cyber world is the new battleground for serious competition between politicians and voters as well. The techniques that are being utilized on the digital battlefield include data collection, influencing voter behavior, destroying the public trust, and creating echo chambers for the proliferation of disinformation. All the things that ultimately can undermine a democracy are being employed by the propagandist.

It is crucial to the future of our democracy to develop enhanced capabilities to identify disinformation whether it originates internally or from foreign interference. Censorship is one tool at our disposal to counter disinformation, but it would be more beneficial and less controversial to focus more on the methods utilized by those who seek to manipulate information on media platforms and educate the audience with respect to those techniques that are utilized.

Propaganda is so powerful because it has become a part of our everyday lives. We live in a rapidly changing and complex world. To deal with the constant influx of information, we need shortcuts. We cannot recognize and analyze all aspects of the news in real time. We do not have the time or motivation to process all the information that comes before us. So we concentrate on triggers, how others perceive a piece of news. We either agree if it coincides with our fact bubble or disagree if it does not. This makes the audience highly susceptible to the propaganda. And it has more of an impact if it fits in with our personal fact library of preconceived outlooks.

Propaganda includes the reinforcement of those ideas and attitudes that are so deeply embedded within our own personal view. When it blends well with respect to our fact bubble, we lose sight of just what it actually is. An often-used ploy is to use an "expert" to validate a viewpoint. If the information is analyzed and found credible by an "expert," then surely it must be true. This person has the credentials and experience that make him an automatic source of the truth. It is this outlook that helps to make propaganda such a powerful tool. The ideology and purpose of the propaganda become secondary. The structure and beliefs of the organization to which the "expert" belongs is not part of our processing activity. The focus is on the message. And if it fits into our fact bubble, all the better. It is important to the propagandist that his message has an audience that understands, remembers, and acts upon that message. The bottom-line desired result is the same, whether it is the simple advertising of a product or the propaganda used to reinforce an idea.

Propagandists create acceptance of their message through the use of social proof. We process information by observing what other people feel who are similar to us and share our social norms. We are most likely to accept the actions of others in our own peer group as correct. This allows us to be persuaded by a common cause or ideology not entirely adopted by us at first. People look for justifications to quickly form many of their beliefs. Shared beliefs quickly allow one to assimilate and project the belief in question. We fundamentally like people who are similar to us and share our beliefs, values, and ideas. By instilling this connection, the belief becomes even more believable later even with little evidence or no evidence at all. Being connected with a philosophy or organization is enough to make the assertion pass the litmus test of veracity. Alternately, anything viewed as an unacceptable belief makes not only that belief unacceptable but also the media, group, or organization from which it originated. A statement becomes accepted or dismissed simply through association. This is literally an audience accepting information as truth simply through generalizations. We view the person centered around a news story by lumping him together with a group in such a way that takes away any individuality of that person. This is effective because it systematically blurs any distinction between an individual and the group offered as being associated with that person.

Even an indirect connection between a person and a group affects how we view the information presented by that person. A similarity between an individual and a group is established. There is a preestablished view with reference to the group. The individual inherits the same view as the one associated with the group. We are dealing with establishing social proof through paranoia. The audience is provided with information about the connection between an individual and a group that helps shape the presentation of the information to be more effective and help persuade people to think about the topic in a certain context.

There is always a reason information is presented in a certain format. It is to reinforce the philosophy of the media platform itself. This is not to say that all media information is unfair and unbalanced, but most of what is presented is agenda driven. The crucial point is that although information presented may be correct factually, the format in which it is presented, the specific analysis that is offered, and the connection to a broader ideology are what make it propaganda. This approach by media platforms adds to the ethical, social, and political problems of our nation. Those who control the media control the opinions of the people.

The media often shifts the focus of information reported from something bad to something good when it serves the ideology they wish to spread. It provides a reason for the information presented, despite its validity, in order for it to be accepted in a certain way. The rearrangement of facts and time lines is a significant method used to distort truth. They are good at subtly shifting focus in order to offer a speculation that coincides with their agenda. They often spin a fact or reality in a way that serves the purpose of the propagandist who has control of the media platform. This propaganda tactic of giving a self-serving justification as how to interpret information stems from the fact that most people simply like to have reasons or interpretations for what is taking place in the news.

In today's media, there is more to the presentation of information than the facts one uses. The way a fact is presented can slowly mold the understanding of the fact in a way that is supportive of the presenter's own thoughts on the subject. The audience is basically programmed to view a fact in a very specific light. The media does more than just presenting facts and information. We live in a fast-paced and complex world that is laddered with information. And the media can be very persuasive as to how we define that information. Even a slight, subtle difference in the explanation of a fact can change the context of what is being presented.

There are paths to find the truth. Truth can only exist when it's supported by verifiable fact. The best verifier is you. If it cannot be verifiable by you directly, then it should not be considered an absolute truth. It should be only considered a viewpoint or speculation. We should try to utilize a systematic, multisource approach to truth verification based on a process that enables us to effectively scrutinize numerous sources of information and separate factual truth from speculations.

Finding and sharing truth and solutions to restore integrity and trust in our country's economic and political systems have a most direct and meaningful impact on the lives of every human. It is important to be aware that the agenda or perspective of others can frame the problem or issue being presented. Accepting the specific framework of the presenter gives them a powerful advantage. Be aware of situational examples such as group beliefs, group norms, expertise of authority, polls, and slogans. Don't believe in simple solutions to a complex problem whether it be social or political. In the end, it must be remembered that it is okay to disagree with how a media story is framed.

An important aspect of all propaganda is the way information from media platforms is interpreted. How we respond to media is varied according to the mind-set we have prior to viewing. In other words, other factors intervene in the way the audience uses, perceives, and processes what they consume in the media. The interpretation of the content of a message is influenced by the "fact bubble" we all carry with us. As previously discussed, governments, corporations, and political parties have the unprecedented ability to process a copious amount of data about the individuals in their audience and then, through sophisticated algorithms, broadcast messages and images to influence that audience.

Our cultural references, fact bubbles, values system, ideology, family, friends, and other groups influence our interpretation of media messages and play a role in how we decipher information and entertainment on social networks. To some extent, we are a prisoner of the above factors which chain us to view digital media through a very narrow lens.

Debates about the influence of Facebook and companies like Cambridge Analytica reveal the importance of emotions not only in our private lives but also in our public outlooks concerning social issues and politics. The problem is magnified in terms not only of emotional manipulation but also in how those emotions come into play in how we relate and understand the world around us. Our feelings motivate us to select from the media presentation that which reinforces our preconceived notions. As previously mentioned, the use of algorithms is the media tool used by media platforms to better understand their audience. We expose our feelings on social media, sometimes with a strong need for recognition. The information gleaned by media about our "self-outlook" is quantified into a data network and transformed into affective algorithms.

Intellectual and emotional compliance is transforming us into addicts of our own emotions. We are at a point where technology is doing the thinking for us, and we are becoming very comfortable with this subtle change. We are losing the ability of introspection when it comes to why we watch and react to media platform information. Communication through technological outlets is more important than direct communication with family and friends. We rely more on technology than those around us. We are seeing, as a result, more isolation, individualism, and less social cohesion, which do not favorably forecast the survival of our democratic institutions.

The expansion of social media does not make us more intelligent or rational. We have more access to information and observe more public debates about issues that affect us both as individuals and as a society, but that doesn't mean we're looking at the big picture more logically or based on arguments that are accurately factual. So ask yourself, Are you open-minded or imprisoned in a *propaganda bubble?*

Diversity, Conformity, Purpose, Organization

There is an obvious dichotomy of ideologies ranging from an extreme in viewpoint to a more moderate stance. We hear very little about the moderate stance and much more about the extreme. There is quite a bit of dialogue about the preservation of diversity. But diversity has become less and less achievable. The coexistence of different ideologies is at stake. On one hand, there is a move to foster international integration even if it means our national security may have to be compromised. On the other extreme, we have the "America First" ideology which includes the semiembracement of isolationism.

In this ideological climate, the preservation of diversity faces quite a challenge. The social influence of media platforms on our culture cannot be ignored. With the mass interconnection of individuals within a social platform or platforms, one's feeling of individuality is at stake. Culture converges on the homogenous consensus of a society and individualism seems to be neither accepted nor fostered. The intent here is not to argue the pros and cons of international integration and cultural individuality. The premise is simply that social diversity is a cultural positive that should be preserved. And given this premise, which is not universally accepted and may never be, media should be looking into ways to somewhat preserve social diversity. Over time, our culture has fluctuated between embracing cultural individuality and homogeneous integration.

The media goal with respect to its audience is to create a more homogeneous viewpoint among its individual membership. This is fostered through programming concentrated on values, opinions, and ultimately attitude change. Common sense dictates that this is a much easier goal to achieve when individuals in the audience are more similar than dissimilar in their value systems. When a group has a similar value system, there is the added component of influencing and reinforcing each other. Add to this, the fact that the media is concentrating on the two extreme opposites and mostly ignoring the centrist area altogether. Research has shown that this is the sector where there is a mix between similarities and dissimilarities. Up to a point, in this grouping, there is both an achievement of similarity, as well as some conduciveness toward cultural diversity. This phenomenon is most observable in smaller group settings rather than larger ones, for example smaller neighborhoods rather than clustered megacomplexes.

Media has the ability to either foster cultural diversity or expand cultural homogeneity, and it mostly depends on the messaging. The idea that messaging comes from specific central authorities has an impact on acceptance. They act as central coordinating agents for the message. Digital media has become an information center on a variety of topics but centering mostly on political, social, and economic beliefs. Individuals can feel varying levels of loyalty to the media they view especially when the audience, for example, is part of a political party that shares the value of the media message.

Cultural diversity can only be sustained when media platforms are accepting of alternate viewpoints. Our democracy and democratic ideals still exert enough influence to slow down cultural patterns that would otherwise lead to a complete monoculture. Allowing influences from other ideologies and viewpoints to permeate media platforms would go a long way in promoting a healthy level of cultural diversity. It is unclear exactly how much diversity currently exists in our democracy, but what is easily observable is the amount of social change and attitude within our society.

The more the media exerts an influence on the way information is slanted and presented to an audience, the more it controls interactions between audience members with respect to beliefs and values and how they socially influence each other. Strong influence by a media platform can keep people with one belief system from associating with those who have a different belief structure which is what our society is currently experiencing when we talk about a "divided" country. The people are not divided, but the belief systems are. This leads to isolation and reduces assimilation. It becomes particularly obvious when we look at the impact on the institution of family. People are much less likely to interact around cultural or social beliefs with other family members who disagree with those beliefs. They relate more positively with the strangers within their peer audience and develop a distrust toward the general public and alternate political outgroups, causing an increase in social isolation and an unacceptance toward alternate outgroups.

In summary, media platforms show a tendency to adapt their message toward audience majority beliefs reinforcing the emergence and persistence of homogeneity among the audience. In the same instance, individually held beliefs are strengthened due to institutional reinforcement including the use of fake news and propaganda. The information feedback essentially becomes a symbiotic loop of social influence. The frequency and consistency of the message reinforces the desired outcome at both ends of this spectrum.

The purpose of propaganda, in general terms, is to directly influence opinions or actions and is initiated by either a group or individual to achieve a predetermined end and may also include the use of psychological manipulation. It is both psychological and sociological in construct. The first intention is to present an interpretation of a reality, and, most importantly, the second is to obtain a certain reaction.

The recipe for organizing propaganda requires a few choice ingredients—prepare a little disinformation, utilize the Internet, sprinkle a few social bots and blogs, top it off with some media platforms, and allow to simmer. The long-term effect of a continuous diet of propaganda is the altering of one's personality in various degrees. The idea behind it is to "convince" the audience or "influence" a specific way of viewing an event or situation. In today's media, propaganda most often is utilized as a weapon to foster political or social change.

The most effective force used is continuous repetition—hearing the same analysis over and over again. It attacks not only the way you think but also the way you feel. It targets your emotional sentiments. The most effective time to use it is when the audience is caught up in a national or world event where a mass interaction of feelings is predominant. If you allow it, it has the ability to consume your entire day and over time weakens resistance to the message. The goal is mass participation with the message either passively supporting it on a psychological level or actively if it mobilizes the audience to foster some form of response.

As previously discussed, the "fact bubble" of audience participants, when in agreement with the fundamental aspects of the message, makes the job of the propagandist much easier.

With propaganda, timing is everything. What is news today is forgotten tomorrow. I sometimes envy those in the audience who are either apolitical or have no opinion on a current event. They remain outside the grasp of propaganda. There is another group which can be labeled as undecided, and they form a large segment within an audience. They are very susceptible to control through propaganda. Since it veils the truth with falsehoods, interaction with this audience is a way of spreading the falsehoods.

Political propaganda involves methods utilized by governments, political parties, or pressure groups with the intention of changing the behavior of the media audience. The purpose is to foster a political ideology through specific tactics and strategies. Cultural propaganda, on the other hand, affects the audience through more of a shotgun effect—through movies, the arts, and literature.

Cultural propaganda seeks to develop conformity within an audience by an increase in the number of individuals whose behavior spreads the intended message, and thus imposes itself on even larger audiences. Essentially, it increases conformity within the audience that effectively will develop an increase of compliance with the social message or idea. The propaganda element is further generated and enhanced by the individuals in an audience who choose to further perpetuate the message either consciously or subconsciously in film, literature, or art. There is a certain degree of spontaneity with this type of propaganda. Most times, the aim is to simply have an effect on one's lifestyle. Again, the audiences' personal fact bubbles play an important role in the acceptance or rejection of the cultural message.

A person's lifestyle, as well, comes into play in determining the reaction. But here again, repetition of the message goes a long way in convincing an audience. With both political and cultural propaganda, there is a linear graphic correlation between the repetition of a message or idea and its acceptance. But one important stipulation for acceptance is that the message is a rational one. It should not be too far off the "beaten track." But most "good" propaganda do address common sense, reason, and experience when they present a belief to the audience furnishing supportive facts along the way. The ideal scenario is to have the belief remain in one's fact bubble long after catalyst for the belief has disappeared.

All types of propaganda require one important ingredient—organization. Be it violent or peaceful, organization is involved. There is always a catalyst. Most times, permits are required, advertising has to be put in place, literature has to be printed, signs have to be made, and transportation has to be organized. This kind of organization requires leadership, financial backing, and time. A question that we must be concerned with when witnessing a demonstration on media whether it be violent or cohesive is who was behind its organization.

There are some forms of propaganda, as witnessed in the media, that can lead to violence. This type is essentially an attack on established law and order and is almost always seen as a negative reaction by the masses. It is an attempt to provoke a movement in the masses through reaction to what is perceived as a crisis. The goals of this type of propaganda are often off the "beaten track" for most of the audience. There is an attempt to make the goals appear reachable, to draw individuals out of their fact bubbles, to influence people to act.

Listeners are not always consciously aware of their motivations, and quantitative approaches have yielded divergent findings that identify the harmful effects of hate speech. When either an individual or organization calls for revenge, reinforces extreme nationalist sentiments, utilizes negative stereotyping of other groups, or uses dehumanizing language in their demands for justice, they elicit either positive or negative acceptance.

At the psychological level, those who believe the world is an unjust place are more extreme politically at either end of the liberal conservative spectrum, and those engaged in watching violent media on a regular basis are more predisposed to justify violence. Male viewers are more susceptible to the effects of propaganda than females. Propaganda has demonstrable conditioning effects that lead to a greater liberal or conservative solidarity and opposition toward the other end of the spectrum, as well as promoting a greater tolerance toward violence against the opposing ideology.

Though the effect of hate mongering is difficult to assess, the goal is not to integrate society but rather to agitate society. This type of propaganda is usually short-lived. If the goals are not quickly obtained, enthusiasm quickly fades. The propagandist uses the emotion of hate to foster violent emotions and to act upon them. At the opposite extreme is the type of propaganda that brings society closer together. Cohesion propaganda as opposed to violence propaganda adheres closely to law, order, and cultural norms. It acts as a stabilizing force for society. It promotes an acceptable approach as a reaction rather than a violent one. This type of propaganda is the norm in our society; however, the violent type gathers more attention from media.

Conformity is a type of social influence involving a change in belief or behavior in order to fit within a group. This change can be a response to real or imagined group pressure. It can also be defined as being a positive or negative adherence. Group pressure can take different forms, for example bullying, persuasion, teasing, and criticism. The term conformity is often used to indicate an agreement to the majority position. Compliance occurs when an individual becomes "influenced" because of a hope that it will lead to a favorable reaction from another person or group.

A conforming behavior is internalized when an individual becomes influenced because the ideas and actions that compose the influence are intrinsically accepted. The ideas become part of their value system. Internalization always involves public and private conformity. A person publicly changes their behavior to fit within the group while also agreeing with them privately. This is the deepest level of conformity where the beliefs of the group become part of the individual's own belief system.

Not everyone conforms to social pressure. There are many factors that contribute to an individual's desire to remain independent of a larger group. Those who value their independence and self-sufficiency are more likely to participate in nonconformity. As a member of a free society, we are allowed to indulge in a certain amount of nonconformity, and yet we must remain within certain parameters of our general culture.

We are individuals in a mass-oriented society, and as such a certain degree of commonality must be adhered to. There are various structures in place within our society that help rein in and support the individual. In our present culture, local structures and organizations are fairly strong (political groups, environmental groups, religious groups, sport affiliations, and the list goes on), but this was not always the case. In the early nineteenth century, the individual felt more defenseless and on their own.

Propaganda has been a component in creating what I call a psychological unity. It can be a force for uniformity especially when the intent is to organize individuals into groups that share a specific mind-set. Make no mistake, public opinion can be swayed and plays a role in group organization within our culture. Through media platforms, it is instrumental in helping individuals form their own personal thoughts on an issue. Public opinion is mainly expressed through the venues which are created and provided for by the mass media outlets. Once a specific opinion is reinforced over and over again on media platforms, it is more easily assimilated into our individual fact bubbles. Media outlets with opposing messages garner very different individuals in their audience makeup. Already formulated cultural opinions on the part of the audience help determine which media outlet they will gravitate to.

Individuals in a free society have a lot in common with others which acts as a reinforcer for our culture, but ideologies can vary greatly. Those most affected and influenced by media platform opinion are the middle class. There is little impact on the extreme ends of our society—the wealthy and the poor. The wealthy enjoy a comfort zone of materialistic freedom, and the poor are too busy struggling to make ends meet. But they are the groups most vulnerable to violent propaganda. When looting and vandalism occurs during a riot, the perpetrators do not come from Beverly Hills. The mental outlook of those in poverty is much narrower than the norm. Their fact bubble is centered around facts passed down from generation to generation rather than media outlets. For example, for the last eighty years, the message to the poor was that the "democratic party is the party of the poor." Where has this belief been of any help to the inner-city communities, yet it is strongly adhered to up to the present time.

The rationale of media platforms is to get its audience to buy into their ideology. They do not want you to discover an ideology on your own. They want you to listen to them and take their analysis as the gospel truth rather than think on your own. A large portion of our society is feeding into their ideological propaganda. Our society has become more comfortable with a media platform interpretation of facts rather than doing the research necessary to come up with a more scientifically based conclusion. The information that we receive from media platforms and *their interpretation* is what the general audience believes.

Now add to this the fact that cultural propaganda seeks to develop conformity within its audience. By increasing the number of individuals whose behavior spreads the intended message and imposing it on even larger audiences helps develop a self-sustaining ideology no longer of individual origin but rather the media audience. Propaganda has as a focal point the addressing of a particular problem within our society. A scientific analytical approach to finding a solution to that problem would go further than the repetitious dialogue we are subjected to through mass media platforms. Propaganda is created through the interpretation of a factual event. It is not the event that causes propaganda but rather its interpretation or what is currently labeled as "spin."

This is where the problem lies—in interpretation. The audience is not allowed to interpret the information on their own. The main goal is to undercut the truth and distract the listeners. The conversation is framed with false terms and misinformation. The main goal is to cloud the very idea of truth and convince the audience to conform. Propaganda tries to eliminate the reasoning process from the equation as much as possible. It appeals to the heart rather than the mind of an audience. Biased information is used to energize an emotional response in the audience which in turn helps gravitate it toward both the opinions and conclusions of the propagandist.

Propaganda is considered a success when it results in a high degree of uniformity in how it is positively accepted. In any case, the main requirement for its success is an effective "interpretation" of the truth. The acceptance of that interpretation leads to compliance, which is an observable component of conformity. This further leads to identification with the propagandist's ideology and the internalization of ideas and behavior associated with it. At its worst, it is social pressure to influence an audience to accept the ideology that the propagandist beliefs are based upon. At best, conformity gives us a sense of comradery, belonging, and group identity with others in the audience.

Conformity is important when it comes to doing what is expected by social norms. Groups have the ability to influence individual behavior and attitude. However, a desire for cooperation and consensus can sometimes lead to a radical point of view and course of action. It is sometimes labeled groupthink, wherein individuals reach a determination without critical evaluation or the exploration of alternate ideas. In all cases, social influence is utilized to attain a level of compliance on both cultural and social issues.

Information Assimilation

We receive knowledge through its *assimilation* or absorption as a believed concept. Some of the knowledge we receive is in direct contrast to our already existing beliefs. In this case, there is an *accommodation* of new information which replaces the originally held belief. But most times, when we receive a new fact, it is assimilated into our existing belief system.

As an example, when a political figure you admire is accused of an illegal activity and this incident does not change your opinion of this politician, this is assimilation. But when you learn of the conviction and the sordid and grievous nature of the crime, which in turn cause you to reevaluate your feelings concerning this politician, this is accommodation.

By far, assimilation is the easiest way to incorporate information because it does not really alter your existing belief system. Propaganda tries to exert pressure on both learning intake modes—assimilation and accommodation.

Facts may initially be presented in such a way to already be infused with a predetermined slant. When a set of facts becomes a problem in the eyes of those who represent public opinion, an opening is created for the injection of propaganda to occur. In an education environment such as a university setting, the audience, comprised of students, is there to consume information. That information often has a reference to cultural, political, or economic reality. Disseminated facts often come with a generous supply of informed opinion by the professor. In this setting, raw unadulterated information provides the basis for propaganda and gives the instructor the means to an end by generating problems that their opinion or interpretation explains.

Their "spin" has as its goal, to motivate the audience into social or political concern. With respect to the information shared, the less concrete and pin pointed it is, the more susceptible it becomes to spin. Information becomes focused on quantity rather than quality. The more general the presentation of cultural, political, and economic facts, the more susceptible it is to accommodation. What is being created with this approach is an increase in the use of stereotyping. Through its use, it becomes easier to manipulate public opinion toward a targeted response, and the more that an individual is exposed to it, the more susceptible one becomes to its use. Propaganda is often used to assimilate citizens into society, to disseminate information that increases participation and involvement of the audience in that society. Sometimes, people want to take part of their own volition. However, propaganda is utilized as an insurance policy to maximize involvement. A democratic society cannot be sustained without the support, involvement, opinions, and knowledge of the people. The goal is to foster opinion to be in agreement with government or cultural goals desired by that country's leaders. It is a situation where you want the audience, in this case society, to demand what has already been decided by those in power. This makes those in power appear that they are very concerned about the needs of the people.

The general purpose is to make society feel more involved and in control or at least have a voice in their destiny. Propaganda becomes a symbiotic relationship in which the goals of the leadership are implemented, and with the audience deriving a degree of satisfaction in feeling, they are truly involved in the decision-making process. Quite often, this is a created illusion of artificial involvement. The end result is that individuals will become less and less capable of forming their own opinions. The audience becomes more eager to accept a propaganda that allows them to feel they have an opinion when in reality they have been given a preconceived mind-set with respect to decisions. The audience derives a sense of belonging and comfort from the propaganda itself.

It has specific objectives, and the audience is cast as a player in a system where ideology or viewpoints are furnished in all areas. Both prejudices and beliefs are reinforced. Individuality is sacrificed for the greater good of society by uniting audience members. Critical and personal thought analysis are subdued and replaced with the ready-made opinions fostered through propaganda.

The audience's ability to judge is affected, making them dependent on the propagandist viewpoint. They become unable to discern truth from disinformation within the presentation. The individual becomes fully integrated as a member of the propagandist's audience. He becomes part of a collective thought process.

All societies have at its foundation a set of core beliefs. The possibility exists that propaganda may be used as a tool to alter those beliefs. Powerful groups and lobbyists influence opinion. Without any use of force, core beliefs can be manipulated. Propaganda must work within a given framework, but that framework can and is presently being chipped away. A point of view can be altered through the use of propaganda.

Media platforms currently enjoy an extensive influence concerning what views and belief is fostered with respect to current cultural, political, and economic issues. They have become a communicator of opinion about the facts that are presented as public information. When there is interaction and disagreement about a viewpoint, the media platforms head for the bunker in an all-out war to shape and mold the public opinion that best fits their own personal ideology. The individual's fact bubble of inner opinions helps externalize and spread the viewpoint most closely aligned with ones already existing fact repertoire.

There are always two entities associated with propaganda—the propaganda developers and the propaganda recipients. Division and isolation can develop between different recipient audiences by promoting allegiance to the audience one is in and suppressing conversation with audiences that have alternative beliefs. A partition or barrier develops between opposing audiences who have different opinions and ideas concerning a specific issue.

We see this most prevalently in the current state of our political system. It has gotten so bad that it is limiting progress in dealing with problems facing our society. The more each audience listens to their propaganda platform, the stronger their beliefs and the greater their disdain for the alternate beliefs of other groups and audiences. Divisions among individuals escalate when it comes to political cultural, economic, or national and world issues. This occurs to some extent within our learning institutions. A free speech issue is raised in debates on college campuses about whether schools should prohibit speakers whose messages are offensive to student groups. This is nothing new, as it also occurred in the late 1980s and early 1990s. On balance, there is certainly a vastly freer exchange of ideas that take place on campuses today than the relatively small number of controversies and speakers who were banned or shut down by protests. For the most part, there is a dissociation between educators encouraging the free pursuit of learning for students and what those people outside of higher education judge to be happening.

Campus controversies may be an example of freedom of speech in flux. Whether they are a new phenomenon or more numerous than in the past may be beside the point. Some part of the current generation of students, population size unknown, believe that they should not have to listen to offensive speech that targets opinions and ideas they are diametrically opposed to. This segment of the student population does not buy into the open-dialogue paradigm for free speech when the speakers are targeting, as an example, gun rights or illegal immigration. Whether they feel that the closed settings of college campuses require special handling or whether they believe more broadly that free speech has no place on a college campus remains a question for future consideration.

Where public opinion exists, propaganda is not too far away. Currently, our very democracy has become a target of public opinion. There is a conflict between the principles of democracy and the principles of socialism. Our nation was based on the development of a government for the people and by the people. But our democracy has already developed, to some extent, a footprint of socialism.

Our democracy is based on the economics of capitalism. Our financial philosophy is free of any socialist agenda. However, we have in place a number of social programs that are to some extent socialist in construct. We have welfare programs, Medicare, Medicaid, food stamps, and even Social Security. But make no mistake, there exists a symbiotic relationship between these programs and democracy. They are able to coexist and flourish. The American people enjoy a level of freedom found nowhere else in the world, but the influences of socialism via social programs exist as well.

As mentioned earlier, propaganda has both a psychological and sociological component. Both are crucial aspects when thinking in terms of media audiences. They are comprised of individuals, but in terms of propaganda, what is most crucial is the audience as a whole both for the sharing of emotional feeling and the psychological pressure exerted by other members of the audience.

The propaganda recipient, as previously stated, brings to the audience a preestablished fact bubble. The propagandist builds on what is already established in the recipient—the fundamental thoughts that are already part of their psychological component. A successful propagandist understands the current value systems and stereotypes that comprise his audience. His role is not to be confrontational but rather to represent himself as an example and reflection of the audience as a whole. Media platforms are the perfect tool to unify audience behavior to expand a specific pattern of thought. Their ideas and objectives are further enhanced when they are expanded upon through advertisements, movies, education, and magazines.

Capitalism and Democracy

Media platforms generally focus around the topics of social justice, politics, and capitalism. Some platforms have sounded an alarm that our democracy is in a state of crises. We hear that capitalism is in the crosshairs of the radical left. Considering that propaganda has become a major component of almost every issue in our country, the topics of democracy and capitalism are not immune.

They both operate together to varying degrees around the world. They both have had an impact in government, business, technology, education, and media itself. Lately, it seems that both democracy and capitalism have been placed on the front burner and attempts are being made to reshape both into something different from what currently exists. Attacks on both are viewed as a concern that needs to be addressed. It is a covert and an overt goal to bring democracy to those countries where it currently does not exist and to bolster the countries where it does. However, large numbers of citizens are not entirely satisfied with how it is working.

When we reflect on democracy, we think in terms of a government that is for the people and by the people. This means that citizens should play an influential role as to who they want to rule our country as well as an influence with respect to how our current democracy is run. It enjoys many different interpretations as to what it really is. We do not live in a purely democratic society, and I am fairly certain that a totally democratic government would be unsustainable.

We have in place socialist programs, and they act as a relief valve to ease pressure within our society where necessary. It is the first course of action during a fiscal crisis. This was the case in the 2008 mortgage and finance meltdown. It is also being played out in dealing with the COVID-19 pandemic. It was the Chinese version of Russia's Chernobyl and the US Deep Horizon oil spill of 2020 in the sense that all will have long-lasting effects. With the pandemic, a stimulus package among other remedies became the first line of defense. This fiscal response played a very important part in sustaining both our economy and democracy. We take our democracy for granted, so much so that we seldom think about it. It is often shrouded in a cloak of "liberty and justice." That shroud basically puts a limitation on its definition. It fails to take into account the financial system in place which serves as a symbiotic reinforcement for both.

Democracy is not perfect by any means, but for those who came from other countries where it does not exist to the extent that we now enjoy, America is a utopia. One's point of view is affected by background and by class as well. The upper, middle, and lower classes of our country perceive democracy in a somewhat different light. This is the reason for the myriad of opinions on how it is functioning. Political gridlock, corruption, inept politicians, the lack of political cooperation, and the lack of problem-solving anger those across the entire political spectrum. Do they really feel, outside of voting, that they have a real voice in their government? For many, our democracy appears to be more by the people than for the people.

Our leadership for the most part is not accountable, and voters rightly feel their choices are limited by the candidates who choose to run for office. This point is exemplified by the fact that not every voter in our country takes the time to voice their opinion at the ballot box. The issue of "trust" in government is prevalent on media platforms with dialogue revolving around suspicions, conspiracy theories, and outright mistrust. Many actually feel that their vote and opinion do not count. Some think that capitalism is actually a barrier to better democracy.

In the media, we are witnessing an increase in social fragmentation and an uneasy feeling about the stability of our democracy and the survival of capitalism with blame often directed at either the most liberal or conservative on the political spectrum. In my opinion, democracy, in the true sense of the word, has a fight on its hands. So the question arises: are we really a government "for the people"? There are many voters out there who would beg to differ.

However, we must keep in mind that democracy is not a straightforward and simplistic notion. The concept is currently in flux and always has been. We all are experiencing the major change in democracy after the attack on the World Trade Towers and the 2020 pandemic. The premise that has to be recognized and considered is that there are revisions and changes to the degree of democracy in government. It has slid to a different level as the definition of democracy continues to be redefined out of necessity. The World Trade Center attack ushered in a different reality with respect to civil liberties and global freedoms. The relationship between our economy which embraces capitalism and democracy is under scrutiny, and they are fundamentally interconnected.

There is a direct correlation between the amount of change in our culture and the amount of change in the meaning of democracy. In an attempt to bolster democracy, there is the concept of "the American Dream" coming to the forefront of conversation, as well as one's ability to get ahead with our form of government. This speaks more to capitalism rather than democracy; although one does not exist without the other.

Opportunity matters to many of our citizens, especially our younger ones, and many feel a nagging uncertainty about the future. There are those in the upper class of our society who value our democracy and our capitalistic system. And to them I say, why not? Their meaning of democracy concerns itself with economic opportunity, free and fair elections, and the peaceful transfer of administrations as the result of the election process. But not every class feels the same way.

Our founding fathers plan was to establish a republic in which the citizenry had specific rights and a strong voice. The *Encyclopedia Britannica* describes a Republic as a "form of government in which a state is ruled by representatives of the citizen body." Modern republics are founded on the idea that sovereignty rests with the people, though who are included and excluded from the category of the people has varied across history. Because citizens do not govern the state themselves but through representatives, republics may be distinguished from direct democracy, though modern representative democracies are by and far large republics.

The term "republic" may also be applied to any form of government in which the head of state is not a "hereditary monarch." It is undisputable that the United Stated fits this definition extremely well. But in our country, the financially well to do have a decided edge in running for the highest political office in the land. So one can argue that a financial monarchy is currently in place. The reality is that democracy, for those of us who think about the term, may have a difference in definition, a difference that is often exploited on various media platforms.

Many students in our country view democracy as a questionable institution. The goal of attending college has become more and more materialistic. College has become the students' stock market. They are gambling that their education will produce an abundant financial reward. Unlike past generations, students seem to attend college not so much to foster the common good but rather to foster a financial gain for themselves. Our democracy and the ideals that are a part of it are currently under attack in the media. The opinion and propaganda involved in that attack are adding fuel to the fire.

As mentioned, it is not possible to discuss our democracy in the absence of capitalism. There is a symbiotic relationship between the two ideals. Democracy is a major contributor to capitalism as well as other fundamental human values. It encourages humanitarian values such as worker rights, freedom of speech, and civil liberties. Capitalism ensures the right of citizens to establish and run a business under their control and ownership. It establishes a secure and stable environment for all business activity.

Governments that establish a democracy enhance peace rather than war, encourage development, promote capitalism, and act as an advocate for the rights of its citizens through the passage of laws. Democracy can be spread within a country through the ratification and embracement of capitalism. The United States values democracy and protection of the rights of individuals along with a strong defense of our capitalistic system.

Government involvement in private business corporations is limited, but regulations are put in place that allow for partial and democratic government oversight. Some of these approaches are based upon, among other things, taxes, business permits, safety, health, and insurance concerns. The stock market is another way in which the government controls and benefits from private corporations through capitalism. The importance of the roles played by the stock market in supporting capitalism is directly related to democracy and free markets.

Capitalism involves itself in the determination of wages, the labor force, and competitiveness. Up to a point, citizens have a democratic right to decide on business prospects within their country and business relationships with other countries. Capitalism establishes and nurtures economic goals. This is indicative of the relationship between capitalism and democracy. We can say that capitalistic policies of most countries are democratic in nature. Democracy seems impossible to sustain in the absence of a capitalist economy. It enhances the concepts of free markets, which is a considerable aspect of any democracy. A free market system is one in which there is very limited or no control by the government in the supply and demand aspect of business.

Individuals are allowed to freely buy, sell, and transact business activities within a framework of law. The business decisions of a country should be made democratically so as to open the market for various investors. This provision is only possible in a capitalist economy which in turn helps to bolster democracy.

Some media platforms are at the helm in the attack on capitalism or at best the encouragement of attacks on capitalism. The main criticism is that it deepens inequality and enriches the smallest group of citizens in the upper class of our society. The facts offered to sustain these attacks are "liberally" sprinkled with propaganda. Corporations are being accused of focusing only on maximizing shareholder value and at the same time ignoring social and environmental challenges.

The average American citizen is being exploited and damaged by our capitalistic economy. The solution offered as a remedy for this concern is punitive taxes on the wealthy which would be used to enhance the lives of the poor. Corporations should serve not only their shareholders but also the broader community of Americans by meeting the challenge of poverty, political influence, and climate change. Many believe that government should intervene to ensure this happens.

Since there exists a symbiotic relationship between capitalism and democracy, when you attack one, you damage the other. The fact that capitalism is not perfect does not deter one from arguing that it is a better system than all the others. But the media platforms paint quite a different picture. They argue that big corporations are increasingly dominating industries as a result of changing technology and misguided policies. Competition is being destroyed. Business startups are negatively impacted. Consumers have fewer choices and less influence on corporate behavior. Complaints against market capitalism are directed not only as being the result of the institution but also to the system itself.

Social democrats view capitalism as a malignancy. Their truth is that it is a tumor that is causing most of the ills in our country. Economic gain concentrates wealth in fewer and fewer hands, and the political system is viewed as unresponsive to the needs of the people.

But under healthy capitalism, democratic government policy encourages and promotes competition, new products, and companies. There is room for improvements in our sustainable capitalist system. But there is an attitude of laissez-faire when it comes to antitrust change and direction. Competitiveness is one element of our antitrust system that is currently ignored for the most part but must again become the major role of antitrust.

Rather than burn down the whole village, a solution may be found by enforcing antitrust legislation combined with innovative financing to level the playing field, ease the red tape for business startups, and encourage risk-taking and entrepreneurship. Market capitalism is being challenged by radical liberal ideas and at the other end of the spectrum a complacent conservative attitude that all is well with the world. By imposing antitrust legislation, consumers and investors who are increasingly concerned with social, environmental, and governance issues in an economy driven by limited competition will produce entrepreneurs who will be motivated to come up with business models that can serve both business and society in general.

However, antitrust is not a topic of conversation on social media. Platforms are more comfortable with spewing a general disdain for the entire system and those at the helm of corporate empires. Some may argue that antitrust is antithetical to the concept of capitalism.

It interferes and places restrictions on private business development. It restricts or prohibits unpopular but, nonetheless, legitimate growth of corporations. Another area of concern with respect to antitrust legislation is mergers. Most economists dislike mergers, particularly large ones, since they result in the limiting of competition. The assumption is that the number of companies in competition or the relative size of the company is a crucial determinant of competitive behavior. Since mergers reduce numbers and increase the relative size of companies, some economists argue that they automatically reduce competition.

Most economists feel that a capitalist economic system improves with antitrust to protect it. Free-market capitalism has a tendency to dominate the business they are involved in. One of the detriments or flaws in capitalism is the desire to limit or destroy the very essence of its own economic mechanism which is competition. It's competition that keeps business costs and prices level and reduces greed which is detrimental to the general welfare of the public. Government intervention, although not opposed in principle, is only necessary in situations where competition is being hindered or neutralized. Where there is no competition, the defense of a free market collapses. But it is an issue that can be addressed without attacking the entire system.

So why aren't major economic goliaths currently being scrutinized as anticompetition? These companies enjoy protections maintained by the Interstate Commerce Commission, the Federal Communications Commission, the Federal Power Commission, and the other numerous state regulatory commissions and authorities

which are too numerous to mention. The mega companies and corporations that these governmental agencies protect and shield from
competition could not last a week without such protection. The only
citizens that really seem to matter are the shareholders.

Ideology and the Media

Currently, when viewing the news platforms, we see what can best be described as a difference of opinion. In actuality, the same set of facts is often described in a fashion designed to lead the audience to a specific conclusion. In simplistic terms, that conclusion either favors the conservative or liberal agenda. Both are guilty of using propaganda techniques to get their points across. The information or facts presented by the media is of less importance than the "spin" that is used to reinforce a specific agenda. Many longtime viewers of news media feel propaganda has never been more problematic than it is now.

One of the areas that stands out as an example of the different agendas is wealth. Basic, evidence-based economics are interpreted purely on media platform political beliefs. I cannot think of a better argument for teaching economics in schools starting at an early age. Children would discover that political beliefs contradict a great deal of convincing evidence that we now have about how our economy functions. We could possibly avoid turning these truths into a vicious battle between liberals and conservatives on media platforms, social platforms, education institutions, and elsewhere. It's okay to dream of or desire a utopia, but students should be equipped with knowledge of economics and the reality of the world as it really is.

Another example of the differences in agendas is political stance. Never has the dichotomy been so blatant and obvious. It can be argued that FOX News has crossed the lines of journalistic integrity and is currently functioning as a conservative agenda propaganda machine. CNN and other mainstream media have a very liberal bias, and it is supported by evidence that journalists who work for these outlets are overwhelmingly more likely to identify as Democrats than Republicans. In other words, political bias is alive and well throughout all media outlets. Factual material is compromised through the use of opinion. As the result of one media study, with the exception of Bloomberg News, Reuters, and Associated Press, most other outlets are guilty of reporting varying degrees of slanted, inaccurate, or fabricated information. Media platforms present political information in a light that coincides with their own political prejudice. Both liberals and conservatives continuously point fingers at each other with accusations of outright bias. The partisanship on both sides of the political spectrum has separated them into two camps of hardened red and blue positions. The difference incorporates not only economic philosophy but also issues of cultural and social beliefs. For example, conservatives feel that the current economic system is fair and equitable, and liberals feel just the opposite.

Ideological differences are reflected both explicitly and implicitly in attitudes and are directly related to personality. Humans possess specific traits that have a direct effect on behavior and thought processes. For example, one trait parameter is conscientiousness in which conservatives tend to score higher, and another is an openness to new experiences in which liberals hold the lead. It is my opinion that liberals and conservatives are equally biased in their acceptance of another point of view. Both sides, to put it mildly, are in the bunkers and ready to battle. The propaganda of media platforms reinforces both ideologies according to the political views they champion.

It is not unreasonable to be skeptical of information if it contradicts one's "fact bubble" background knowledge on the subject. Propaganda combined with an individual's "fact bubble" unite to elicit a specific bias that seems to be justifiable and rational but is actually based on purely political prejudice. On some topics such as economics, conservatives may have an edge with respect to knowledge levels, and in general, current political research contradicts the concept of similar knowledge levels with respect to both ideologies. It depends on the topic in question. But what stands without argument is that there is an abundant amount of bias on both sides of the aisle. Rather than focus on the issue of political prejudice, it may be more helpful to investigate how propaganda is used to alter and slant factual information.

It is essential in a world awash in misinformation that we learn as much as possible about the issues of the day, and propaganda hinders one's ability to think intelligently and critically about the facts that are presented on media platforms. There is enough ignorance on both sides, with intelligence and critical thinking becoming subservient to a partisan view of the facts.

Humans are prisoners of the preexisting facts they hold to be true. When they see a media story that confirms their preexisting fact bubble, they think it to be true, actually want it to be true, and they very quickly "like" it and then share it on Facebook. This behavior takes the news story to a whole different level of acceptance. This applies not just to politically based "fake news" but to scientific facts as well. A day does not go by without the term "fake news" being used. The use of the phrase has exploded. Researchers have found that people on both sides of extreme liberal/conservative agendas are equally likely to believe political news that is consistent with their ideology and to disbelieve news that is inconsistent with their side of the aisle. If you are extremely conservative or extremely liberal, you are even more likely to cognitively fool yourself into believing a news story (if it supports your agenda) or reject/disagree with it no matter how logical if it disagrees with your ideology/agenda. People determine news accuracy in a way that appears motivated by their own ideological positioning. To sum up, liberals and conservatives are similarly motivated to avoid exposure to one another's viewpoints and are similarly motivated to even deny scientific findings that are inconsistent with their ideology.

On a more positive note, both liberals and conservatives are equally adept in sniffing out news as either being a legitimate story or one of dubious fact. A healthy majority on both sides of the aisle are not completely susceptible to fake news. Some people tend to think with their head and are motivated to seek out and process information, whereas others tend to think with their gut, motivated to action by their emotions, fact bubbles, and agenda bias.

To further extrapolate, you would think that those who consider themselves logical thinkers and superrational would be less likely to succumb to motivationally illogical reasoning. Quite the opposite, for when highly cognitive thinking individuals were presented with fake news stories that were in agreement with their ideology, they were even more likely than everyone else to view the story as true. And when they were faced with fake news stories that were inconsistent with their ideology, they were less likely to consider the news to be truthful than everyone else. One possible explanation is that logical thinkers and superrational people are not only more likely to disbelieve political news stories that disagree or are inconsistent with their ideology but also more likely to seek out further information that reinforces their stance. This is consistent with research showing that people who score high as logical thinkers and as being superrational tend to communicate more with ideology-supporting social networks, but of course, this is understandable when social networks operate in an echo chamber of solely their own supporting rhetoric.

Propaganda and disinformation are both guilty of being catalysts for further polarizing society. In the past two decades, more than ever, media's coverage of presidential elections has fanned the flames of disinformation, fake news, and deception, and at the same time pleaded ignorance in doing so. If you think the country is divided now, imagine how fractured we may be in the future if allowed to continue unchecked. We must become a more media-literate electorate, able to discern true facts from destructive propaganda by analyzing information before we place it in our fact repertoire. Media coverage is ever increasingly emphasizing the character of party leaders rather than the issues that we should all be especially concerned about. Elections have become more involved with the political marketing of candidates rather than the substantial issues currently plaguing our nation.

Fake news and propaganda engage both liberals and conservatives through a motivated and biased reasoning lens, and both liberals and conservatives can fall prey to fake news, even though the underlying motives may differ within each group. This is consistent with an ideological or fact bubble approach to the understanding of politically biased processing with respect to fake news or propaganda. The spread of political, social, and cultural misinformation through media can have a tremendous impact on the political landscape. Asking people to think more critically about political views is not the complete answer. There is a need to facilitate greater levels of communication between those with opposing political outlooks. Social media has the potential to divide audiences, and we must keep in mind that it also has the potential to expose people to ideologically diverse viewpoints and to point out fake news and propaganda.

Why do some people lean toward liberalism while others lean toward a conservative ideology? That's almost like asking, what is the meaning of life? The question is quite complex and involves a myriad of variables. The audience most likely did not read a plethora of ideological policy statements that helped them form a political ideology. Differences of ideological political opinion are shaped by a person's life experiences, where a person lives and lived, the kind of family situation a person is raised in, whether you or your family were wealthy or poor, whether you are young or old, and—let's not forget—nationality and race. Emotion comes into the picture as well with emotion having a partial biological basis. All of this and much more combines into a formula that helps make up your world outlook. And how one views both positive and negative national and world events has an impact on political ideological reinforcement.

Campus Bias and Partisanship

Media platforms present factual information served with a fairly good amount of bias, propaganda, or, at best, opinion. Besides media platforms, colleges have been at the center of news topics with respect to liberal conservative slant. Many news stories depict college students as politically and environmentally concerned, while others depict the students as championing radical left-wing ideologies.

So the question is, Does going to college turn students into political liberals and at the other end of the spectrum political conservatives? We can start with a premise that we may all be able to agree with which is that attending college can have an impact on value systems.

Conservatives have used media platforms to argue that universities brainwash and pressure students into believing a liberal ideology. The rationale used in supporting this assumption is that universities are mostly staffed with liberal professors. Liberal college professors are telling students what to think and are creating a barrier to prevent other opposing ideological discussion. Some state lawmakers are suggesting that universities should consider political affiliation with respect to hiring practices in order to better balance out political representation of the faculty.

Campus conservatives are depicted in the media as being not only outnumbered but not in touch with the concerns of the nation. This imbalance has an effect on student relations, stifles open discourse, and impairs the overall educational climate. The media platforms often pick and choose incidents that support their college student ideology. Studies have shown that first-year and sophomore students do demonstrate an increase in positive attitudes toward liberal ideologies after a year or two of schooling. But studies have overall shown that college attendance has produced gains in appreciating political viewpoints across the spectrum and not just liberal philosophy.

Studies have also shown that the development of negative attitudes toward liberal and conservative ideologies were about the same for each viewpoint with about 30 percent of students developing those feelings. Background and prior feelings are an important factor in determining the ideology most adhered to. In other words, students who begin college really disliking liberals or conservatives carry that dislike into their college experience. But the same studies point to a general softening of opinion later in the college experience. Similar results were found in both private and public college settings. Students gravitate toward liberal ideologies when they first come to college and after their first year, but while students still favor liberal ideologies over conservative ideologies, studies have shown that this gap does not widen over the first year.

The studies point to a conclusion that choice of political ideology may have little to do with the faculty directly, and instead it may be the climate that campuses try to create for the expression of different viewpoints, political and otherwise. Students may come to college never having met someone with a different political stance, and it is difficult to avoid doing so in college. One objective of higher education is to encourage communication, debate, discussion, and exposure to political and social viewpoints from many different collegians.

News stories on social media exaggerate the examples they use to prove a point and end up making one feel that college campuses are a hotbed of radical political ideology on both sides of the aisle. Nothing increases ratings like sensationalist stories especially when your audience is already predisposed to believing the story in the first place.

The American college campus, on the contrary, is not a dangerous place. If you have a conservative ideology and say what you really think, a group of young liberal thinkers will come forward to challenge your position or invitation to speak on campus. But the idea that political correctness is dominating American universities and threatening both higher education, and the broader right to free speech is not as prevalent as the media would have you believe. The crises you view on social media is more than a little exaggerated.

There have been relatively few incidents of speech being squelched on college campuses, and there's, in fact, limited evidence that conservatives are being unfairly targeted. Free Speech Project researchers had cataloged more than ninety incidents since 2016 that fit their criteria for a person's free speech rights being threatened. Of those ninety, about two-thirds took place on college campuses. These incidents range from a speaker being disinvited to a faculty member being fired over allegedly offensive comments to a student-run play being canceled over concerns it would offend.

These numbers should raise questions about the so-called political correctness anticonservative epidemic. Free speech attacks are extremely rare incidents that dominate media platforms and do not define university life in the way that critics suggest. There's a consistent pattern in the data when it comes to conservative ideology. Most of the incidents where supposedly conservative speech has been challenged in the past few years seem to involve the same few speakers. Conservative student groups usually invite speakers who have made a name for themselves for their extremely conservative stance. In doing so, the liberal campus groups are provoked into action. When students react by protesting or disrupting the event, some media platforms use it as proof that there's a real intolerance for conservative viewpoints. To a lesser extent, there are incidents where left-leaning speakers have been challenged as well. In mostly all cases, protest involved a presentation by an individual speaker rather than an organization. That is not to say that this behavior is not troubling, but it hardly reaches a point that can be considered a crisis. The fact is that there are some incidents that reach media platforms and are exploited and used as a propaganda talking point to reinforce the platforms ideology.

Campus free speech critics aren't showing the audience the complete picture. The real reason behind this kind of attack is to color universities as completely and dangerously liberal, which has the effect of undermining higher education for the purpose of reinforcing a specific partisan platform. As previously mentioned, the reaction to these types of stories has prompted the creation of legislation to counter attacks on free speech.

Because of sensationalized attacks on conservative speech, state governments have established new rules and guidelines for political speech in public universities. And this trend seems to be growing. In Wisconsin, one of the strictest states to enact legislation, rules have been ratified by the state university's board of regents that allow for students to be expelled if they are found guilty of having disrupted the speech of other students three times. This kind of legislation is the antithesis of just what the First Amendment is all about, and it is my opinion that it will be facing a constitutional challenge moving forward. The presidential order to withdraw funding from colleges and universities that are accused of not allowing or permitting free speech on campus is in itself a threat of government intervention with respect to speech on campus. The question is, Who will it be that determines free speech on campus? This looks like a solution looking for a problem. The purpose seems to be not so much to provide protections for free speech but rather a way for state and federal governments to monitor campus speech. It appears to be a dangerous solution and one that will hopefully be challenged.

Some media platforms would have you believe that there is an increase in campus ideology that supports the rise of totalitarianism on college campuses. The term "social justice warriors" has become a commonly used term to describe both left-leaning professors, liberal student leaders and college administrators that support the suppression of free speech and has become a commonly used phrase in mainstream media political discourse. What is being created is a viewpoint that is out to make free speech appear less free. Left-wing college students, faculty, and administrators are labeled as the primary threats to free speech. Students on the left are seen, according to conservative media platforms, as the ones who find the most problematic concerns with allowing all viewpoints to be expressed on campus. But the question arises as to why this kind of reporting is gaining traction in the first place. Let's look at this story line from a propaganda viewpoint. Conservative politicians and conservative media platforms are not only amplifying the problem but exploiting it as well to solidify their own political ideology. The scenario that there is a free speech crisis on political campuses for the most part is overblown. We should be careful not to fall into a mind-set, as some media platforms suggest, that there is a free speech crisis on campus.

The point that must be emphasized is that free speech on campus is not a simple matter. The fact is that while there are a small number of free speech controversies on college campuses, the conservative media platforms would have you believe that they are the norm. The point here is not to determine which ideology is the worst offender in free speech controversies but rather to propose that it is not as commonplace as the media would have you believe. Creating an open learning environment should take precedence over creating a learning environment that attempts to protect students from hearing offensive or biased speech that is not a norm on campus in the first place. The use of state or federal power to monitor speech is a scary proposition.

Democratic-leaning voters have maintained a positive attitude toward academia, while their Republican counterparts hold a more negative viewpoint. This is a difference that is fueled and reinforced, as mentioned, by the various media platforms. In general, conservatives remain suspicious of the intentions of university professors expressing concerns that they do not act in the public interest. And their most common diagnosis of what is most problematic with the American higher education system is faculty bias. Most are convinced that liberal educators are force fueling their liberal political and social views in the classroom. They feel that the system is overrun with professors who are unfair to those with differing opinions and are guilty of creating hostile classroom atmospheres while discouraging open debate, and even employ the power of the grading system to discourage political disagreement. In other words, progressive professors are making life more difficult for right-of-center students. But this is, by far, not the college norm. Most college professors adhere to a standard that is extremely fair and supportive of all students in their charge despite their own political affinity. It is true that left-of-center views are particularly common in the humanities, fine arts, and social sciences, where political subjects are most likely to enter class discussion. But most educators are not trying to indoctrinate their students with a liberal-leaning philosophy. What is presented on media platforms is not the norm but rather the exception. The majority of college professors have no intention of forcing their students to think as they do. Quite the contrary, good educators will do exactly the opposite, by challenging and debating their students to examine an issue and maybe attempting to persuade them to recognize their personal point of view but never abusing their position to demand an ideological conformity to what they believe. Many professors look for constructive student participation that encourages thoughtful engagement even if it includes a serious political difference with what they believe.

To sum up, educational misconducts that make the news are the unusual incidents that are presented for their propaganda value. In a nation with more than four thousand colleges and universities, there is an extremely low rate of documented professorial bias in the political arena. Again, this is not to say that today's campus faculty is not more liberal than conservative. It can be said that the difference in ideologies is expanding but the impact on student populations is being exaggerated. If students are changing their politics because of teacher influence, the change most often is a shift away from conservatism. As previously mentioned, there is an increase in the politically liberal viewpoint, but it is by no means indicative of a national crises or a radical change in ideological world view. What can be stated is that as far as higher education goes, the diversity balance favors the liberal ideology. However, conservative students can likewise grow in their own beliefs even at very progressive schools. It helps them to clarify values and ideas about different issues and provides an opportunity for them to test their own conservative beliefs. With respect to social media, there's plenty of evidence that the views professors bring to class are disproportionately liberal; but, contrary to what social media would have you believe, the good news is that there is no reason to believe that those who try to force those views on their students is of epidemic proportion.

Issues: Second Amendment, National Debt, Censorship

The *Second Amendment* gives all American citizens the right to own guns. The propaganda and debate surrounding this amendment is exhaustive. In 2008, the Heller decision by the Supreme Court defined a specific method of determining meaning. The ruling stated that the purpose of the amendment is irrelevant to understanding the intent and must, therefore, be ignored in determining whether a given law that has been passed violates this amendment. With a five to four decision, the right to purchase and own firearms was unequivocally reinforced.

There are many antigun activists who are extremely unhappy with the way the amendment was interpreted. Their stand is that owning a gun is not a constitutional right citing purpose within the amendment itself. In the Heller decision, purpose was eliminated from the equation. To the antigun crowd, this was nothing more than a distorted interpretation of meaning. The argument used is that there is doubt with respect to the amendment's purpose.

But one has to ask, Does the argument against gun ownership go beyond a reasonable doubt? My personal opinion is that it does not. I am basing my opinion solely on common sense since I have absolutely zero background in law. This being the case, I'm not sure my common sense rationale holds water. But here goes. Let's use a redundant analogy. The purpose of a driver's license is to add safety and security to the act of driving. Regulation is an important part of securing safety on the road and documenting drivers as having the necessary practice, knowledge, and skills necessary to driving. One cannot imagine allowing someone the right to drive without a certain degree of regulation with respect to the process. The idea of driver regulation has nothing to do with the passing of a law giving citizens the right to drive. The purpose of regulation is to ensure that safety and accountability are embedded into that law.

I view the Second Amendment in the same light. It gives our citizens the right to own firearms, period. What seem to be more confrontational are regulations and just what kind of firearm is allowable under the amendment. The right to "keep and bear arms" is quite a general statement. And to be sure, at its proposal the ability of weaponry was quite limited. I'm not sure whether or not they ever envisioned the invention of the AK-47 or the machine gun. But this is where regulation comes into play.

With the Second Amendment, "a well-regulated militia" suggests accountability in dispersing a right to bear arms. But the entirety of this argument hardly ever comes up for discussion on media platforms. What is presented is that the right to bear arms shall not be infringed. The naysayers counter utilizing the purpose rationale of the amendment. But is it actually a purpose clause or merely a stipulation that regulation is an important aspect of this right?

Citizens have a right to bear arms. Felons convicted of murder are citizens. When released, do we continue to allow them that right, or do we regulate that right? The propaganda on the left employs the argument that the conservatives are reading their own interpretations into the meaning. But the conservative wing counters, and rightfully so, with the same argument. The most important question here is, Has either side proven their point beyond a reasonable doubt?

The propaganda flows easily on both sides with respect to individual gun incidents that occur regularly in our culture. Mass shootings are caused by guns. Ban guns to end mass shootings. Car accidents and deaths are caused by cars. Should we ban cars as well? And when a good guy takes out a bad guy, the conservative wing makes sure it does not go unnoticed. Both claim incidents as reasons either for or against gun ownership. How ridiculous is that?

What would be more constructive is a conversation revolving around regulation. The better the regulation, the better the safety—both in gun ownership and driving. All the propaganda statistics being bantered around by both sides are really meaningless when it comes to a discussion of the Second Amendment. Statistics are only as good as the source from which they come which is another propaganda problem in itself.

Many arguments favoring gun control cite instances where the wording "common defense" was written into several state constitutions at the time as a rationale for the individual right to bear arms. The argument proceeds that if the intention of the Second Amendment was to stipulate that right as well, why was it not included? However, the wording "necessary for the security of a free state" in my opinion goes beyond "common defense" and encompasses common defense as well as the reason for such an action whether it be an internal or external assault on freedom. The first parts appear to be the rationale for both managing and allowing the last part which adds very strongly and in no uncertain terms "shall not be infringed."

It appears as well that some detractors place emphasis on the word *militia* arguing that the right applies only during times of war and was not meant as a sanction for the individual right to bear arms. But the definition of *militia* (a military force that is raised from the civil population to supplement a regular army in an emergency) implies that it is created by individuals to supplement regular armed forces.

The regulation of gun control is done by law, and that is where emphasis should be placed. By regulation, I do not mean control but rather management and responsible supervision. There is room for improvement in the system especially when it comes to background checking. States have been given broad rights in the area of regulation. There are state laws where guns are not allowed to be carried in certain areas such as school zones. *Regulation.* But attempts to "ban" handguns in Chicago was struck down in 2010. *Not regulation but a ban.*

In reality, the pro and con arguments concerning gun ownership and gun rights may never be adjudicated in the court of public opinion. The conversations on this subject will never abate. Truth be told, in the real world, there are bad actors out there. These actors do not give a hoot about antigun laws and will continue to be a dangerous menace to society. So when confronted by one or more of these actors, the choice is to call 911 and hope they respond in time or afford yourself the opportunity to protect both yourself and your family through the legal possession of a firearm. The American citizen should continue to be afforded the right to choose when it comes to defending the precious gift of life. Constitutional rights are a crucial aspect for the security of our safety and freedom.

In summary, the Supreme Court through the Heller decision recognized and reinforced the concept that the Second Amendment is entirely compatible with strong firearm regulations. Some argue this is the beginning of the end for gun ownership. But while it is true that the Heller decision was far from the blanket endorsement of unlimited gun rights, the decision reinforced the belief that essential gun safety laws are constitutional under the Second Amendment. It is an affirmation that critical gun safety laws to improve public safety and reduce gun violence are compatible with the Second Amendment. This will be an ongoing confrontation between those who will be dammed if they agree by those who are dammed because they don't.

*****

There has been very little deliberation concerning the rapid rise in the national debt. And not talking about it will not make it disappear. The economy from 2016 to 2019 had been highlighted almost constantly and praised as a great political and national success. However, the national debt is never included as part of the highlight. In fact, it is very seldom a topic of national conversation. It is mentioned in passing and mostly relegated to being an obscure topic.

This underreporting should raise serious questions about fiscal responsibility and where to draw the line between appropriate communication and propaganda. I believe a nationwide national debt discussion is long overdue. Praising the economy is all well and good, but there seems to be a burying of heads in the sand when it comes to balancing the budget or discussing the national debt. If we all had an unlimited financial credit card resource which we do not have to readily pay back, we would all be in a happy financial place. But we are on a road that sooner or definitely later will lead our country to a dead end with nowhere to turn. Recently, the financial stimulus package as a response to the devastating impact of COVID-19 has dealt another problematic blow to the establishment of fiscal responsibility. And sooner or later, we will be told that our country's credit card is closer to being maxed out. Eventually, we will run out of road to kick the can down.

With respect to fiscal health, government spending is being utilized for the purpose of forwarding a public relation campaign of "Don't worry. Be happy." Some of this money goes toward legitimate public communication purposes, but much of the spending is probably wasteful and is used to promote propaganda. There is a vagueness in defining publicity, propaganda, and lobbying. The Government Accountability Office (GAO) does not routinely research and report on agency communications, unless specifically requested to do so. Lack of oversight and vague restrictions mean that many agencies waste taxpayer money on frivolous and inappropriate communication, sometimes to promote a positive spin on government expenditures.

As one example, the State Department spent over a half-million dollars to convince people to "like" the department's Facebook page. The federal government is the second-largest public relations firm in the world. This kind of spending not only is wasteful at a time our national debt is reaching record-breaking levels, but much of it is used inappropriately for propaganda. Greater transparency and supervision will help make agencies more accountable for such spending. Cuts in allotted public relations funding, although a very small part of the equation, and the propaganda it utilizes may help to not only curb some waste but more importantly focus attention on the fact that our country will have to face a very serious concern in the future.

The biggest problem is not PR expenditures which in reality are a "drop in the bucket." It is the presentation of a slanted viewpoint. The funding is geared to making everyone believe that all is well with the economy when in fact the country is inevitably heading toward a day of reckoning and the dead end I previously mentioned.

Nevertheless, one recurring budget topic has to be placed on the front burner sooner rather than later—debt and deficit. Simply put, the country cannot continue to spend more than it is taking in. This will eventually become an economic terminal illness. The presumption of ongoing economic growth is a risky proposition to depend on as a lifeline for the economy. This message became all too clear with COVID-19. Additionally, the reduced size of the baby boomer generation means the nation simply cannot expect continuous high growth, because a smaller segment of the population is contributing to the economy as workers.

The propaganda of upbeat economic assumptions is leading the country to a complacency with respect to national debt that will eventually bite us in the butt. The continuous assumption of ongoing growth does not account for a possible and inevitable recession or natural disaster or any other crisis, such as COVID-19 that recently impacted our economy, and that will negatively impact the national debt. The budget cuts discussed, past and present, have done and will continue to do little to get at the humongous debt and deficit. More structural and dramatic change is necessary in order to have a substantial effect in the development of a balanced and healthy budget. I believe it must involve global cooperation and, as a result, most all nations will benefit. But this is a discussion for another time.

Debt and deficit reduction are difficult, since the most dramatic ways to reduce both are raising taxes and cutting popular programs, both of which are unpopular choices. It would be very difficult to make changes in entitlement programs such as Social Security, Medicare, and Medicaid. Even now, economists worry that there will not be enough money to pay retirement benefits in the near future. You can stretch a rubber band just so much until it eventually breaks. And the propaganda presented on media platforms do almost nothing as far as warning the public of the impending crises.

Lawmakers will remain very reluctant to reduce the Social Security benefit people are expecting, especially when the benefit is offered to virtually everyone that comes of age. Medicare as well is judicially guarded. Budget calls for a reduction of $846 billion in Medicare cost achieved by reducing wasteful spending and requiring that prior authorization before treatment be in place and by looking more closely at providers who consistently charge more than others have been immediately criticized by members of Congress. After all, sooner or later, it will be reelection time. Through media propaganda that everything will be "worked out," Americans have less interest in helping pay down the soaring national debt than any previous time in history.

The tax cut of 2017 has come with a price that also has be paid down the road. And that leaves the nation with a pretty dismal outlook for addressing either the deficit or the debt. Ignoring the problem is the best way a politician can ensure their reelection and retaining their seat. A strong economy is an essential foundation for growth. But our nation has to be put on a fiscal diet in order to assure a positive environment for growth, opportunity, and prosperity in the long-term future. With a strong fiscal foundation, the nation will have more access to capital, more resources for future public and private expenditures as well as improved consumer and business confidence.

If the country fails to act, long-term fiscal concerns will remain unheeded; and our economy will eventually weaken as confidence is diminished, access to capital is reduced, and interest costs destroy the implementation of key investments in our future. More and more federal resources will be diverted to interest payments, and there will be less available to invest in areas that are important for economic growth. Although we are in a low-interest-rate environment, we cannot expect that situation to last forever. If interest rates rise, the federal government's borrowing costs will increase markedly.

With increased-interest-rate atmospheres, federal borrowing competition for funds in our nation's capital markets increase as well, and rising interest rates would curtail new investment in both business equipment and expansion. Entrepreneurs would face a higher cost of capital, possibly limiting innovation, employment, and reducing the advancement of new breakthroughs that could improve lives. If allowed to continue, there will be a point where investors might begin to question the government's ability to repay existing debt which could become the catalyst for an added increase in interest rates, thereby further raising the cost of borrowing for government, business, and households. Over time, this will lead to a loss of confidence and a reduction in investment and, as a consequence, slow the growth of productivity and wages in America.

Additionally, higher interest rates, because of an increase in federal borrowing, would result in a housing market slowdown and an increase in cost to finance car payments and pay for college. A reduction in investment would result in fewer education and training opportunities and leave workers without the skills necessary to keep up with the demands of a more technologically based global economy. A reduction in research and development would make it harder for American businesses to remain on the cutting edge of innovation, as well as hurt wage growth in the US. Slower economic growth would make our fiscal challenges even worse, as lower incomes lead to a reduction in tax collections that will further the negative effect on the federal budget. Important and much-needed entitlement programs would come under even greater budgetary pressure, threatening support for those who are most in need. However, this front-burner issue has been relegated to the back burner of economic topics. With this looming problem, the future is on shaky ground.

High-debt levels also reduce government flexibility in responding to future emergencies, natural disasters, war, and recession. One of the reasons the United States was able to recover from the Great Depression more quickly than other countries was that the national debt was relatively low. The US debt was at about 35 percent of GDP before the financial crisis started. As a result, US policymakers had considerable flexibility in addressing the situation. If the national debt was significantly higher at the start of the crisis, as it is now, it would most likely have been more difficult to remedy. Additionally, the United States had the fiscal ability to meet the enormous demand of fighting World War II because debt was relatively low before the war.

A strong fiscal outlook is essential for a growing, thriving economy. Putting our nation on a sensible fiscal path creates a positive environment for growth, opportunity, and prosperity. With a solid fiscal foundation, a nation gains an increased access to capital funding, resources for public and private investments, and a healthy consumer and business environment as well as a strong safety net. In the foreseeable future, there will also be the impact from AI on employment which will have to be dealt with.

As the federal debt increases, the government will spend more of its budget on interest payments with diminished funding in public investments. Over the next sixteen years, the Congressional Budget Office projects the possibility that interest costs could total $1.2 trillion a year (with the assumption that interest rates remain low) if the current situation continues to go unchecked. As of now, the US spends more than $1 billion per day just for the payment of interest on the national debt.

When more federal resources are diverted to paying interest, there will be less available to invest in areas important to economic growth. Not if but when interest rates rise, the federal government's borrowing costs will increase sharply. By 2049, projections by the Congressional Budget Office estimate that interest costs could be more than twice what the federal government has historically spent on research and development, nondefense infrastructure, and education combined.

The tax cuts of 2017 are doing exactly what could have been predicted: a phenomenal addition to the national debt. To cover expenses, the United States government has had to borrow a substantially larger amount of money to pay for the cost of tax cuts. This is something that is constantly underreported in media and is also being relegated to a back-burner issue. Much of what is presented on media platforms, and what I consider propaganda for its lack of presenting the complete picture, is about just how great our economy is. The main media focus mostly concentrates on either attacking or praising the president depending on what platform you were watching. A presidential campaign promise is always to reign in the national debt. When the Democrats took control of the House of Representatives in 2018, you would think they would aim their sights on this spiraling problem. But to the contrary, they became fixated on the president and impeachment. The implications of the 2017 tax cuts add a need for immediate austerity somewhere in the budget perhaps in the form of cuts to Medicare, Medicaid, and Social Security, to get some debt under control. Good luck with that.

There is a faction among economists who believe that the debt is not out of control but rather in a healthy place. They argue that underborrowing is just as dangerous as overborrowing. They argue that debt payment is half of what it was in the early eighties. Of course, they do not mention the disparity in interest rates between the early eighties and current interest rates. They feel there is strong evidence that the United States has enormous running room to borrow. That is because it is a huge and wealthy country that borrows in a currency it can print, with a large internal market, and it controls the global reserve currency; plus, it is the key world financial center. All that means is that there is a huge demand for US debt, and thus insuring modest interest rates. We could run up trillions more in debt without risking even a slight negative consequence. But the question is, Will the low-interest-rate environment continue forever? If I wanted to negatively impact or destroy a countries economy, I would cheapen the cost of borrowing to increase that countries debt as well as reliance on borrowing and when this is achieved simply start increasing the cost to borrow. All without firing a shot.

It is also true that slashing borrowing to zero would impact the world's economy and could easily create an economic crisis. That is not being proposed. Foreign countries need dollars to settle their international accounts, and if they aren't readily available, then they might strangle their domestic economies with high interest rates that would be needed and required as payment to borrow, initiating a worldwide recession.

Too much austerity can make a debt burden more problematic by cutting output and thus the nation's ability to pay. Other countries, such as Greece, have actually hurt their economies through too much austerity, by causing their debt-to-gross-domestic-product (GDP) ratio to increase because of the recession produced by the austerity. There is some truth in the philosophy that in times of economic weakness, the responsible thing to do is borrow and spend. But that does not mean to spend yourself into an abyss that will be very difficult to emerge from.

In the early eighties, price increases were regarded as so harmful that the federal government increased borrowing costs to bring down inflation. The Fed could have stabilized borrowing costs by printing money and buying up government bonds, but that would have just pushed even more money into the economy, further fueling a problematic inflation index. The first priorities in economic policy should always be full employment, maximum production, and price stability.

In summary, if we fail to reign in the national debt, our long-term fiscal challenges will continue to escalate, and our economic environment will become weaker as confidence in the economy continually diminishes and access to capital is curtailed because of fiscal fear. Higher interest costs would diminish key investment opportunities moving forward, and conditions for growth will continue to be under stress. Our nation would be put at a greater risk of an economic crisis. If our long-term fiscal overspending is not addressed, our future economy will be diminished, resulting in fewer economic opportunities for all and less fiscal flexibility to respond to future needs.

*****

There are opinions held by some that censorship in the United States should be used to curb propaganda. It currently exists, and it is labeled "censorship for the common good." For example, censorship with respect to TV ads, movies, and pornography. But the censorship I am talking about is that which is utilized in the media. In reality, media censorship may be the worst propaganda of all. Yet it occurs today on a regular basis in the news, and most times we do not realize it.

Media platforms decide every day what to run and what to restrict. Censorship is a tool of propaganda as much as propaganda is a tool of censorship. Their purpose is the same—news manipulation. Simply by editing a story you are opening the front door to censorship and the back door to propaganda. A subconscious decision to keep information from becoming public is an act of censorship as well as a path to propaganda. Sometimes, there are important grounds to justify the use of censorship; some of which are reasons of national security or protecting the privacy of others. Sometimes, the rationale is less moralistic such as protection from negative fallout either corporate or political.

The decision of what to share in a story and what to hold back is a difficult one and is often made more difficult when outside pressure is applied to censor a story or part of a story. Sometimes, the source of a story is protected in the name of either safety or privacy. This perhaps is the most benign and understandable form of censorship as is omitting lurid details involved in a story. This is done not to sanitize a story but rather to avoid horrifying the viewer with explicit details of a violent nature.

It is much more sinister to allow censorship whose purpose is to protect corporate or political interests. When the outcome of censorship is the propagandizing of a story through deliberate omissions in the defense of a political bias, we are describing a common practice of media platforms. With the onslaught of citizen journalism and Internet platforms, the "interpretation" of truth has an easier way of getting out. But these very avenues of information through the interpretive process bring forward their own challenges in the era of "fake news."

The problem of disinformation can never be solved through censorship. It has proven to be an ambiguous concept ranging from explicit legal prohibitions to more subtle forms of economic and social control. Currently, there are forces willing to restrict various types of communication. By doing so, we are replacing one evil with another. Even the suggestion of dealing with disinformation or fake news through the formulation of protective or restrictive law is a slippery slope.

In my opinion, the best defense against disinformation is a healthy investigative instinct. The audience has a responsibility to avoid being misled by questioning the information presented. Media platforms deserve some of the blame for allowing information to be presented to the audience in distorted fashion. If we are, in effect, going to have these enormous platforms that were meant to present honest and factual news decide what gets listened to with respect to a news story and what should not be included in the presentation, there's no limit to what could happen to divisiveness among viewers.

The impact of disinformation and propaganda is that it interferes with democracy in two ways: they both dominate and distort the public conversation concerning an issue and corrupt the process of democratic decision making, and when this process leads to the political success of one candidate or political party over another, the political force that wins the elections through manipulation might go on to further damage or deconstruct the constitutional system that is in place. This process is very difficult to stop once the winning political entity is in power and can only be prevented or slowed down by the tools of a judicial democracy—the self-defending constitutional state.

But currently, there is a vacuum when it comes to the control of propaganda opening the door to all sorts of political opportunists. The content of media platforms and the architects of this form of communication leave us with many existential and political uncertainties. We now reside in a postfact era which leaves us with the questioning of trust and a state of unreliability. A complex array of collective strategies exists through which fear, anger, and anxiety are created and presented in an extremely repetitive manner.

At their inception, Internet platforms maintained that they would hold a neutral stance when it came to information exchange. But over time, the manipulation of user attention through the use of algorithms, among other methods, has been determining what an audience sees and hears first. They have become curators of information. So, in essence, we have private companies with governmental, dictatorial like powers of censorship. Perhaps a remedy lies in exploring ways to require that platforms decentralize become more diverse and competitive through the development of alternative media markets. They have a responsibility to all users to be platforms for both multipolitical and multisocial discourse.

Propaganda Prisons

Newspapers, magazines, news channels, radio stations, advertisements, or any other types of mass media contain some level of propaganda. It is often seen as having a negative connotation due to its history of influencing power and control during the world wars. It is defined according to *Webster's* dictionary as "information or ideas methodically spread to promote or injure a cause, movement, or nation, and the deliberate spread of such information or ideas." The purpose of propaganda is to convey the only way to look at a particular situation or idea.

Sometimes, it results in no important change in audience position or viewpoint. The topic does not have much effect, because it may be insignificant to the viewer. Sometimes, it is presented in a humorous form to dull the fact that they are actually viewing a source of propaganda while making the viewer oblivious to the fact that what is being viewed is actually propaganda. How common is this type of presentation? It is a part of almost every late-night show on media.

Propaganda in the media coverage of a war can have a lasting effect on an audience and may result in changing the way society reacts to a conflict. This was especially evident during the Vietnam era. Its influence on public opinion can be the difference between continuing and ending a war. There is a significant effect with the use of propaganda, misinformation, or disinformation in a rationale to even go to war. This was evident with respect to the Iraqi War. Media was caught up in a rally round the flag spiral through the use of foreboding unease. By using fear of more terrorist attacks against the US, the government targeted a war-directed campaign through media. Other major countries were less convinced about the various claims to justify war. Since they did not directly experience 911, their level of fear was much lower. Propaganda itself can be an evil entity. For example, Hitler's Germany. Its methodology was used to persuade people to think and more importantly react in a certain way; and with questions of war, that usually means getting them to either reject or support the endeavor.

Whether the propagandist works in a peacetime or wartime situation, certain tools are utilized to mobilize ideas, opinions, and attitudes. An important one that is commonly used is *insinuation*. What is presented comes with an accompanying interpretation that fosters the premise of the propagandist. They try to motivate others to accept without challenge their own presumption and to react accordingly. Insinuation draws an unproven conclusion from the facts and tries to lead the audience into accepting a supposition even with the lack of logical detail to support it. The propagandist usually tries to sidestep critical reactions from their audience to strengthen their insinuation even further. What come to mind are the insinuations made during the impeachment hearings of 2019–2020 and the Justice Kavanaugh debacle which the public had to endure.

How does the propagandist effectively use the tool of insinuation? By making broad and overreaching statements. By presenting their statements in simple and familiar language. By refusing to admit, and will not even suggest, that there is another side to the issue. The media presentation on the topics mentioned is an excellent example of propaganda. Another example is the repeated assertion that the president of the United States was involved in a collusive partnership with Russia.

There are several ways in which the power of *suggestion* can be used: by bringing a concern or product to your attention, by creating an opinion about an issue or product through a reference or comparison, and by instilling a lasting emotional bond with either a topic or product by creating a symbiotic association. Worried about climate change, then just suggest turning the discussion to the lack of political will to reduce carbon emissions. But keep jobs, the economy, and financial costs out of the discussion. It's all the fault of politicians. The use of suggestion is also extremely useful in commercial advertising. Go no further than the advertisement of beauty products. People have a tendency to believe what they hear in advertisements. No one fully understands why suggestion is so influential. Researchers believe it is rooted in a subconscious brain process, that part of our brain that works unconsciously and on instinct. Suggestion is so powerful that it can even affect the way we see ourselves. Think of a beauty product. As long as you're convinced enough of the effect of a product, the way you view results is with a positive reaction.

Technology has also evolved to use another power of suggestion which is to analyze our behavior and suggest other related concerns or products. It's the "people who bought this also bought" strategy or "the people who viewed this movie or documentary also viewed" approach. It's an attempt to influence decisions.

Another method of suggestion is the appeal to the already formed thoughts of the audience being targeted. As previously mentioned, one's *"fact bubble"* plays a critical part in how propaganda is received. It's easier to preach to the choir. Psychologists say that preconceptions are an important factor in belief. Therefore, some members of an audience may support some unsound economic idea because they desire security in their old age. This is one reason so many socialist ideas have taken root in our country. Some people will believe an outrageous idea to improve their economic situation even if it sounds too good to be true. The concept of free college tuition comes to mind. The propagandist will study public opinion to find out what issues people are either in favor of or not in favor of in order to decide on the method that they will use to bring about a desired outcome. They fully understand that such terms as "economic equality," "social justice," and "law and order" arouse favorable attitudes and would serve as an important device to use in getting their message across. And just the opposite, the propagandist may use certain other vocabulary such as "violent," "anti-American," "radical," "socialistic" to influence their audience to reject an idea that they view as contrary to their own interests.

Lately, in the media, left-leaning politicians have been presenting some pretty outrageous suggestions to cure the ills of such issues as climate change. But there is little in fact to back up these ideas and suggestions. The appeal is mostly to discontented or unhappy groups. There is no concern for the truth, only the formation of a catalytic response that favors the ideas of the propagandist. In a given situation, it will accept any idea that might prove useful, and it will abandon that idea as soon as the situation changes. Ideas on national socialism and economic reform have been received as either positive or negative depending on one's preexisting fact bubble.

The skilled propagandist also knows other techniques of insuring that you conform to their way of thinking. They resort to the use of *key words*, *slogans*, *memes*, or other symbolic forms. Advertisers appeal to desire as the main interest of their audience. The desire to be strong and healthy, to be socially acceptable, to be beautiful sells everything from clothing, cosmetics, dieting programs, drug products, soaps, to perfumes. Anyone who views an advertisement, either on social media or in print, will instantly understand exactly what I am talking about.

An advertising slogan packs meaning into short sentences or key phrases. The purpose is to get the message noticed. The skilled propagandist insures in every way possible and by all the means at their disposal that their message will find their way into the minds of people. When a person is deciding on the purchase of a particular product, it is the slogan accompanying the product that first comes to mind. Many years ago, advertisers discovered that appeals to the rationale as to why a product was a good purchase were not always effective. Appeals were then shortened and emotionalized, since most audiences will not take the time necessary to thoroughly investigate explanations of why one product is better than another.

International political propaganda is full of examples of the use of striking slogans. For example, Brexit was used as a description of the separation of England from the European Economic Union. Fake news describes media stories that are laden with personal opinion and innuendo. Add to this the fact that if something does not agree with your partisan narrative, it is fake news. Compelling slogans have been devised to win support for a cause and many other such activities. Slogans have been a rallying point of people in the past and continue to influence to the present day. If a slogan or term catches on correctly and objectively, its influence can certainly be long-lasting.

It also makes effective use of symbols. A *symbol* is a concrete representation of an idea, action, or thing. The American flag is truly a symbol of importance. When the flag is disrespected, the philosophy and ideas associated with it are disrespected as well. The flag conveys a common message to masses of people. It is a symbol of the kind of cohesiveness that holds a social group together. Symbols can be used to develop both favorable and unfavorable attitudes. Symbol usage will create images that are used much as a deaf person uses sign language. Cartoonists have stereotyped symbols to represent the president, various ideologies, the economy, and many other issues. These symbols are effectively used to convey a stereotyped message that is near and dear to the propagandist's heart.

Stereotyping is another tool in the arsenal of the propagandist that is easily exploitable in order to achieve a specific reaction especially when emotions are running high. We are all guilty of prejudicial feelings in one form or another. Most times, those feelings involve likes and dislikes about everyday choices we all have to make and are mostly inconsequential. However, the prejudice and stereotyping that is most alarming involves groups of people who have a specific belief or ideology. A prejudiced individual draws a conclusion about a larger group of individuals on the basis of a much smaller sample. The use of smear tactics is at an all-time high, involving outright lies, distortions, out-of-context quotes, and innuendo. The "apple does not fall far from the tree" is the kind of thought process at work here and which is being exploited through propaganda. We have especially been experiencing this in the world of politics. Democratic politicians are evil. Therefore, all Democrats are evil. Republican politicians are evil. Therefore, all Republicans are evil. As we should know, nothing could be further than the truth. There are good and bad actors in every group or organization. Media platforms love to take the words of the worst that belongs to an organization or adheres to a specific viewpoint and parade them in front of the public as if he or she is representative of everyone in that group. And then we wonder why there is a continuous and increasing divide within our country. The media takes a statement from a group member and turns it into an emotionally resonant stereotype that becomes associated with everyone else within that group. This feedback creates a distorted perception of reality and at the same time puts us in a heightened emotional state, making us open to further manipulation. The propagandist builds up a solid and rationally constructed argument and then presents an irrational conclusion and opinion, which is especially effective when our emotions are already at a heightened level. People can be better manipulated when their emotions are at a peak.

Another less widely used strategy of the propagandist is to create a reaction through *deceit*. This occurs when the propagandist invents an incident or exaggerates an incident in order to provoke a specific response. As an example, what come to mind are Jussie Smollett and Tawanna Brawley, who both faked assault in order to achieve a specific outcome. The resulting wave of indignation was used to support a preplanned effort against the group targeted and labeled as the causal factor.

Another area exploited by the propagandist is *statistics*. They are very adept at taking a statistic and interpolating it to fit nicely into their own agenda. Most of us are not great at dealing with numbers at the best of times and are worse when the numbers are presented in a way that confirms our preexisting worldview. There are many variables in statistical reporting: randomness of the sample, who is in charge of the polling, mathematical ranges of error, bias, degree of competence, untruthful participants, and fluctuation of opinions. Many polls and statistical analysts have as a goal simply to persuade someone to accept a specific point of view or philosophy and not to simply determine public opinion. The polls for the 2016 presidential election come to mind. When viewing the polls, one would think that having the election was a mute issue.

Another form of propagandist manipulation is through the use of *slogans*. Slogans can either be used to inhibit or advance a cause. When repeated regularly on a continuous spectrum, they become a kind of truth in and of themselves. The term "fake news" is a powerful way to use two works to debunk all information coming from a particular source. The term in itself is thought terminating. Media stories are compressed into a very short, highly emotion-inducing, and authoritative-sounding phrases, easily remembered and easily defined. The phrases when in sync with one's point of view become the beginning and end of any further constructive analysis.

An effective method of spreading propaganda is to allow it to spread and grow quite organically. While there are, indeed, professional propagandists out there, much of what you encounter online is much more subtle. Propaganda is gently introduced and touted as an ethical outlook and is viewed as a representation of a much bigger acceptance without any proof that it is no more than the thoughts and philosophy of a small minority. It is introduced as a dangerous extreme but in a benign form, penetrating the subconscious very slowly but eventually leading to a false conclusion that this outlook is widely accepted by the entire group in question. It is basically the extrapolation of a single incident as the defining viewpoint of a much larger entity. This type of propaganda is not only very common but very insidious. It is presented through social platforms and gains a life of its own from multiple sources and through the use of specific phrases and emotionally charged statements. It develops from those sources into a more cohesive form, ultimately creating a view repeated over and over until it becomes part of the subconscious and distorts a person's perception of reality largely before it reaches a conscious level. If liberals are allowing the homeless problem to escalate in certain cities while doing nothing to remedy the situation, then this must be the position of all liberals. If conservatives feel that climate change is not exacerbated by society, it is because they all have plugged their ears to the controversy. This type of sociological and insidious propaganda is leading to greater division within our country. The fact is that not all liberals think alike and not all conservatives think alike.

The media outlets are acting as information-processing systems designed to propagate worldviews by controlling the flow of information and expanding incidents into a defining aspect of a much larger group. It is my contention that conservative and liberal philosophies are aligned along a continuous spectrum and that people exhibit different degrees of both. Looking at media coverage, you would not think that we have a large number of independents as part of our political system. Yes, terms such as "left of center" and "right of center" are used by the media, but how often? Sociological propaganda fogs our thinking and penetrates the subconscious very slowly leading to a false conclusion that this outlook is widely accepted by the entire group in question and does little but stir up prejudices and hatreds. People need to become more sensitive to sociological propaganda methods if they are to protect themselves from manipulation.

It is no longer just a tool for changing your opinion. Now, in our digitally oriented society, propaganda is a pathway to immediate buy-in and participation when it comes to political conflicts. This is accomplished from the safety and comfort of your living room sofa. It has become a catalyst in the breaking of relationships and connections between friends and relatives whose opinions are different from your own. Participation in this kind of socializing propaganda helps to increase conflicts and make them part of everyday life. This increasing degree of participation can also lead to an internalization of conflict. Instead of encouraging you to reach out and investigate alternative sources of information, socializing propaganda has as its goal to actually change the way you cognitively process information besides changing the way you emotionally interact with others in your environment.

Use the Internet to challenge and find alternative sources of information. These days, however, it seems that even a huge diversity of voices does not help to challenge propaganda or increase critical thinking. In order to address the dangers of propaganda, we need to focus not on its content but on its delivery and to ask how the new technological tools used for its proliferation changes the relationship between users and their environment. Propaganda has always been more at home in a closed environment where it does not need to compete with alternative sources of information and where it has cornered the market in shaping the perception of the audience. What would be most useful are counter propaganda programs to break through the walls of deceit. Many dictatorial regimes have disconnected their local Internet from the global infrastructure in order to maintain thought isolation. Our country has no forms of threat to limit alternative avenues of information beyond the control of traditional political institutions. The commitment of media platforms to disinformation and manipulation when coupled with the easy access and repetition of the new digital age gives particular advantages to the propagandist whose purpose is to actively shape the media narrative.

Propaganda, simply put, has as its goal to communicate ideas and viewpoints designed to manipulate a target audience by affecting its beliefs, attitudes, or preferences in order to obtain a thought process that is in harmony with the political or social philosophy of the source. Make no mistake, it is the intentional manipulation of news, specifically through the use of misleading information and has as its purpose to support a political or social goal by manipulating behavior. The challenge is to analyze a media story to ascertain what elements within it are misleading or manipulative. This is an extremely difficult behavior to instill in an audience.

Politics, Media, Democracy

The use of semitruths to influence the electorate is to a large extent affecting decision making at the polling booth. Political decisions are being influenced by the disinformation that is not only reaching a somewhat uninformed electorate but is leading to a decrease in critical thinking. The media supplies analysis. Its ultimate purpose is to support and provoke a political action on the part of the audience. Propaganda offers interpretations for conflict-related matters. Unfortunately, the interpretations are based on a mixture of truth and falsehood, and it is becoming more difficult to distinguish between them.

Propaganda is capable of not only changing an audience's perception of social and political issues but is also a way to change the audience's behavior. In this sense, it always acts in two ways. It changes the attitude of the audience and shapes the activity (for example, voting or, for that matter, not voting) in relation to the issue.

We can find some sort of propaganda technique being utilized in most aspects of both media coverage and media advertisement. The "infoslant" actually depends on what media platform you are watching. The opinions and news coverage of the various platforms are so different that sometimes you wonder if they are talking about the same country.

The divide in America is not only along the liberal and conservative line but also along the choice of media platforms currently involved in presenting the news. Political opinion, as well as those political viewpoints in our fact bubble, is fostered by the media platform we choose to watch. If you watch FOX News, building a border wall is both necessary and important. If you watch CNN, building a border wall is a waste of money for a nonemergency situation and not a good idea. So we can see that media platforms directly affect and exacerbate the current divide. Why do these slanted platforms exist in the first place? Part of the answer is revenue and plenty of it.

The so-called mainstream media has a ripple effect that reaches out to the entire American media ecosystem in varying degrees. The platforms have divergent attitudes toward the same stories. They often do not report on the same stories if they are not in line with their political agenda. What is being created and fostered is not only partisanship but a partition or divide as well.

One of the major aspects of the various platforms is that their audiences, both liberal and conservative, are consuming entirely different viewpoints on the news, as well as different news stories. This partition or divide extends out to the powerful influence wielded by various TV and talk radio hosts and other increasingly aggressive online sites. Politics has been turned into prime-time concern and anxiety for both conservatives and liberals worried about the state of the nation.

Stories in opposition to the political slant of a media platform are unable to cross the partisan barrier. The reason given for the obvious nonreporting on both sides are that the stories in question just do not add up. They do not pass the litmus test of fact—that what is being presented is a false theory. It is almost as if we live in alternative universes. There are two separate spheres of news coverage that respond to different incentives and operate in very different manners. One of those spheres is comprised of conservative media coverage as well as conservative talk radio hosts, and the other is the liberal composite from radical to left of center.

The legacy and reputation of the newscasts of the old broadcast networks of the fifties and sixties are a thing of the past and have been replaced by infoslant Internet and media platform coverage. Right-leaning audiences concentrate to a large extent on right-leaning platforms while left-leaning audiences focus their attention toward more liberal media outlets, thus reinforcing and encouraging a divide. What is being created and fostered is an ideological, racial, and ethnic division that is damaging American free speech and cultural unity. Both sides like to hear the news that reaffirms their deeply held fact bubble. That's just a natural predisposition to hear information that reinforces what one believes.

Many committed liberals gravitate toward stories that promise to expose conservative wrongdoing and hypocrisy. Many conservatives are continuously entertained by talk radio hosts who preach that liberals want to establish socialism in America. On both ends of the spectrum, there is an abundant amount of false information and outright conspiracy theories without strong traditional fact-checking mechanisms in operation.

Viewpoints are being established through the use of singular examples and most time that does not give us a clear understanding of the total picture. At the extreme right, conservatives are generally more staunchly anti-union, religious, and supporters of capitalism. On the left, there is strong concern for individualism, the environment, and both social and cultural problems. Both sides feel that neither position receives enough attention and support from establishment newspapers and radio networks.

Both liberals and conservatives believe that the creation of left- and right-leaning media organizations is the answer to getting their beliefs and ideas in circulation. Without such media platforms, there is a real belief that their ideas just would not be circulated. Prior to the creation of biased media platforms, a belief was gaining strength that existing media was ignoring the real concerns of the American people about particular issues by hiding behind a veil of objectivity. Thus, the remaking of American journalism was put into motion. In the fifties, the reporting that we now experience did not exist. An unemotional neutrality in broadcasting was the order of the day and at the center of news broadcasting.

The corporate responsibility of all business enterprises is minimally to tell the truth. Perhaps it is time for legislative intervention to ensure that platform operators tackle the problem of information manipulation, disinformation, and propaganda while at the same time promoting and protecting the right to freedom of opinion and expression.

This may offer a glimpse into the future of an Internet in which more online messages, videos, and posts may be deleted due to legislative law or through the preemptive censorship on the part of tech companies caused by fear of legal reprisals. Call it a necessary evil or a rule for the preservation of truth. But the question of free speech will come up sooner or later (most likely sooner). And more importantly, the question of just who the censors would be must be addressed.

The monitoring of free speech should not be left up to tech companies alone for obvious reasons. In both cases, self-censorship and legislative censorship will lead to free speech constraint and a much narrower range of issue-oriented expression. It is one of the least advantageous ways to combat propaganda. It has become a systemic problem and can only be best resolved through a systemic solution.

Propaganda is maneuvering public opinion. New technology has transformed both the way information is disseminated and the structures in our democracy used as venues to spread misinformation, disinformation, and propaganda as a means to manipulate public opinion. The intention of propaganda is to generate insecurity, hostility, and polarization. It will continue to be used to influence the democratic process. It is utilized to amplify discord and foster agreement with the information being presented. The correlation between disinformation and its effect on political and social opinion requires more quantification. The effect of media content on the audience is being largely contested and in truth has not been scientifically proven. However, platform providers should at least be more responsible for third-party content.

Social media platforms have claimed neutrality when it comes to technology and messaging, but that does not seem to be the actual case. There is a yin and yang occurring between free speech advocates and those wanting to take down a few nefarious posts or online content that is infuriating to specific politicians or political ideologies. Do not put the blame on politicians alone for a possible era of increased online censorship. We cannot forget the role tech companies played in getting us here in the first place. The problems down the road have no easy solutions.

We now have like-minded emotional newspeople and audiences gravitating to their respective corners in the boxing ring of platform media news. It fostered an alternative, exclusionary media environment in which the truth of a story is judged not only on its content but also the media platform from where it originated. What is being fostered and reinforced is a separate political reality, a reality that increasingly does not reference opposing platform ideas in a positive analysis.

It's easy to criticize the divide with respect to news and news consumption from the different media platforms in our country. Those of us who consume a lot of news experience it each and every day. There are those audience members who, indeed, question what they view on news echo bubbles. There are those viewers who routinely criticize the other side's "fake news" and also seek out information through their own investigation that reaffirms their own fact bubble. And there are those who feel that selective exposure to like-minded political news is less prevalent than one may think. Their argument centers around a belief that politically slanted media platforms are not reaching most of the US population. The feeling is that political programming is not a main course in viewer participation. At the same time, one cannot ignore the fact that media is contributing to the existing divide. I do not believe that anyone can argue that it is helping to reduce cultural and political friction. The problem is exacerbated by the fact that the stories, ideas, and beliefs gain a life of their own by spreading among friends, relatives, and colleagues.

The political audience hears something within their favorite media sphere that confirms their existing "fact bubble" or their partisan viewpoint. They talk about it repeatedly to people who are not mainstream avid news listeners. The biased, generalized, or outright false information spreads far beyond the initial audience to those who do not participate with respect to the media platform in question. The audiences play a key role in fueling misinformation to a bigger nonaudience base.

The different media platforms convey not just different viewpoints but also different reactions, different realities, and different emotional feelings. The viewer comes to the inference that one side of the news is either uninformed or incapable of telling truth from fiction. What is being presented is not so much news as a blatant public relations campaign. I understand that propaganda is far more complex and problematic than merely misinterpreting or generalizing about the facts. Its aim is to deceive but not with an "in your face" technique. And the consequences appear to be much worse than most producers of propaganda and their audiences realize.

Both liberal and conservative propaganda are having a negative effect on democracy itself. In our democracy, where propaganda is commonly used by media platforms, audiences believe they live in a liberal democratic culture where free speech is protected by our Constitution. But this belief is to a point a fallacy; and the behavior of the media is actually reinforcing the concept of intolerance, which is basically an antiliberal, antidemocratic concept.

Political propaganda uses one political ideal and pits it against an alternate ideal. The ideologies, as well as the financial interests behind those ideologies, do unrepairable harm and undermine what should be a neutral presentation of fact within both science and news reporting. Propaganda introduces itself as the end-all of a story and fosters what is basically, more or less, a political speech. This infoslant presentation runs counter to all democratic ideals because it shuts down the possibility of any democratic dialogue which is truly what constitutes the meaning of free speech.

The propagandist is obsessed with attempts to force their belief system or reality on an unsuspecting audience who are "sometimes" reminded that what they hear as factual is being interspersed with personal opinion. Ultimately, they would like you to believe that their "truth" is the only truth. This behavior is a far cry from any definition of democracy that is "worth its salt." The propagandists themselves appear to be losing touch with reality by interpolating news stories into something that better fits their agenda. They operate in a world of conspiracy rather than factual news reporting.

A real investigation into actual fact rarely has the ability to gain traction in this kind of environment, thus resulting in a failure to bring mass attention to the flaws in the reporting of the story. If we do not understand how propaganda actually works and the purpose behind it, democracy falls victim to what has essentially become a battle of ideologies using any means necessary to gather new recruits for the cause being espoused.

The strategy to undermine confidence in free speech is similar to what we see in college and university settings. Although it is not the norm, we have witnessed instances where there is an intolerance to any opposing view that contradicts the populist college agenda and the fact bubbles of those students. The very institutions that democracies rely upon to mediate competing versions of the truth sometimes exhibit an authoritarian approach to discourse and stifle opposing points of view. When this occurs, and it is not often, there can be no academic competition when it comes to a discussion of opposing ideologies.

A true democracy requires rational debate. With the ever-expanding division within our country, the opportunity for dialogue is getting slimmer and slimmer. "Either think the same way as I do, or don't think at all." What is happening is simply an attempt to shut down open-minded thinking. A true democracy values not only the liberty and political freedom it enjoys but is also defined by a wonderful and healthy tolerance for difference. There is a lack of respect for difference of opinion, difference in cultural values, difference in social ideologies, and difference in how we prioritize the importance of scientific concerns and how best to remedy those concerns. Therefore, our form of democracy is under attack as well.

The view that a collective thought process and intellectual sharing and deliberation is superior to an intolerance of certain viewpoints seems to be lost in the current divisive ideological culture that currently exists. Free speech and a public reasoning for the common good is losing ground by the diminished sharing of ideas and the exclusion of certain groups in the conversations.

In order for there to be a catalyst of change, it is important not only to understand what propaganda is but also to identify the underlying rationale for its use and to recognize it for what it really is: an exploitative attempt to spread a one-sided ideology. To be fair, both political ideologies are "guilty as charged." In attempts to stifle democratic deliberation, both sides of the ideological divide are conspirators. The sole purpose is to divide opinion and protect and enhance those divided opinions by any means necessary. Propaganda becomes a tool that discourages an audience from participating and sharing their ideas concerning how best to address the problems our nation currently faces. Both sides are obsessed with how to best "spin" the news to strengthen their personal philosophy.

It's difficult to have a real discussion about an issue when the story is filtered through a specific spin. The idea of a "fair and balanced" media platform is an insult to one's intelligence. A true analysis of the dialogue exposes the real agenda, and it has nothing to do with "fair and balanced" but rather "unobjective and manipulative." It is very easy to acquire the philosophy of not being able to believe what anyone is saying on the news, and therefore, it is fruitless to even be part of a media platform audience. Unfortunately, not everyone sees this and use the "opinions" fostered by their favorite platform to reinforce the ideas and point of view they already hold. And in doing so, they are adding to the destruction of democratic autonomy, intellectual equality, and higher-level reasoning.

Propaganda is an attempt to "darken a room" rather than shed light and improve rational discourse. To truly be objective requires openness, and the possibility of openness is limited with propaganda in play. What are truly being reinforced are one's personal biases. Propaganda eases you into an armchair and hands you a drink and some chips all while offering to do your thinking for you. In the long term, it does irreparable harm to the public's trust. It is truly a polarizer when it comes to ideologies.

We are all victims. We all become prisoners of the media platforms that espouse "our kind of bias." It is a divider. In essence, anyone who has a political ideology can become a prisoner of propaganda. It creates a one-sided viewpoint which in turn creates an enemy of anyone who does not share that viewpoint. The reality is when somebody wants to prove they are right, they do so by pointing out that somebody else is wrong. There is nothing inherently wrong with this except when the means used go far beyond the factual information to make one's point in the first place.

Media platforms are doing nothing to ameliorate this problem. They have a great potential to act as a greater good in reducing social and cultural divides. They are in a position to actually alert the public about the dangers of propaganda manipulation. They have the platform and ability to correct fabricated information, research authoritative unbiased sources, and, in general, curtail the spin they place on reporting. Instead of analyzing media messages and producing an influential spin, simply present the story, and allow the audience the power to analyze. This is especially important when it comes to politics, elections, and voting.

Seventy years ago, the studies in this area pointed to the conclusion that the message of the media had a minimal effect on voter preference, that the voter's mind was made up long before the messaging. The prevalent result of research at that time was that those most likely to change their vote choice were those who were least exposed to politically oriented media. This rationale sort of made sense since those most interested in politics are most likely to already be highly partisan and highly resistant to information aimed at changing their thought process. I believe we can establish with certainty that "most" voters know whom they will vote for long before an election takes place. Therefore, the main target of political reporting and propaganda are those that are not die-hard partisan voters which is a smaller percentage of voters compared to the whole. However, presidential elections can be decided by very small margins. This group is the least involved or influenced in media messaging. But what has changed in my opinion is how the messages themselves are promoted.

The way we receive information has drastically changed since the fifties—the Internet, computers, laptops, cell phone technology. It is becoming more and more difficult to not be influenced by technology. Media presentation ranges from the use of direct persuasive influence on public opinion to the more subtle and indirect means of altering political processes. It now has more varied platform hardware to directly persuade people to support one candidate over another in the context of an election. It has the ability to direct attention to a particular issue that supports their ideology and ignores the issues that would minimize that support. Campaign-directed media stories emphasize an issue that is perceived as one candidate's strength or another candidate's weakness. It is a purposeful attempt to either alter or reinforce a voter's decision-making process by shifting emotional feeling more positively toward evaluating the candidates in question on that particular issue, which, of course, favors the media platforms choice.

There are very few people who are single-issue voters, but issues when used in conjunction with other issues paint a picture of a candidate which is in stark contrast to their opponent and can have the ability to shift a candidate's overall favorability in the eyes of some audience members. This process can be either subtle or in-your-face direct; but to be sure, we are constantly exposed to it day in and day out. Because of the consistency of the messaging, the influence of competitive media platforms in the political environment is tremendous.

When viewing opposing media platforms, switching back and forth with the remote, you have to wonder, as mentioned, if you are moving through alternate universes. You might conclude that the messaging of opposite ideologies and platforms cancel one another out. To some extent, that is true, but it is not the most important point here. The most crucial point is the effect it has on reinforcing the divide. Recent studies have produced the conclusion that there is very little evidence of media persuasion in the political arena due to the slanted reporting of the various media platforms. But the point that remains unquestionable is that division in our nation is reinforced and the healing process is nowhere in sight.

Political advertising and advertisements from opposing candidates that appear in commercial form during a show or movie presentation are more likely to have a cancelling effect than the continuous philosophy presented on a media platform. Media platform ideology story lines are basically political advertising in narrative form. In summary, although these presentations and theme choices may or may not have a considerable influence on voter preference, they certainly negatively influence the divisional polarization currently taking place. Contributing to this division is the fact that media is literally everywhere in our physical environment.

They influence people when they are driving, walking, on mass transit, at the gym, on vacation, and basically every time they search for something on their iPhone. The more the audience views, the more they are influenced. Its presence dominates all aspects of life and reaches all kinds of people. While it is true that most Americans are well aware of media platform persuasion and there exists a long-term loyalty to one ideology or another, negativity can have the effect of altering one's perspective of an opposing ideology and not in a good way. Although platforms may not have much effect on a well-established political point of view, I am not so sure the same can be said as to how platforms change tolerance to opposing viewpoints and ideas.

Delivering the Message

Mass media does have the power be it to influence the audience that is "sitting on the proverbial fence or to reinforce an opposing ideology up to and including taking action." The prevalence of advertising speaks volumes about the strength of media platforms. And if that is not convincing enough, one need look no further than the prevalence of political consultants and talk show hosts that dot the landscape of both ideologies. There are large amounts of money being spent on multifaceted attempts to influence audience viewpoints.

The effect of all this may not lie in the message being espoused by the different strategists but rather in how the message is publicized. When a political candidate holds a rally, what is actually more impressive: the message itself or the venue of how it is delivered? When rallies are held and overflowing crowds are in attendance with thousands unable to participate because of overwhelming audience response, that becomes the message.

The development of computerized voter targeting, sophisticated communications technology, and the formation of extremely knowledgeable and effective public relation firms all add to campaign effectiveness. Not so much the message but rather how it is formulated and delivered. Although one can never be sure with accuracy why one candidate is perceived as a better choice over another, we can be certain that there are a multitude of factors that go into achieving a victory, and one of the most influential is public perception.

So in 2016, two perceptions stood out: the positive media platform polling numbers of one candidate ("Why go out and vote? She is a sure winner") and the massive attendance at rallies and overwhelming emotionalism of the opposing candidate ("If we support this guy, he may actually have a shot"). To be sure, there are many other factors involved, the discussion of which could probably fill another book; but years from now, these two variables will probably be brought up the most.

Although it is true that a combination of factors is in play during elections to influence public opinion, it is difficult to assess the effect of any single one. The accumulation of empirical results is difficult to interpret, because of the various factors in play. However, certain ingredients stand out as most likely more influential than others. These factors can either have a positive or negative influence on voting. When this occurs in combinational form, where they are counterproductive for one candidate and productive for the other, the results could be quite surprising, such as what occurred in the 2016 presidential election, where one ideological group thought the outcome to be obvious to the point that voting was not that crucial and the other ideological group was reinforced by media coverage of overwhelmingly supportive campaign rallies. This is not to say these were the only factors involved but stand out as quite influential in producing the outcome.

Another contributing factor was the impact of the Clinton e-mail scandal and doubts about her honesty. The Clinton e-mail scandal received detailed scrutiny. The timing of the investigation created a perfect storm. The damage was based on the supposition that facts, at first, is an "either-or" process. Either you believe the fallout surrounding the nonprofit organization, the e-mail and Haitian scandal, and the cover-up theories; or you did not. Both fact and supposition remain a constant until further information is brought forward that may alter both. But the questions and doubt remained in place even up to the week of the election. The messaging became controversial, and it was the reports concerning the left that became problematic. The rally messaging on the right was also an observable phenomenon. They both resulted in a stronger verification of the scandal message rather than its dismissal. Visibility has become an important factor, as well, in political propaganda, from the perception of how much a candidate receives in donations and spends on the election campaign to the visual success of political rallies.

Sadly, none of this has anything to do with the issues, and none are indicators of a successful presidency. The election process itself is what confers legitimacy on an election outcome. But if the process is believed to be a function of media coverage or political consultants or costly advertising, then it becomes very difficult for those on the losing side to see the election outcome as fair. For this reason, many voters felt "the fix was in."

The general public associates campaign propaganda advertising as a deterrent in choosing a candidate. This is one instance where advertising may not deliver the desired effect. When first viewed, expensive television advertisements attract a great deal of attention, but because of overuse, they may be one of the least effective means of persuading voters. Over time, and quite naturally, these ads lose their intended effect. Assessments of the extent of influence from any given message often exaggerate the amount of influence of that message. The media platform assumption is that political opinion can and is changeable, but the media influence of ad campaigns in elections remains questionable at best.

The audience gravitates toward messaging that reflects like-minded feelings and, therefore, reinforces their preferences more than change them. To what extent these "observations" of unimpactful advertising will be scientifically upheld has yet to be observed. Many researchers have speculated that audience exposure to ideas they do not already agree with is increasingly limited by the choice the audience makes with self-selection. Viewers look at some of the media content offered today and find it to be heavily biased, more so than in the past, toward one ideology or the other. However, the potential to be a reinforcing influence is greater than ever before. Without taking into account the audiences for these programs, the content itself seems more geared toward persuasion than news programs of the past, which at least attempted to achieve "fair and balanced" reporting. Media personalities now view themselves as a political force, and they increasingly cover their own self-importance in their programming. Their reputation is built upon their prowess in "propaganda analysis. They have become the media superheroes whose job it is to prevent the unwitting public from becoming victims of political persuasion.

Media coverage of politics encourages us to be among those who know the "real" facts behind an issue. But in reality, media views audiences as gullible and easily manipulated. We, as Americans, are truly not being well served by news platforms in general. The one-sided approach to covering politics is a disservice to the American people because the coverage, strategy, and tactics displace more serious reporting of the issues at hand. The entire purpose of election analysis is to provide politicians with opportunities to expose the public to their persuasive arguments rather than issue debate. Media political coverage has exposed some pretty serious problems with the issues of fairness and objectivity.

Artificial Intelligence (AI)

After WWII, a number of people independently started to work on the creation of what at the time were considered "intelligent machines." In the late 1940s, English mathematician Alan Turing may have been the first. He strongly believed that artificial intelligence (AI) was best researched by programming computers rather than by the construction of machines.

By the late 1950s, there were many researchers on AI, and most of them were basing their work on the programming of computers. Artificial intelligence (AI) is an area of computer science that emphasizes the creation of intelligent machines that work and react like humans. One of the activities computers with artificial intelligence are designed for include speech recognition. The next time you talk to your TV remote, consider you are interfacing with a form of AI. It is the science and engineering of making intelligent and comprehending machines based on intelligent computer programing. It is related to a similar field of research aimed at using computers to understand human intelligence.

The advance of artificial intelligence (AI) and the effect it will have on human interaction both on an interpersonal level as well as the assimilation of information and news will have a continuing impact. The area of concern here is not so much the creation of machinery to replace manual labor but with the creation of systems to actually affect our way of thinking. One may immediately infer that with AI, there would be a decrease in disinformation as well as misinformation.

If you want a vision of the future, imagine a world where AI becomes an integral part of our everyday lives. In addition, when it comes to exercising our right to vote, the threat that AI can have on the process is an ominous concern. The term "bots" when discussing AI describes the social media manipulation activities of both domestic and foreign origin.

The 2016 election brought to the forefront the power of foreign intervention in our election process. In the past, to be successful, human beings manually created and managed accounts, used handwritten posts and comments, and spent countless hours reading content online to reinforce a specific narrative which they intended to advance. Recent successes in artificial intelligence (AI) is enabling the automation of much of this work, thereby amplifying the disruptive potential of both domestic and foreign online influence. AI is proving itself to be an effective method to direct and amplify the sentiments and interests of affinity groups that lean toward a specific ideology.

Therefore, AI may not be a death knoll for the problem of propaganda but actually quite the opposite. This emerging threat draws its strength from naiveté in our society by lack of public awareness, by an ill-prepared legal system and laws, and finally by social media platforms that are not, in reality, sufficiently concerned with their exploitation by outside influences. Addressing the problem will require a multiprong approach that involves both the attention of lawmakers and the moral obligation needed to inform and enlighten the public.

Additionally, and just as important, social media platforms have to be held accountable. Basically, information AI is a combination of emerging technologies which are capable of creating and implementing the advancement of both false and convincing disinformation. As previously discussed, propaganda uses both misinformation and disinformation. Misinformation is sharing information by someone unaware of whether it is true or not. If the person who is sharing the information knows it is not true but is sharing it anyway, that is disinformation.

The ability to distinguish among news, opinion, and propaganda becomes particularly important when the viewers become engaged in a social, economic, moral, or political cause. As they learn more about an issue, they will need to be able to distinguish reliable and factual sources and to ignore misinformation and disinformation. However, AI has the ability to create very convincing false realities. The information agenda used in AI actually promotes a personal connotation to what is basically "news via machine." It is capable of enhancing propaganda and influencing opinion as well as possibly being used as an effective system to unmask and detect propaganda.

The terms "Siri" and "Alexa" are pseudonyms for basically what are actually machines that mimic the behavior of live users in the service of either answering questions or promoting narratives on a particular topic. They manifest themselves quite often in the realm of customer service. As far as customer service goes, most times, one has to do a "novena" before finally getting to speak to "a real live person." They are the witnesses to the incredible breakthroughs in the area of speech recognition.

Most recently with the development of a project called Open AI, founded by Elon Musk, computers have actually been able to generate a story using just an opening line. The results were quite remarkable, and the resulting stories though not completely believable were in the realm of being somewhat credible. Language processing is being used more and more to automate an ever-increasing share of the customer service and information technology workforce which in turn has resulted in decreased labor costs and loss of jobs. The situation will inevitably get worse before hopefully getting better.

Additionally, advancements in image recognition and generation can now produce faces that are almost entirely indistinguishable from that of a real person. AI technology also has a more inconspicuous but no less important application in influencing what audiences see online. Social media platforms identify trending content and add that content into the feeds of other audience participants. While the use varies from media platform to media platform, these trend algorithms tend to produce results associated with "likes," "dislikes," "tweets," and "retweets," which heavily influence audience interaction. "A-eye" is not only watching you but is determining the probability of decisions you will make based on specific intel. In addition, the responses to one small interaction are all that is needed to catapult it into the feeds of thousands upon thousands of additional users.

To appreciate the threat at the intersection of misinformation, disinformation, and machine personas, all one has to do is review your use of machines to acquire online information. You probably are aware enough to avoid suspicious accounts on platforms such as Twitter or links to sites which you deem as suspicious. You probably do not accept Facebook friend requests from people you've never met. However, the Internet is a system that virtually can act as a "virus" and can have an impact almost anywhere. A fake video or news story is often picked up by unsuspecting audience members who, unaware of it being a fake news scam, spread the story across media platforms reaching an audience of millions in a very short time. Conversation concerning the story is shaped and molded by the originators of the fake news, and anyone who claims the news or video is a fake is targeted with accusations of supporting a cover-up. A fake public consensus of belief in the story make those who question it feel like a minority. Often, news outlets fall prey to the story or video as well and vouch for its credibility which lends a sense of professionalism to an outlandish lie. AI technology could put this power into the hands of anyone with some degree of computer expertise.

There is no easy way to determine if the information received is authentic and not fake. AI presents challenges that necessitate a national discussion of its possible malicious use, and much of the conversation will result in first amendment concerns that will lead to a legal discussion, which in turn will add additional consequences that will require considerable reflection. Solutions are best discussed in terms of vulnerability, social and national malignance, and the law.

Currently, there is a lack of public awareness or challenge toward content that audiences view online. With respect to politics, AI has become a prime mover of disinformation and confusion. A concerted effort should be made by government legislators and media platforms to bring mass public attention to AI-generated misinformation and, worse, disinformation. There must be a nonpartisan approach to addressing this problem if progress is to be made. To be sure, methods used to "fake news" the public will only become more sophisticated over time. Currently, quite a bit of fake news is more easily identified, but with improved sophistication and technology, this will not remain the case.

Everyone should question what they see online. The audience will be continuously confronted with the ease with which deception is made possible. Alleviating the problem requires us to avoid that first impulse when we see a fake or questionable story or video, to engage in spreading and sharing it, but rather to question its authenticity and truth. Another major problem is that the legal system is not keeping up with passing the laws necessary to prevent malicious propaganda.

One tactic used by the propagandist is to register an unlimited amount of e-mail addresses to establish better control of a story or video whose purpose is to deceive the audience into accepting a fake news story as gospel truth. The problem is with media platform regulation, monitoring, and inspection. We are in a mind-set that this kind of behavior is low in seriousness and is simply a minor violation of a service agreement. But the potential for damage is mind-boggling. For example, there is a fairly well-known media site that allows more than one account with your e-mail and encourages the use of throwaway e-mails. The repercussions of standards such as this are obvious. Perhaps legislators should not leave regulation to social media platforms alone. Pressure should be put on platforms to ensure their users are who they say they are. It is without question that anonymity is an important aspect in Internet usage, and attempting to alter this would go over like a lead balloon. However, minimally, there should at least be a better vetting process in the area of account creation.

Questions involving identity protection and personal freedom will become major talking points. We are all living with a certain amount of "invasion of privacy" that has surreptitiously entered our lives and is being used to monitor both emotion and attitude. Every solution will require painful change. However, regulators will not take any significant steps in implementing the above until the problem reaches opulent proportions and magnitude. AI can become both an effective tool to combat propaganda and also be used to effectively generate propaganda. In addition, research has shown that "fake news" readily and easily develops a life of its own more so than real and legitimate news. In the very near, future computers will be able to develop and generate very convincing news content that a regular audience will find difficulty with assessing its credibility.

Machine learning algorithms, one type of AI, are used successfully in the detection of spam e-mail. Messages are analyzed to determine whether or not they are real communication from n real person or a spam-type message. This type of text analysis is helpful in detecting malicious e-mails and messages. An unbiased analysis of how different media platforms frame and present a story would add to the clarification and separation of fiction from nonfiction. A major variable is that the propagandist, over time, will increase their level of sophistication to improve the look of authenticity and changes their method of approach in presenting fake news. With the passing of time and improved technology, spam e-mail and deception appear to be a problem that the media audience will deal with well into the future. Some fake news could become so sophisticated that the stories become very difficult to dismiss as a deceptive fake story or video. The best way to combat the spread of fake news may be public awareness. The consequences are almost always an attempt to socially polarize, increase political partisanship, and damage trust in mainstream media platforms as well as our government.

In summary, investigate the veracity of a story before moving it forward on an Internet forum. Democracy is under an attack that would have been unimaginable in the fifties. Technology has altered the very foundation of news and media platforms, and trust in media coverage continues to decline while machine learning artificial intelligence and algorithms are playing a more critical role in threats to media accuracy and integrity. Through the use of algorithms and personal data, AI can become a source of whatever information it is programmed to forward.

Artificial intelligence and automation are having an impact on political and social concerns. AI is perceived as a threat to democracy from its impact on election hacking to data surveillance. On the flip side of the coin, the development of strong AI can become the basis for a decision-making process that can far exceed our current political and partisan politics. It could be used to investigate every alternative and possible long-range outcome to reach the most perfect decision available. But this will be a consideration for the future.

Currently, technology is being utilized to create divisions within our country, which are just as important factors as the actual political and social concerns we face. Aside from pointing only to technology and media platforms as dividers, we must also understand the scope and impact of the issues themselves. This is a crucial start in implementing discussion centering on corrective measures.

Both social and political problems are a fundamental part of every society. Deeply polarized media sources add very little to the solving of those problems but instead spend most of their airtime and Internet platforms on the "blame" game. They move in a pernicious circle of hate and attack with the sole result of acting as a magnifier of the problems we face. It is long overdue for mainstream platforms to begin exercising significant constraint on the bias and at best "point of view" that they continue to spread on stories covered.

Platforms on both the left and right extremes of the ideological spectrum are prone to sacrificing accuracy in favor of biased messaging, making them also prone to the spread of disinformation. The accountability and fact-checking mechanisms of media platforms closer to the center on the spectrum provide a barrier against unchecked proliferation of disinformation and a check on the biased reporting from both extremes. Media platforms close to the middle are far more objective and balanced than far-left and far-right ideologies and are less vulnerable to the practice of spreading disinformation and misinformation.

The platforms that concentrate news on the extreme right and left have as a strategy the repetition, amplification, and magnification of news interpretations that strengthen their political and social ideologies rather than correcting the bias-confirming rhetoric and misleading interpretation of facts. Both conservative and liberal platforms at the extremes of the ideology spectrum lack the desire or willingness to adhere to objectivity and accuracy in their reporting of media news and events. The larger the audience that is held under the sway of these extremes, the much larger the amplification of the conspiratorial and deceptive stories. This reinforces the significant gap in information quality for audiences and does nothing to remedy the political, cultural, and social division in our nation.

Today's media platforms are, of course, inseparable from technology, and through technology, the bias and disinformation of the extremes are catapulted to much larger audiences. Technology is not at the core of the disinformation problem but acts as a catalyst in its dissemination from both ends of the spectrum. The symmetry in the structure and practices of the extreme platforms in our country is evidence that the dynamics and problems in modern day media cannot be explained by technology alone. The platforms develop the ammunition of disinformation, and technology is the gun that shoots that disinformation far and wide. Algorithms are an important facet of information dissemination. Both algorithms and machine learning impact media manipulation and disinformation. In large-scale digital media platforms, algorithms serve an important role in spreading disinformation and are used to manipulate the way an audience perceives a story. Twitter is littered with bots spreading disinformation and false accounts. Its spread is just as bad, if not worse, on Facebook than on Twitter. Add to this, all the disinformation on the open Web. The impact is devastating in terms of creating an open-minded, fact-oriented researched approach to media coverage.

Media platform propaganda has to be addressed in order to reduce the polarity we see in our country. Their behavior adds fuel to the fire. Platforms need to research the stories they air and stick to a nonbiased script. The American people do not need biased explanations along with the reporting of news. Let the audience be the interpreter of the news presented. This would go a long way in mitigating some of the polarity which continues to take place. The temptation to leap to assumptions in news reporting is a negative that media personalities find hard to resist. All with ratings and ego as the catalyst for this divisional behavior. We are naturally drawn to the attacks as a form of entertainment and a reinforcer of our personal "fact bubble."

Add to this, the use of trolling, clickbait strategies, social media algorithms, pinpointed advertising, and psychological media profiling, and the problem of polarity continue to escalate.

Questioning and inquiry are actually at a minimum with the added opinions and interpretations that go hand and hand with media reporting. The instances of this kind of behavior are extremely obvious. Some researchers feel that the impact cannot be scientifically assessed as to the influence this phenomenon actually has. However, it is impossible to not recognize that this behavior and strategy, even though not scientifically assessed, is of importance in determining and reinforcing audience attitude. It is of utmost importance to defuse this activity based on the fact that it is an observable and dangerous form of propaganda.

Audiences reached by misleading and false articles and media sources number in the millions. As mentioned, the impact that these stories have in changing behavior may be unable to be scientifically evaluated, but that does not affect the stated observation that this behavior serves no positive purpose. The observation of both misinformation and disinformation in the news, regardless of the lack scientific impact studies, is a serious disservice to the audience that has to be addressed.

The rapid advancement of technologies that digitally manipulate media will only exacerbate the problem. Deceptive media has no place in a democratically healthy society. Disinformation is a sickness that is affecting the well-being of both culture and society. Media platforms have an enduring influence on news interpretation.

There are a number of ways in which artificial intelligence (AI) may help to address media platform propaganda. It could be used to detect and flag false stories on a large scale. Algorithmic tools can be put in place to improve fact-checking and act as a propaganda deterrent. It could also be used to suggest places to find other viewpoints on the topic in question. But this will have no impact on the news reporting taking place on mainstream media platforms. Growing an entire story and adding personal embellishment from a single seed of fact has to be curtailed. Framing and interpreting a story in misleading ways is actually more dangerous than espousing a completely preposterous and readily identified false claim. News stories and their media interpretation or misinterpretation have an impact on existing social and political attitudes and analysis.

So what do we do about all of this? There is no easy answer, but the best thing we can do is to continue to work to make the public aware of the problems undermining today's media platforms and the quality of the information they provide. By focusing attention on the education of media audiences, the negative effect of disinformation can be lessened, and an aura of trust can rebuild and strengthen political and civic media reporting which is essential to a well-functioning democracy. Once the American audience understands how the mainstream media platforms function, the vulnerability to their effectiveness should diminish over time and may even act as a catalyst to restoring unbiased and unopinionated reporting on both political and cultural stories.

Strengthening media accountability is vital in reducing disinformation and manipulation and will play an important part in establishing a stronger democracy where news is judged on facts and not the spin interpretation that is currently presented along with the news. Hyperpartisan news sources, factories of disinformation, and a deluge of fake news on social media are no basis on which to inform the American public. There has never been a greater need for a robust, independent press guided first and foremost by the truth. *I'm not saying that opinion has no place in the news, but opinion should be presented in an unbiased platform where all sides of the opinion spectrum are presented.* Then let the audience decide. Placing constraints on political reporting and taking a careful and cautious approach to regulation is essential if we are ever to get a handle on both misinformation and disinformation. It's time to end the process of audiences receiving media news that is allowed to go unchallenged and is basically an attempt to either reinforce audience ideology or change one's political inclination.

Media platforms are designed specifically to bolster addiction potential and entertainment value. They attempt to eliminate conscious thought on the part of the audience other than blatant agreement or disagreement. Turning political tides in favor of who is best at presenting a biased ideology has to be challenged in the name of reducing cultural polarity.

Organizations such as Cambridge Analytica and Facebook and their use of both AI and psychology to predict ethnicity, religious and political views, personality traits, intelligence, age, and gender, as well as the funding practices of such ideologists as the Koch Brothers and George Soros, have to be brought out into the open. Money and predictability have become the drivers of election campaigns, and democratic principles have been put on the back burner. The philosophy is "We do not want to know what you think, but rather we want to shape how you think." Of particular concern are the data-collection activities of Facebook and Twitter. The extent of their information mining is incredible, even encompassing areas such as sexual orientation and recreational drug use. It is an incredible amassing of personal data. The use of "liking" and "sharing" and how long you remain on a page as well as scrolling and purchases are very predictive factors in developing a fairly concrete profile of a user's personality.

Your profile is sold to data analysts, businesses, or election researchers willing to pay for it. Between that and pursuit of personal history data and credit reports from companies like Experian, analysts get a pretty good idea of your personality and financial profile. Based on your profile, some advertisers may be equipped with paid for information which may give them an edge on getting you to change your mind about a product. The goal is to look for persuadable personality types whether it be for a product or for political purposes. One has to develop a certain amount or common sense to recognize when there is an attempt to sell you on a product or an issue using information about yourself in the process. This tactic will only become more and more refined over time.

One way to counteract this behavior on the part of data analysts, businesses, or election researchers is through the passing of strong privacy regulations. They would require a strong oversight and have very serious consequences for those who break privacy regulations. However, when the government tries to ban something through law, a court challenge most likely will ensue. New laws have to be written in such a way as to minimize a legal challenge. Nonetheless, this type of activity affects your privacy and is a legal concern. There are groups and companies out there whose sole purpose is to mine for information about you, to gather intimately personal data in order to conduct large-scale and yet individualized marketing of the information to any interested party willing to pay for it.

Tech giants like Facebook and governments around the world are struggling to deal with disinformation, from misleading posts about products as well as cultural and political information. Engineers at Facebook are currently working to identify and suppress online disinformation. As artificial intelligence (AI) becomes more sophisticated, there is a growing concern that disinformation and misinformation generated by AI could make the problem of propaganda dissemination even bigger and more difficult to deal with.

This technology can, over time, help governments, companies, and other organizations spread disinformation in a far more efficient manner. Rather than hire humans to write and distribute propaganda, companies, governments, and organizations can use machine technology to compose believable and, more importantly, a varied content and method to make propaganda look more factual by coming from different sources. If this is done on a large scale, the impact can be enormous.

A fake post seen by millions can, in effect, be tailored to a political agenda using different simplified AI or machine created changes. This level of propaganda dissemination can be in place in a few short years. AI technology learns about language by analyzing vast amounts of text written by humans, including thousands of books, articles, and other Internet content. After analyzing all this data, it can develop a variedly written story line all leading to the same analysis.

Machines can generate images and sounds that are indistinguishable from the real thing. This could accelerate the spread of false and misleading information. Some media platforms are currently working with technology that will completely understand the natural way people write and speak. These systems are a long way from being perfected, but they are constantly improving with time. There is a real threat from unchecked text-generation systems, especially as the technology continues to improve. Once fully developed, this will have the capacity to be used as a propaganda catalyst. It will be able to target people individually and lure them into believing in an idea or a cause.

This research has the potential to create a weaponized machine to manipulate both opinions and behavior to advance specific social, cultural, and political agendas. Our nation may be faced with a sophisticated voter-manipulation machine that has the potential to become a game changer and the deciding factor in elections not only in our country but around the world as well. No one ideology will corner the market on this manipulation. As Henry Wallace aptly put, "Their final objective toward which all their deceit is directed is to capture political power so that, using the power of the state and the power of the market simultaneously, they may keep the common man in eternal subjection."

The new propaganda with its insidious techniques is essentially an addictive con machine. The end result is digital dependency. The future of constructive, civic dialogue and a free and open exchange of viewpoints especially with respect to politics is most certainly at risk and in danger of being lost forever.

Companies are acquiring and amassing tremendous amounts of personal information about our likes, dislikes, and personality traits, and are able to develop programs to translate that data into a fairly accurate personality outline used to predict and or ultimately change one's behavior. Currently, your choice of what you "like" on Facebook can actually be used to determine the following: sexual preference, gender, political ideology, and specific traits with respect to personality and personal character. In some cases, the profile actually exceeds even what you think about yourself. If you really want to know a person's true character…check out their Facebook page.

Data about your shopping habits, property ownership, the church you attend or if you don't, what stores you shop in, the magazines you have a subscription with, and other forms of information about your lifestyle can be used to formulate a very predictive personality model that can be used to influence social, cultural, and political attitudes.

We have essentially become a victim of the technology we use. It is not an exaggeration to say we are prisoners of technology and, therefore, prisoners of propaganda. We have built a propaganda prison for ourselves. This prison has no bars but rather keystrokes, apps, and remote control buttons. Our free will is basically less free now than at any other time in history. The prison we created isolates us more and more from one another. Cell phone rules have to be put in place to make dinnertime a moment to share with other family members. You dare not be without your cell phone. Laws have been put in place to limit cell phone distraction while driving, a serious activity where concentration has to be kept at the utmost. Personal interaction has been limited through cell phone use. What we view on this technology is quite often accepted as gospel truth without any verification taking place.

The personality profiles for every adult in the US obtained through technological information mining contain up to five thousand data inputs. And those profiles are being continually updated and improved more and more each day. Both Twitter and Facebook are being used to collect a lot of personal data because people are obsessed by the technology. The reply, the tweets, and retweets include basically the entire argument and the entire emotional feeling you have about a specific cultural, social, or political concern. When a bad actor or terrorist is either killed or apprehended, what is one of the first things that are looked at? Their computer and Facebook page. This occurs even before canvassing friends and neighbors.

The collection of personal information about your personality, viewpoint, thoughts, and concerns are disconcerting; but what is actually more troubling is what they do with the data collected. Your behavior can actually be predicted by your personality, and the more you know about an individual's personality, the more you know about their psychological makeup and the choices they would make if presented with a very specific flow of information. You can actually predict with a fair amount of certainty the decision of that person based on the information they receive and ingest. Therefore, we are all becoming more and more prisoners of the technology we use, the information we receive, the personality profiles and database established through our choices and actions, and especially the propaganda and misinformation we are subjected to. Your personal information and psychological profile not only can be used to predict your behavior but can be used to go one step further—to alter your future behavior. We are discussing a very serious concern here and one that we should all be aware of. The tactics used for the most part to gather information and to alter decision making are secretive at best, if not completely unknown, by the audience in question. For example, with regards to the election process, remember the days when you would receive a phone call, be asked to answer a short survey, and then be asked the most important question, "How do you plan to vote?" That might be the point where you hang up the phone. Well, folks, you can't hang up the phone anymore. Technology and the tracking of your online movements and interests and your reaction to political ads and information designed to change your behavior by preying on your personality trait profile say volumes about your political feelings and subsequent reaction. What you say is just not as important anymore.

We have arrived at a point where a handful of billionaires and corporations can massively influence an election. There is no transparency or accountability. They are able to manipulate voters in a way we are not aware of. They have the ability to influence up to ten million voters through bias and search results on a massive scale. This can be done without the knowledge of the voter and without leaving a paper trail. Without monitoring systems in place, we will never know it even happened. The methods used are invisible and subliminal. The number influenced can range from 2.6 million to 10.4 million depending on the level of aggressiveness used. Something as simple as a "Go vote" reminder on election day to one political party and not the other equates to 450,000 votes. And a "Go vote" reminder does not cost a dime.

Much of this is done through Facebook dark posts, which are only visible to those being targeted. Dark posts are also used to depress voter turnout among key groups of voters. Posts have been used to try to suppress the African American vote. Hillary Clinton once referred to African American youth as "super predators." The statement was used by the opposition in ads reminding certain selected Black voters of her words. Miami's Little Haiti neighborhood was targeted with messages about the Clinton Foundation's troubles in Haiti after the 2010 earthquake. In the Little Haiti neighborhood of Miami, the head of a local women's advocacy group had questions for Hillary Clinton. Marleine Bastien, executive director of Fanm Ayisyen Nan Miyami, believes that Clinton-backed projects helped global investors more than they benefited poverty-stricken Haitians. The more Hillary Clinton refrained from responding to the concerns and questions from the people of Haiti, the perception became that she was trying to evade responding to the issue. To be clear, dark posting was used or attempted by both campaigns in 2016 with the sole purpose of depressing voter turnout. Democrats and their operatives sought foreign help on a number of occasions during the 2016 election to discredit the opposition. It included the fabricated Steele dossier and allegations concerning misconduct and conspiracy by their Republican opponent. To sum up, Democrats reached out to foreign sources to collect what was political disinformation on their opponent and their aides, and Republicans used issues with seeds of fact in their dark post activities.

But it must be noted that the Republican campaign used it much more extensively and were decisively better at it. They have historically taken more advantage of dark posting in political campaigns. Because dark posts are only visible to the targeted users, there's no way, with the exception of the ad originators, to track the content of these ads. There was no oversight or public scrutiny of the many attack ads used in this manner. Just the "rapid eye movement" of millions of individual users scanning their Facebook feeds. Political campaigns can identify and influence potential voters more effectively by gathering as much information as possible on their identities, beliefs, and habits, and continues to drive both Republican and Democratic data firms, which are currently hard at work on the next generation of digital campaign tools. When it comes to politics, there just aren't any angels out there. The philosophy is "Win at all costs." And propaganda along with misinformation plays a leading role in the scenario. It is without any doubt that fake news and propaganda played a role in the 2016 election. The spread of false, biased, and political agenda information was used against voters on both sides where information mining was used to track voters and also utilized highly personalized political messages that would resonate with specific personality targeted models.

Another question that needs to be studied is the extent to which the audience's already existing "fact bubble" plays in determining the information choices the viewer was making. Nonetheless, the technology community needs to address the problem of how AI propaganda is being used for emotion manipulation in mobile messaging, virtual reality programs, and augmented truths.

If fake news is the fuel used for the new automated AI political propaganda machine, bots or fake social media profiles are the lubrication used to ensure a perfect running machine that would control conversations on social media and silence or intimidate journalists and audience members who might question the messaging. Bot propaganda campaigns amplify the messages of political actors, spread messages counter to those of their opponents, and silence those whose views or ideas might threaten those same political actors. Bot developers can be categorized into three groups. They may work for a government sponsor or a consultancy agency or may actually be an individual that is either motivated by their political beliefs or is looking for an opportunity to sell their networks of digital influence to the highest bidder.

Not all bots are created equal. The average Twitter bot is little more than an AI robot that is programmed to retweet specific information to help forward specific ideas or viewpoints. They frequently are programmed to respond automatically to Twitter users who use certain keywords or hashtags. The more sophisticated bots, on the other hand, are more analog and are operated by a real person or group. Fake identities with distinct personalities are their disguise, and their responses to other users online are very specific with the intention of changing their opinions by directly attacking their viewpoints. They have online friends and followers and are sophisticated to the point that they're also far less likely to be discovered and deactivated. As a result, these high-quality botnets are often used in political campaigns. This is one of the activities Russia has been accused of. However, I believe it is safe to assume that most major countries, if not all, are involved to some degree in this activity.

Weaponized AI propaganda machines are only going to become more sophisticated, and improvements in accuracy and influence will allow it to become an even more important problem to deal with. And in dealing with this kind of messaging, keep in mind that the problem is compounded manyfold by the number of bad actors involved. They represent the arrival of a new era in political messaging. All fueled by the gathering of more data, development of better personality analysis, and an increased deployment and engagement of AI technology. It will be very difficult to counter or fight back against this system of messaging both in the court and with the public as well. Predictive-personality targeting becomes even more dangerous with breaches and the potential access to data on US citizens from such government organizations such as the IRS, the Department of Homeland Security, or the NSA. This use of AI has the potential to develop precision and power and becoming a very threatening propaganda technology with the ability to shape major aspects of global politics for the foreseeable future. The distinguishing factor between those who win elections and those who lose them will be how a candidate uses data to refine machine learning algorithms and automated engagement tactics. Elections may very well be decided by which party has the better AI technology.

AI has found a place in the determination of future elections which will involve on a larger scale the use of machine learning. It will be waged online, either covertly or overtly, with the unwitting help of all of us. Anyone who wants to change the use of AI for propaganda and disinformation has to be cognizant of how it works. It's only by this understanding and by developing better safeguards both through technology and laws coupled with a sincere passion to hear unbiased information rather than a manipulated version of the truth that elections will be decided upon through reason and thought rather than emotion and untruths.

The concept that text-generating AI software will eventually become a major tool in the manipulation of online information needs to be addressed through education and legal reform. Just as AI can be used as a tool for propaganda and deceit, it may well have a place in helping to expose and clean up disinformation campaigns. AI can be formulated to act as disinformation detectors by detecting machine-generated text.

With financial markets, algorithms influence large portions of public stock and commodity trading that no longer requires true human analysis. Like politically used AI, they involve the use of trading algorithms attempting to influence price or leverage in the trading arena. In both cases, politics and stock/bond trading, algorithms are used to gain an edge with respect to public sentiment. The relationship between AI and the effects on public opinion is indisputable and will most likely continue to evolve in even more sophisticated ways. Couple that with the ever-developing and reinforced "fact bubbles" or ideological matrixes all of us have, and those propaganda prison bars become more and more difficult to break through.

Propaganda can be used to create distractions or develop a smoke screen to blur focus on more important issues. This technique consists of having the public focus its attention on a topic that is more convenient and less volatile. It is the practice of presenting a news story to the public at a time of turmoil to manipulate the media to look in another direction. This kind of manipulation occurs quite often in our current culture. As a possible example, the announcement of the creation of a space force may have had as its purpose to act as a distraction.

On December 20, 2019, the announcement was made designating the creation of a "space force" which would be charged with the responsibility of protecting America. It would, in fact, become the sixth branch of the US military. The air force would relinquish all of its space duties to the space force, including war preparation in space and protecting US satellites from harm. In listening to media reports, one would get the impression that this is a done deal. In reality, the space force has become the sixth military branch. But in the wake of budget constraints, all that really has occurred is that Air Force Space Command personnel have been predesignated as space force personnel. So why bring the space force topic to the forefront?

The answer could be as simple as a way to deflect concern for some very real and obvious problems facing our country. This was a positive story for the American people.

So the question arises. Even though a subject is based on fact and truth, could it still be a form of propaganda? Could the propaganda reside in the reason for the story in the first place? My contention is that information based on fact could have a propagandist rationale behind it. It is not my intention here to say that the space force story has a propagandist function. That would only be true if the probability of it becoming a reality were slim to none. After all, why announce the creation of a space force if the chances of its creation are dubious at best? Given that the air force currently is involved in space activities and based on the cost for the establishment of a separate branch of the military, one may say that the creation of another branch of government may not be necessary especially at a time when fiscal constraint is of the utmost importance.

The subject of "space force" is being used as an example to point out how real and factually true news story lines can possibly be utilized for reasons unconnected to the story itself. Getting back to the "space force" announcement and the fact that there are clearly several obstacles in the way of its development, the announcement at best appears premature. So much so that the resulting end product of this initiative may be a few years away at best. For one thing, the air force is not completely in favor of a space force or sixth military branch. The reason given is the added complexity to what is already in place. A transfer or new layer of authority would have to be established along with rules of responsibility and governance. The additional overhead and maintenance issues would add an extra burden on the US taxpayer at the least time of affordability.

The argument for maintaining and enhancing a closer scrutiny on the domain of space is without question. The Pentagon already had a space-war and space-operation agendas to counter threats and which will need to be transferred. Both Russia and China have already taken steps to insure a role in space for their cyber, electronic, and warfare activities. It is not beyond reason to infer that they may be working on activities that would be able to cause American satellite disruption. Additionally, Iran successfully launched what it calls its first military satellite on April 21, 2020. There is a tremendous amount of military equipment in space, especially satellites which help the US, Russia, and China navigate and communicate with one another. On top of that, satellites in space help to track enemy equipment, perform intelligence operations, and even help to control missile deployment and accuracy. There is also the question of the multitude of commercial satellites and other communications equipment that is currently in place and being added on to. An additional problem is added by the concern that, with modern technological advances and knowhow, all the equipment that countries are putting in space are subject to being hacked, thus interrupting a satellite's normal activity. The effect on credit card transactions and phone calls would be incredible to say the least. And finally, there is the concern of the tremendous amount of space debris that could also inflict damage.

So the idea is that creating a new service will add a layer of protection to space concerns by establishing a military branch whose entire job is to focus on space. That would give the US a force to counter Russia, China, and other threats while giving space-focused staff a seat in the Pentagon. The obstacles to the creation of a sixth military branch, a space force, are possibly surmountable; but the rationale of creating a new branch of the military and the ensuing cost and increased bureaucracy when it is already incorporated into an existing branch (which is currently in place) may be an argument that is hard to defend.

So why the announcement? One reason is presidential style, and I offer the other reason to be for the purpose of issue deflection—to deflect from the problems in play at that time. In addition, the announcement of a space force has unleashed and fueled propaganda surrounding the issue of Unidentified Flying Objects or UFOs. Many believed this announcement to be the first step in the acknowledgment of the existence of extraterrestrials and technology accumulated from crashed alien spaceships. "Ufologists" applauded this announcement and praised the president because this was considered a first step in bringing to light what they believe to be a conspiracy of secrecy in government bureaucracy. The belief is that this move will unmask the secret space programs currently in existence. The main point here is to establish how even a blatantly factual story can either be used as deceptive propaganda or as a generator of unproven allegations, disinformation, and misinformation on a completely separate issue.

In summary, some of the most effective propaganda techniques work by misdirecting or distracting the public's attention away from other mainstream issues. It's important to see how the repetition of a news story plays out and evaluate what isn't being reported or what is reported just once and not followed up. In an age of information deluge, distraction techniques can be an effective propaganda tool because of the purpose it serves. One way to test for distraction is to see how a story is received in the foreign press and to ascertain its importance there.

One-Sided Approaches

Propaganda is a partisan affair presenting one side of an argument surrounding a news event, a cause, political stance, or ideological position. Its creation can be the result of a government, an organization, or an individual. It is in direct contrast to the impartial reporting of information. The purpose is to present information in such a way as to influence an audience and either attempt to change the thoughts of that audience or reinforce the thoughts that already exist. It is usually repeated and dispersed over a wide variety of media in order to create the chosen result in audience attitudes. It is everywhere—from the reporting of media platforms to advertising the necessity of getting a flu vaccine every year. It often involves simplistic ideas, beliefs, values, and attitudes already in the audience.

The following propaganda techniques, which were previously mentioned, are also a part of the propaganda prison that we should all be made aware of:

- psychological warfare (propaganda between nations);
- public relations (management-controlled information);
- propaganda laundering (report a story through a dubious source);
- astroturfing (the creation of illusionary support for or against an idea, cause, or issue);
- photo and video manipulation (use of technology as a method to influence);
- using professionals for collaboration purposes (use of experts to influence thought);

- straw man and scapegoat incriminations (information-deflection techniques);
- clickbait methodology (using curiosity and sensationalism to attract Internet choices); and
- hoax.

It occurs so routinely that we fail to question the real reasons and purposes behind their use. *Psychological warfare* is the planned strategical use of propaganda to mislead, intimidate, demoralize, or influence the thinking or behavior of a group, an organization, or a country. With respect to war, the purpose is to deter your opponent's will to fight. It is used to gain the upper hand in a conflict by winning the support of a friendly group within an enemy territory. As one current example, in January 2020, protestors in Iran's capital, Tehran, demanded the resignation of Iran's leadership following the admission of the government of Iran, after days of denial, that the Iranian military accidentally downed a Ukrainian passenger plane, killing all 176 people on board. It happened hours after Iran launched missile attacks on US forces in Iraq in retaliation for the US assassination of top Iranian commander Qassem Soleimani. The president of the United States expressed full support and encouragement for the protestors in their defiance of the regime in power. This is an example of using White propaganda through overt psychological warfare to weaken an enemy by supporting an action detrimental to the enemy in question, all without firing a shot. The president supported and influenced the morale and attitudes of the Iranian people. Using knowledge of their beliefs and dislikes, he supported the driving of a wedge between the Iranian people and their government. An incident involving an accidental action was weaponized and deployed to reinforce the values, beliefs, emotions, reasoning, motives, and behavior of the target group.

In this case, the media and Twitter were used to reinforce a message of unity and support for the Iranian demonstrators.

In his 1949 book, *Psychological Warfare against Nazi Germany*, Daniel Lerner separates psychological warfare propaganda into three categories:

- *White propaganda*: The information is truthful and only moderately biased. The source of the information is cited.
- *Grey propaganda*: The information is mostly truthful and contains no information that can be disproven. However, no sources are cited.
- *Black propaganda*: Literally "fake news," the information is false or deceitful and is attributed to sources not responsible for its creation.

While grey and black propaganda campaigns often have the most immediate impact, they also carry the greatest risk. Sooner or later, the target population identifies the information as being false, thus discrediting the source. As Lerner wrote, "Credibility is a condition of persuasion. Before you can make a man do as you say, you must make him believe what you say."

The main focus of psychological warfare is to destroy the will of the enemy. That will can be broken by reaching out and supporting the enemy of your enemy or actually encouraging them to become an enemy of your enemy. In today's ongoing war on terror, the Jihadist terrorist organization ISIS uses social media websites, as well as other online outlets, to promote its psychological campaign designed to recruit believers to their ideology and take action against those considered enemies.

Both *public relations* and propaganda have been used to shape public opinion and action for centuries. They both use mass communication to generate a targeted public perception. Propaganda, however, deals with disinformation and other negative communication to achieve an objective related to an issue, cause, or political agenda. Both propaganda and public relations employ techniques to alter or reinforce a thought process. Both the propagandist and public relations person use techniques that can influence a viewpoint or feeling by manipulating others to act or respond in a certain way. However, public relations are more geared to the interpersonal relationship between individuals, companies and individuals, or companies and other companies or groups.

Various interpersonal techniques are utilized to influence thought and behavior. The simplest technique is to convince the public to think, speak, or act in a particular way simply because others are. The desire to fit in with others has long been used as a motivating force in society. A public relations person's responsibility is to successfully sell an idea, opinion, product, or action by provoking audiences to expend their energy on interpretation rather than critiquing or by convincing the public through the use of positive terminology.

In summary, the area of public relations is propaganda with a different technique. Both seek to shape perceptions and influence public opinion. Since their claims can be checked, public relations utilize truth. It relies on logic, facts, and sometimes emotions to disseminate information between an organization or individual and its audience. The underlying philosophy is to build. It relies on one-way communications and seeks to eliminate negativity within its target audience. But within the realm of social media, it relies on two-way communications that encourage different points of view so companies can better serve their clients and customers. It is an attempt to maintain goodwill and understanding between a company or business and the public.

The term "propaganda laundering" certainly carries with it a blatant negative connotation and rightfully so. We are all aware of criminal activity labeled "money laundering." Just as money can be illegally laundered, the media information we receive can be laundered as well. A story posted on a dubious media outlet, blog, or social media platform is received with much less trust in accuracy and truthfulness than one published by a reputable media outlet. When picked up by a reputable platform, it gains credibility. Fake news stories, disinformation, misinformation, and propaganda can all be laundered. As money laundering is a corrupt activity found in the financial world, news laundering is a deceitful activity found in the world of information. In many respects, it is a much worse crime than money laundering. It is used to sway thought processes and public opinion and influence the conclusion you derive from information input. The true corruption occurs when it is picked up by a reputable platform and used to mislead or misinform. There is a direct correlation between the effect of laundered information and the reputation of the media outlet disseminating the information.

The more reputable the news source, the more effective the news believability. The conspiracy theories concerning President Trump's ties with Russian operatives started out as an unverified and unprofessionally created news story and wound up making its way to the mainstream media. The laundering process of the story kept it moving up the ladder of credibility without any professional verification taking place. It was the growing popularity of the story through the laundering process that gave it a life on its own. An unverified misleading story made its way onto mainstream media platforms; and at the same time, the laundering of the dubious connection of being created through a foreign government with malicious aims was subdued. A media audience has a right to know where the information they are viewing comes from. The original news source and its rating should be immediately available. More and more people in various countries get their news from social media, and it is important that the viewer knows the rated reputation of the source. It is extremely easy to launder news in our current environment. There are few checks and balances in place to verify the reputation of a news source.

Letting governments regulate the Internet is not the answer we should be looking for. Instead, we need to create a self-regulating ratings system which would serve the public's best interest and improve the viewer's right to know exactly the origin of a story as well as the reputation of the originator. Media ratings based on reputation, ranking, and past record should be placed at the beginning of each and every news article presented. This would also be a motivator for the various outlets to improve safeguards for their reputation. The cost of mistakes and loss of reputation would add another level to the responsible reporting of a media story.

This would certainly boost and add transparency to all news stories. Both transparency and an informed public may be the best possible ways to ensure that news laundering remains at a minimum and, when it is used, it is recognized for what it is. The American people deserve real and factual news about war and peace, inequality, housing, racism, education, climate change, poverty, taxes, and any other news that affect our lives or the lives of others. The laundering to influence the quality of a news story for the purpose of legitimatizing the story and disconnecting it from its origin has been occurring far too often in the media. This has led to the growing lack of trust in media outlets.

Not only is *astroturfing* a propaganda technique, but the term can also be applied to the technology used to create an artificial support group that appears to publicly be in favor of a given issue, philosophy, or idea. In reality, it is a managed and artificially created group of a propagandist interested in creating the impression that the stated issue, philosophy, or idea is supported by a large number of independent viewers and, therefore, generates a stronger impact, influence, and effect on the viewing audience. On the Internet, it is easy to create and manage support groups that fight for one or another cause in large numbers. There is software available that literally allows you to create an army of followers. The software allows you to fabricate Internet-based identities which have a complete history and all the necessary background information. It is literally the creation of fake grassroots coalitions. This can easily be accomplished within social media where a number of false identities, also called sock puppets, can be set up with posts and actual conversations. Supporting evidence can be created in the form of leaflets and posters.

There are instances where actual events may be staged using volunteers, or even inviting members of the public to join in using a false pretense. The hardest part about astroturfing is making sure the "cat is not let out of the bag." The lie is an animal with very short legs. Sooner or later, you catch up to it. Media platforms are always looking for stories, and they are vulnerable to accepting news reports and images that are actually disinformation. There are groups that can actually be hired to perform this illusion while the financer of the operation is able to maintain a safe distance, lest he be accused of being the catalyst. When outside funding is involved, beware of astroturfing. When you observe a well-organized demonstration using professionally made signs, ask yourself, "What or who is funding this action?"

An astroturfing effect may even be created by the use of language with exaggerations such as "the American people," "everybody," or "always." It can also be utilized to quell any contradictory viewpoints. I wish I had a nickel for every time I heard the term "the American people" on a media platform discussion. The most successful astroturfing, in time, strengthens the opinion that was its initial goal as people accept the promoted disinformation and actually help to spread the impact by fostering it within their own groups. The way this is accomplished varies. As mentioned, it can make a story appear as if more people support it than actually do or that the issue involved in the story has created a tremendous activist following. It can also brand anyone who disagrees with the story as being in the minority and their viewpoint as not being well received. In the advertisement of a product, astroturfing can make that product come across as more effective and efficient than it actually is. Individuals are actually paid to write good reviews online about a client's products and to criticize any competitive product. The reviews try to make a product appear more necessary to have than it actually is or that something is popular when there is no real interest in it. Astroturfing can become expensive to successfully implement. It is illegal in many countries and in specific areas such as politics and business. Those involved in astroturfing see themselves as business people merely providing a service to a client. However, the purpose of that service is to deceive the audience into believing that an issue, idea, or product is either better or just the opposite worse and that the perception is widely held.

How can you detect a hidden agenda advertisement or story? Examining whether a story, an advertisement, or tweets act in "bot" fashion only detects a very small number of astroturfing sites, since humans, not AI programmers, are responsible for the bulk of astroturfing activity. People are paid to post the messaging involved in astroturfing activities. As such, these people find shortcuts for the task they are involved in to make their job easier. You will notice less variation in message content and timing. The tweets or messages appear very similar and identical and appear in a short time frame. Real, honest, and concerned messaging may appear very similar as well; but the time frame of the messaging is much more extensive. The concentration of similar messaging within a short time period is a pretty good indicator of astroturfing. The identification of political, corporate, or other special interests that disguise themselves as an independent or grassroots movement through published blog posts is necessary in order to filter whether or not the information you are exposed to is truly reliable.

Photo and video manipulation are often used in our Internet-dominated world. The Web abounds in image manipulation. What we are doing here is raising awareness that picture manipulation is alive and well on the Internet. The use of unflattering light, diffusion, and shadowing, as well as framing, can alter a person's appearance and the viewer's reaction to that appearance. Oftentimes, photos are not altered, but the most undesirable one is used to portray a political player that is the antithesis of the ideology of the media platform using the photograph. Bias in the media is not limited to written or spoken words. Images are powerful tools that can be used to advance an ideology. Truly, a picture is worth a thousand words. Very rarely is a photo debated the same way words are. A photo in itself can have an agenda behind it. And images can be much more dramatic and compelling than the use of vocabulary and are an ideal tool to use in manipulation. An image appears as more objective and less debatable than a story line. Words are more easily labeled as bias. Most people view photography as a snapshot of reality. But behind every reality is the photographer's agenda. The photo itself is not as objectionable as the bias and manipulation behind the photo and the underhanded manipulation of the public. Photos appeal to one's emotion and sentiments rather than objectivity and rationality. Emotion is a difficult thing to change once it takes root. We have to ask ourselves if the images we view advance a neutral point of view concerning the accompanying story line.

The use of *professionals for collaboration* purposes has been used in advertising almost forever. It basically is an endorsement, written, spoken, viewable, or a combination of all three by someone with media recognition and expresses either support or opposition for a product, an idea, an organization, a person, or a philosophy. A testimonial is often used to help the cause of a political candidate through candidate support, issue support, or, more broadly, philosophical support. While the support itself may be genuine, they may also include an exaggeration as to the reasons for the endorsement. We all have an idea how this works in advertising. The end goal of a professional endorsement is to get you to buy the product. Many times, an expert, such as a doctor or engineer, is used to endorse a product.

With political endorsements, the end goal is the same except that the product is a person, an ideology, or an entire political organization. The purpose is to sell the point of view of a famous professional or media personality to the rest of the audience.

To be sure, this form of propaganda is, in most instances, less effective than others that are out there. To be blunt, the audience is not stupid, and they see this for what it is. Where it gets a little less clear is when the famous professional is used to recommend an idea or philosophy. The goal is to get the audience to accept the judgment or opinion of the professional in question. The reasoning used by a famous professional does not necessarily have to be false. The presentation can be very concrete and factual as long as it serves the purpose intended. However, it may be a presentation that solely focusses on one side of an issue. And this is where the use of propaganda creeps in. Some believe that well-known film or TV stars have the potential to sway millions and millions of viewers to buy into their viewpoint. The scientific testing of this belief is very much needed. In the 2016 presidential election, the candidate that lost the election won the famous celebrity popularity battle. The question here is, Are celebrities really looked upon as political gurus who really know what is best for the average citizen? The celebrity and testimony of others often fail the test of credibility when it is used outside the arena for their fame and recognition in the first place.

Political parties feel that a celebrity testimonial is worth votes. How many is up for debate? How many people see a celebrity endorse a candidate or ideology and view that as another reason not to support that candidate? Oftentimes, a media platform will use ordinary folks like you and me to endorse a candidate. One media platform uses news commentators to interview folks in a diner. "Those folks are just like us, and they are on that candidate's bandwagon." No one ever questions the political ideology of the part of the state where that diner is located. Testimonials need not be true and honest. You can find people to agree with pretty much anything depending on their geographic location, and some will be happy to say whatever you like. In this instance, testimonial propaganda takes advantage of the goodwill and trust the public tends to feel toward people very much like themselves.

The use of a *straw man or a scapegoat* is an example of propaganda deflection. Straw man propaganda is the use of an unfavorable idea presented as something that the opposition or individual opponent is in favor of. Scapegoat propaganda, on the other hand, is placing blame for a problem on a person, group, organization, race, or religion. Straw man propaganda is the misrepresentation of an opponent's position on a specific issue. The straw man attack is focused not on your opponent's actual position but rather the misinterpreted position created by the propagandist. The actual original meaning and position of the individual being attacked is not even mentioned. Several democratic presidential candidates espoused the idea of Medicare for All. The idea was challenged as to its cost and the health care industry disruption it would cause. But another attack came to the surface—that the proponents of this idea were in favor of all-out socialism which would eventually lead to communism. The jump is quite remarkable. Oftentimes, the originators of the Medicare for All concept were attacked as all-out socialists or communists. The basic structure of the straw man concept involves an opponent making a claim, the propagandist creating a distorted version of the claim, and then attacking this distorted version of the opponent in order to refute his original assertion. Quite often, the distorted interpretation is only remotely related to the original claim.

The opposing argument may focus on just one aspect of the claim, taking it out of context or exaggerating the claim itself. It is meant to distract from the real issue being discussed and is not a logically valid argument. When a presidential candidate or president states their position on secure borders and curtailing the influx of illegal (undocumented) aliens (families) in the name of national security, well then, that candidate must be a racist. When faced with a straw man deflection, there are some options you can use to counter those arguments and place the conversation back on track. You can point out why you believe the objection is a straw man argument by detailing the distortion as compared to the original premise. You may choose to ignore the argument entirely and simply continue elaborating on your original point. That will move the discussion back to the original topic. You can also accept the argument and then state why it is unrelated and irrelevant to the initial point that was the focus.

A *scapegoat* is someone who is assigned the blame or made to take the fall for something that was not their fault or not their entire fault. It is the action of singling out a person or group as a cause of a negative event. Scapegoating may take place between individuals and individuals, individuals and groups, and between a group or groups and another group or groups. Anyone can become a scapegoat. Any organization can become a scapegoat. In simplistic terms, it is a blame game, but it is very seldom a game. It is a serious action and has the power to ruin reputations and involve legal action. By assigning blame to an individual or group, the perpetrators of this action are actually saying it wasn't them. They had nothing to do with the problem and, therefore, have no responsibility to fix it. At best, it is a tool for distraction. Scapegoating allows individuals or entire groups to point the finger of blame at others instead of themselves. The targets of scapegoating usually are outsiders, a person or group who can become the recipient of blame; and there are also instances where the recipient actually belongs to the group pointing their blame finger.

With scapegoating, one blames a problem on another individual, group, race, or religion. The blame can involve a very specific and pinpointed allegation, or it can be a generalized attribution of blame. As an example, undocumented immigrants have been singled out as the cause of low wages in the United States as well as the cause of unemployment. In actuality, low wages involve several causes and are a complex economic problem with many factors combining to reinforce it. The victims of scapegoating are usually chosen because they are the easiest targets to victimize as well as the least likely to retaliate or have an ability to retaliate. The scapegoating individual, group, or organization lashes out at a victim who is least capable of defending themselves.

There is a tremendous amount of hatred on both sides of the political spectrum. The effect of this hatred on ordinary citizens is completely ignored. More energy is put into hatred and scapegoating than, for example, working for the community that elected you into office. There is no effort to improve the community that placed you in office—no effort to create new jobs, improve infrastructure, or quality of life issues. The voter becomes an ignored part of the equation. The height of a voter's popularity begins to diminish immediately after election day. The political focus becomes whom to blame for the problems we face, to scapegoat the blame to others with little concern about exploring remedies. What a waste of talent and energy. What a waste because of the senseless direction utilizing valuable time and thought. The cause of this lack of constructive direction lies with the politicians. We wind up with a political system where some accomplishments are being achieved on a national scale but very little achievement is taking place at the community level where the votes placing representatives in office came from.

Clickbait is the use of curiosity and sensationalism to attract Internet choices of what to look at when on the Internet. Turn on your laptop, and in a very short time, you will be exposed to a number of sensationalized stories presented in such a way as to pique your curiosity. The propagandist uses your natural curiosity to get you to click on a sensationalized headline. Behind the stories, you will find demands for action, created hysteria, or all-out exaggerations. Sometimes, it is hard to differentiate fact and fiction. Many of us receive our news over the Internet. It is a major outlet for many of us to try and keep informed. A good rule of thumb is to treat the Internet like you would treat receiving a negative medical diagnosis—get a second opinion. In other words, find additional sources, and see whether or not they arrive at the same conclusion.

Many times, you come across stories that reinforce your personal bias or "fact bubble." It is not unusual that after a story breaks and, in the days following, additional information is presented that actually changes that whole premise of the original story. The best way to receive information is with an analytical mind. Current media platforms want you to think their thoughts only. Choose the relevant facts only, and draw a reasonable conclusion based on those facts. Do not get drawn into the emotional connotations of a headline.

Many stories are born with a deficiency in factual information and an oversupply of opinion and unsupported conclusions. Do not allow yourself to be manipulated by sensationalism. Recognize signals of poor source credibility such as hyperpartisanship. Do not take the bait. Do not take the *clickbait*. And don't let your biases and fact bubble cloud your reasoning. *Clickbait* stories do have a purpose—to cloud reasoning, disrupt research of facts, and create confusion or anger. And so far, it seems to be working. In some cases, the motivator is the generation of income. Our enemies would like nothing better than to divide our country—to get us to hate each other and to create discontent. They often appeal to a person's preexisting biases. And it looks like they are doing a pretty good job. When the phone rings, do you answer it each and every time? If you are like me, you screen your calls. Perhaps it is time to screen information as well. And finally, always question the origin of the information you receive.

A *hoax* is an action that is intended to deceive or defraud. When a newspaper or the media reports a fake story and it is outed, it is described as a hoax. Misleading public stunts, such as the one perpetrated by *Empire* star Jussie Smollett is an example. A common aspect that hoaxes have is that they are all meant to deceive or lie. For something to become a hoax, the lie must have a purpose or intention. It must be outrageous and dramatic, but it also has to be believable. Above all, it must be able to attract the public's attention. Once this has been accomplished, the hoax is in full effect. But we have to be clear on the fact that this, too, is a form of propaganda.

In summary, propaganda and the techniques employed to promulgate a desired outcome of its use is actually more of a potent weapon than censorship. World governments are moving away from trying to censor social media which is viewed in a blatantly negative light and instead are turning to propaganda to influence public opinion. There is a concentrated effort to shape online opinion through information manipulation. Many of the methods utilized have been reviewed. The future of Internet quality as a source of information rests on people's ability to fix problems with social media such as abuse by propagandists with an agenda. The coordinated use of partisan commentators and media platforms to disseminate false content, often with the backing of a political party, has reached the level of all-out political warfare.

The type of propaganda coming from media platforms is organizational in its construct. Organizations involved in political and social disinformation online are unable to hide their identity. We have a pretty good idea of their philosophy by how they approach their audience and the attitudes they foster. Media platforms should be measured using a classification scale that rates them on several dimensions: ethical versus unethical, mutual understanding versus persuasion, and fact versus opinion. The Internet is used more and more by media platforms to spread their ideas to the public. Media organizations spread propaganda regarding elections and social issues in order to mobilize voter buy-in. One might say that an important part of media platforms has become the business of propaganda. With technological advancement, the nature of propaganda has changed from being a one-way communication process to a mass media event directed at a receptive audience and which allows for communication to become bidirectional. It is a key ingredient in the empowerment of grassroots and protest movements. It is also being blatantly used by media platforms for political agendas and to exact a persuasive influence on their audience. It is as if their main intention is to misinform and spread half-truthful information. It is a tool to spread ideology. The aim is always to either reinforce or change attitudes and behavior.

If communication is biased, has as its intention to influence behavior, simplifies a story or on the other hand exaggerates a story, is ideological, and does not take into account opposing views, then the elements for propaganda are present. It paints a one-sided or misleading picture of an issue. The content of media platforms is often very selective and has as its purpose to manipulate its audience. It does not provide the whole picture, and the audience cannot assess the truthfulness of the information that is presented. Media platforms present information with a liberal dose of opinion with the objective of making you think their thoughts. They are not communication sources with an aim to ethically make you agree to their ideology. We must always ask ourselves if the opinions stated are justifiable. Are the opinions stated reactionary? Do the opinions follow a logical consequential order in leading to a conclusion?

Another form of control can be achieved through *subliminal* messaging. These messages have a motivational objective and can be either visual or auditory. It is a form of messaging input that the conscious mind cannot perceive. It is often associated and used with other media such as TV advertising or songs. It can be used to strengthen or heighten the persuasiveness of a message or can be used to promote an entirely divergent message. Authentic subliminal messaging cannot be perceived or uncovered by the conscious mind, even if you're actively engaged in investigating them. This is because the stimulation that we respond to every day, things that we see and hear, are above the level of conscious perception but subliminal messaging is below this conscious level. Subliminal messaging is like stealth aircraft, and even though we're utterly unaware of its presence, it is there. The stealth messaging that is hidden in what we hear or watch is picked up by our subconscious mind which cannot help but react to this invisible stimulation. In other words, it has an impact entirely devoid of our recognition or approval.

Yes, messaging can affect behavior, but the message does not have to be subliminal. When researchers played music in a liquor store, they found a startling result. On days when German music was played, German wine outsold French wine. However, the reverse happened when French music was played. Although people were not aware of how the music affected their behavior, the messaging in this case cannot be considered subliminal, since it could be consciously heard. Background music used this way is an example of supraliminal messaging—store customers hear the music but are not aware that it has the ability to influence their thoughts. So the next time you find yourself making an out-of-the-ordinary wine choice, like not ordering your favorite wine, check the background music.

Subliminal messaging is different with respect to the fact the stimulus in question is undetectable. For example, an image flashed so quickly that the eyes do not see it or a sound so low that the human ear does not hear it. But both have an equal impact with respect to being registered subconsciously. Can subliminal messages influence your thoughts and behavior? Yes, they can. However, subliminal messages can't make you do something you wouldn't want to do. Mere exposure to an image, even subliminally, can only suggest associations, with a possible effect on your thoughts and behavior.

Propaganda Impact and Influence

Propaganda is a part of our culture, and it will remain incessant. It is believed to have its origin in Europe with the work of Catholic missionaries under the leadership of Pope Gregory XV in 1622. Although the term "propaganda" may have a date of birth, the concept of propaganda cannot. It is not a creation. It is a constant. It is like evil—you can never destroy what was never created. It will always be present. The human race has always been involved in trying to alter or create attitudes and opinions. Propaganda was in existence long before it was given a name and was given a negative connotation. It was looked upon as being self-centered, subversive, and dishonest. The techniques used in propaganda have become very sophisticated and are used in the sale of products and services that we are all told are a must and a necessity. In the world of advertising, the concept of propaganda has a more neutral and positive acceptance. After all, it's part of doing business.

One thing for certain, it will always be with us because it has always been with us. It impacts every area of a culture, and the effects are sometimes enormous. We can grasp the concept better when viewed through the lens of the different aspects of our society. We talked in some detail about its use in politics, ideology, media, artificial intelligence (AI), and advertising. But, as mentioned, its influence permeates all aspects of society. A breakdown of just how propaganda wields its influence in various areas of both society and culture will be briefly reviewed. There is evidence pointing to the conclusion that something in our culture and society is going radically and unexpectedly awry. Much of today's conversation presents America's future as falling from a state of democratic grace, and propaganda is one of the main catalysts.

Attempting to control thought is as old as human history from the story of the serpent telling Eve that eating the forbidden fruit would give her godlike power and knowledge. The battle to control the mind is very old, indeed. Wherever differences exist, propaganda exists as well, all for the purpose of both shaping and controlling human opinion. Any systematic widespread circulation or advancement of particular ideas, doctrines, or ideologies to support a cause or to destroy an opposing one through deception or distortion is the essence of propaganda. It may take many different forms, including speeches; books; films; and visual or artistic venues such as posters, paintings, sculptures, or public monuments.

Its sway can be found in, among other areas, theater, music, art, movies, religion, education, finance, health, fashion, the legal system, race, immigration, freedom, history, war/peace, lotteries, the war on drugs, science, love/hate, journalism, and most recently COVID-19.

Theater

With *theater*, the social, ideological, and political point of view of most playwrights wind up in their work. Most, by an overwhelming majority, are focused within the liberal spectrum. They basically are a venue to explain to us and reinforce what we want to hear about one liberal view or another. A play that seeks to persuade an audience to take a specific point of view on a subject, whether it be political or cultural, is no longer a play but falls into the category of being a manifesto. The purpose of theater is to creatively portray a world but oftentimes becomes obsessed with portraying a point of view as well. It often depicts life as it is and at the same time suggests life as it should be according to the author. For example, in many plays, there is a strong sentiment against capitalism. There is a covert, if not overt, element of moral pressure. The full complexity of a problem or issue that is the main topic is often simplified and painted with the brush of persuasion. The purpose is to make their personal point of view known even if it means taking liberty with how a story is presented. It is as if the playwright has an already preconceived notion of how an audience will think, and their work takes for granted their concurrence. Disagreement with the playwright is not only considered wrong but an indication that you are the type of person who just doesn't get it and should be excommunicated from the genre. The principal goal is to persuade the audience to accept a cause and that the progressiveness of the playwright and their view of the world is all there is. All this is accomplished through a reductionism of truth and presenting only that information that reinforces a progressive principle.

There is beginning to emerge a group of artists who have grown unaccepting of plays fostering political correctness and actually poke humor at the concept. They have become cheerleaders against the telling of a story that only shows one side of an issue. The world of theater has always had a liberal ideology. This is truer with theater found in large city areas such as New York. The focus is usually on a social or cultural issue, and you leave the theater clearly being educated on the only way to think about the subject. The liberal viewpoints on such issues as immigration, sanctuary cities, and open borders are not subtly presented. The perspective being fostered explodes on the stage. One has to look far and wide to find a play with an unbiased agenda. It seems that they are being created to change or challenge one's thought process or point of view. The lives and actions of our forefathers are being examined and criticized using the contemporary standards of today with disregard for the standards that were actually in place and very much accepted in the time frame examined.

Plays that have a conservative perspective are conspicuously missing. Artistic directors of regional theaters and playwriting programs throughout the country are one sided in choosing playwriting themes. If you are looking to find a play that has a conservative slant or, for that matter, a middle-of-the-spectrum approach, you will, more often than not, be very unsuccessful. You really cannot discuss the history of our country and those involved in shaping it without including a discussion of conservative social and political movements.

Doing so distorts reality. Part of the problem may lie in the fact that plays with conservative or right of center material is less likely to make it to the theater stage. Such plays exist, but their popularity is lacking. It limits subject matter and point of view to the extent that it excludes half of the audience. Plays that challenge the predominantly broad-based culture are truly lacking. The liberal philosophy is that everything in society is wrong and needs to be addressed and remedied with no acceptance of opposing viewpoints. So one has a pretty good idea of how this affects motivation to even "right" a play with a "right" of center viewpoint. The question remains, Will there ever be more room for both political and social diversity in American theater?

Music

Music has been used throughout the world as a means of delivering a social, political, or cultural message to a targeted audience. It's the type of message that has the ability to become imbedded in one's memory and to be easily recognizable. Music messaging is a very powerful tool. It can be put to use as a harbinger of good or can act as a conduit for propaganda or a specific ideological viewpoint. It flows through the mind as a leisure activity without any obvious threat or conspicuous agenda, but it is sometimes used to send a political or social message. It can influence our emotions as well as alter the way we view a political or social concern. It is by no means a catalyst for critical thinking but rather for emotional thinking. The music we choose to listen to can affect how we feel about an issue. Therefore, music can be an attractive venue for the dispersal of propaganda. Songs and concerts continue to be used to raise funds and to foster humanitarian aid as a response to a social or catastrophic crisis. Musical concerts continue to be a powerful venue to raise humanitarian awareness and financial support. It speaks to the emotions and can be an effective mobilizer. It can unite people in a common cause.

On the other hand, a protest song is one that is associated with action for social change. One of the common threads uniting protest songs is the opposition to various forms of injustice (human rights, civil rights, gay rights, unpopular wars, and so forth). The purpose is to hold people accountable for their mistakes. There is most always a villain involved whether it be an ideology, a person, or an institutional structure. The object is to point out an injustice or wrongdoing. Music can be extremely influential in the delivery and acceptance of a message. Audiences often find an escape in music, a way to relate to the world around us or simply a form of relaxation. Many view it as a necessity in their lives. Some music contains a message which can be either positive or negative. We all are aware that it can send a message that can actually influence an audience. It does have a capacity to affect how we see ourselves, the world around us, and the culture we are a part of.

We are all aware of the drug epidemic that engulfs our society, and music audiences are sometimes exposed to references and messages promoting the use of drugs. There are some songs that contain references to substances such as methamphetamine and cocaine, as well as references to more common substances such as alcohol and marijuana. Unfortunately, much of this music containing drug references portray a more positive than negative consequence related to substance abuse. As repeatedly established, propaganda is the spreading of information, especially of a biased or misleading nature, which is used to promote or reinforce a particular point of view. In this case, the point of view is that taking drugs is a really "cool thing." Therefore, we can say that substance abuse propaganda is used to extoll the virtues of taking drugs regardless of the harmful effects on impressionable young adults and teenagers. But most music is extremely influential, enjoyable, and comforting, and has become an important part of teen activity. During this crucial stage of personality and attitude development, it can play a big role as a determining influence.

Women are fighting for the right not to be looked upon as subservient to men. Music portraying women as subordinate and promiscuous, capitalizing upon for their looks and their bodies, is not constructive. Musical lyrics and videos that promote young women and girls to meet male expectations instead of their own sense of worth and well-being are detrimental, and impressionable young minds can be easily influenced by these messages. In videos, women are seen in provocative clothing involved in a choreography that centers on acting and dancing in a suggestive manner, all of which is directed at impressing and satisfying men. As an added consequence, a negative stereotype of men is promoted as well. They are viewed as lacking in morals, disrespectful, and callous to women and are only motivated by sex as to the main reason for interaction. At this critical time in their lives, women should view themselves with respect and communicate to others a strong sense of self-confidence as they strive to become recognized as an equal, integral, and valuable part of society. Heavy metal band music has often been given a bad rap throughout the years because of their use of dark imagery. It has been blamed for increased violence, crime, and suicide. It is often described as satanic, evil, and a promoter of debauchery. But there is no verifiable evidence to support this. And there is a flip side as well. Heavy metal bands also write songs that range from fighting drug addiction to dealing with physical abuse or personal loss. Although most people think it is the personification of anger, there are some heavy metal lyrics focusing on love and dealing with pain and sorrow. The message in many of the lyrics is to relay to the audience that nobody is perfect and even if you are going through a difficult time you will get through it. At many heavy metal concerts, the artists will often tell their fans how important they are and that they can get through any of the negativity they experience in life.

The first thing that comes to mind when mentioning rap and hip-hop music, if you are not a devotee, is a negative connotation. It has developed into a prolific form of communicating feeling. Hip and rap promote violence, drugs, murder, and other nefarious activities. Again, the music cannot all be lumped into one basket. Many of the songs have positive messages and purpose as well. It has increased the awareness of issues that many of those living in inner cities face. It has promoted both social and political awareness among young people. Individuality, the importance of education, and believing in yourself are some of the more positive themes. Hip-hop's primary purpose is to express the artist's feelings through the telling of a story or describing a situation. To be sure, there is some positive messaging, but it is far and few in between and has a more difficult time of gaining recognition since they are less recognized by the recording labels. For a recording company, there is more popularity and financial reward promoting a negative lyric than a positive one. For this reason, most artists are magnetized to negative message lyrics than positive ones. The positive side of both hip-hop and rap has to gain more exposure.

America can be considered the birth mother of country music. It is often associated with the red, white, and blue. Songs involve patriotism, country pride, freedom, women's rights among others, and the breaking of hearts as well as the opening of hearts. It has the ability to stir both sentiment and emotion with respect to an intended message. The allure of gospel music is rooted in a deep spiritual belief that Christianity can provide a fundamental message through music. It was a way to answer the counterculture of other forms of music where irreconcilable differences were felt to exist. The desire to listen to music is part of human nature. It provides its own personal perspective on culture and an interpretation of what is happening around us. It is the universal language that is used to deliver a message and point of view.

Art

Art is looked upon as visual creativity. It shares with social media the common purpose of sharing information, ideas, and viewpoints. They are both venues that allow people to communicate emotion, feelings, passions, and reactions. They both have the ability to reach large audiences and can influence both thinking and perception. There is a link between both propaganda and art. For example, during World War 1 and World War 2, art was used as a motivating force to unite our national war sentiment. Conversely, it has been used to depict the horror and misery of war. Works of art have been created that vividly depict the destruction war causes in the lives of those innocently caught in its grip.

There are art movements that feel art should remain a pure construct, that it should be totally separated from an ideology and should be based solely on the inner emotion of the artist. The art should come from the aesthetic outlook of the artist, from within him or herself. It should not encompass an external political or social ideology or reference point. As an example, one need not look further than the art of abstract expressionists such as Jackson Pollock. And even in this instance, freedom from a message or ideology is not completely escapable. His art was looked upon as a response to the rigid, pragmatic, and structured socialist art coming from Russia (Soviet Union) and other countries. To some extent, art cannot exist outside a social or political framework, and attempting to completely separate art from propaganda is futile. It is the eye of the beholder that connects the dots. As long as someone can have a thought about a piece of artwork, a connection can be formed to analyze it through a personal belief structure. Art perception is always discerned by the minds of viewers who bring to it their ideologies; prejudices; and political, cultural, and religious beliefs.

Protest art is a means to arouse the emotional buy-in of audiences and to create a visual representation to be used as a persuasion device. Such art finds a niche in the rollout of demonstrations or causes with a message. They are the banners, signs, posters, and printed materials used to reinforce a message. Any systematic widespread circulation or advancement of particular ideas, doctrines, or ideologies to support a cause or to destroy an opposing one through deception or distortion carries with it the essence of propaganda. It may take many different forms, including speeches; books; films; and visual or artistic venues such as posters, paintings, sculptures, or public monuments. Both graffiti and street art can be utilized in the same manner. It, too, is art with a message.

Environmental artists have been praised for raising awareness about the issues our planet faces. This art form encompasses a broad area that includes a wide range of techniques and styles. The creation of environmentally related art has helped focus concern on substantial issues and has raised the level of awareness with respect to ecological problems. Here again, we have art with a message. Environmental artists help us to understand nature. It fosters a human relationship with it and points out the damage created by man and the need for remediation. One of the main characteristics of this art, with a few exceptions, is that it is usually created for one particular place and often cannot be exhibited in museums or galleries. The purpose of environmental art is to be a catalyst for change in the audiences' mind.

Propaganda art delivers a message. The war posters of World War 2 showing women involved in strenuous male-oriented tasks were an attempt to get women to become involved in the war effort by taking on duties they would normally shun. The idea was to foster a national identity of women as having the ability to be essential contributors to the war effort. Its purpose is not to merely make a political point but to reconstruct and change existing reality as well. History abounds in examples of political regimes that have shaped their world according to their ideology. And today, popular mass movements are forming that introduce and spread messages designed to foster and dissemi-nate ideologies with their own propagandist viewpoints. Propaganda art is present in all societies from the most totalitarian forms to the most liberal democracies. It fosters a dichotomy in either how we perceive our government's actions or in our relationship with govern-ment overall. It uses loaded messages to change an attitude toward the subject at hand. A poster of a presidential candidate utilizing the words "hope" and "change" or "make America great again" is geared to influence perceptions. It may not necessarily be an untruth, but it is a culturally manufactured perception. Most often our discernment is in agreement with our own moral code or a perceived utopia that is fostered by the visual art. In any case, it is there to serve a need. It is there to reinforce an unconscious or conscious emotional reaction toward the subject depicted in the artwork itself.

Movies

Movies can be a conduit for propaganda capable of influencing both behavior and opinions. Their agenda can be to simply influence the audience with the use of subjective and deceptive content. Most influencers can be found in either documentaries or fictional story lines. Movies and serials utilize mostly fictional story lines that are stereotypes of romantic situations or melodramatic content which may or may not be based on truth. One of my favorite serials, *Seal Team*, depicts the courage and death-defying exploits of an American Seal unit. Pretty much every episode winds up being a success story. You almost forget that our country has been spending enormous amounts of money, resulting in casualties and horrific injuries, to fight almost never-ending confrontations around the world. The self-aggrandizement of this serial is in stark contrast to reality. This is not to suggest that there is anything wrong with this story line. It results in a positive outlook with respect to military interventions. It is just that we often do not recognize the propaganda undertone in story lines such as these. In the movie *12 Strong*, the success of a military unit sent to Afghanistan in the early days of the war is depicted. The movie ends on a successful note but the fact is that we have been involved in this same conflict for over eighteen years. The movie sort of makes us forget that point.

That made me think even more about how susceptible we have become to what is being presented in media and entertainment. My point of view is that story lines are oftentimes being accepted without any dissection of the message or introspection of reality and the bigger picture. Movies are a universal medium with the ability to influence both the individual movie spectator and large audiences alike. They are categorized as a form of entertainment—a way to relax and enjoy your evening either at home with family or in a theater setting. Most of the time, there is no need to wear a critical-thinking cap. You are watching a movie as an entertainment venue. Films create an illusion of reality. Even in a fictional movie, the characters are discussed as if they actually exist. Filmmakers can be masters of illusion, and for the viewer, it becomes their reality. They can be a very effective tool for propaganda and can be used to define attitudes for the particular film time line, clarify the issues prevalent at that time and possibly in such a way as to motivate a positive or negative emotional response. It is not always the intent of the filmmaker to stimulate the historical consciousness of the audience, but it does happen and sometimes through the use of distorted events.

Movie propaganda runs the gamut of being overtly conspicuous or discretely insidious in an entertaining way. Television series follow a trend. Currently, a topic of conversation encompasses itself around the question, Are we alone in the universe? So we have quite a few series come out that deal with the same question: an airplane that disappears and reappears five years later, a child with incredible abilities is found at the site of a crash, and others serials. With the inauguration of a new president in 2016 and his focus on increasing both the funding and strength of the military, series such as *Seal Team, Six, The Brave*, and others have conjured a following and interest. Other shows about patriotism focusing on police and medical personal abound. There was at this time a glut of flag-waving shows. Let's be honest here. These shows were a response to audience attitudes and market research. The decision was made based on research that audiences wanted to see story lines involving unexplained events and a positive view of military, police, and emergency personnel; and the filmmakers and TV producers gave us just what the doctor ordered. It basically is a type of propaganda that the viewers themselves have demanded. The use of film can be a powerful form of communication. They develop an empathy and understanding of the characters involved.

Documentaries are factual accounts of actual events that surround an event or story. Nonfiction topics in film have been around for a long time. The most important part of making a documentary is to remain completely objective. If it does not, it can easily revert to semifiction. As with all film, in making a documentary, decisions concerning content have to be made. It is possible to be objective with the facts presented, but by omitting other relevant crucial facts, a documentary can be made to lean in a desired direction. In other words, with the genre of documentaries, manipulation is a real possibility. They can serve a constructive purpose, but at the other end of the spectrum, they can become an exaggeration or a complete untruth depending how facts are presented or unaccounted for in the story. If a documentary filmmaker wants you to believe a specific message or ideology, it can be achieved through manipulation. Films have been produced in documentary form to explain an event or series of events with an explanation suggesting that a conspiracy of unimaginable proportions was involved. The explanation is the manipulation. The term that has been applied to this documentary format is conspiracy cinema. The facts are presented along with the personal interpretation of the filmmakers. They dictate both content and message.

Most of the movies coming out of Hollywood have a liberal lean to them. Some of the liberal story lines are quite obvious, while others may not be. For example, and in broad terms, movies with a story line that require a level of cooperation among antagonists to overcome their differences or a common enemy sends a positive message concerning cooperation and getting along with others. The stories usually end with a "hakuna matata" moment. Movies with story lines involving racism, women's rights, civil rights, immigration, corporate greed, politics, and terrorism all wind up unfurling a message: "We should all be able to get along" or "It is impossible for us to get along because of unsurmountable differences." The messages are theories of how life should be or a snapshot of reality in the eyes of the filmmakers focusing on the causes and circumstances surrounding a difficult situation. But it is rather difficult to turn some theories into reality or to change attitudes. We see a film with a "We should all be friends" outcome and wind up leaving the theater and the message as well. Or we see a film with the opposite message and are either repulsed or strengthened by it. In order to be lucrative, a movie having a liberal bend has an advantage that far outweighs its counterpart. When you see a movie about corporate greed, it doesn't leave you with an enamored feeling about the corporation, or the message may be missed altogether. After all, it's just a movie, or is it?

Cinema has been purposefully used to attract an audience into accepting orchestrated propagandist messages. Film has been used to instill and perpetuate social, political, or religious ideas through manipulated story lines. Propaganda films provide a conduit for the messages of a government, a group, or even a single individual with a particular agenda.

Whether or not you personally agree with the message may not be as important as exposing the message itself to a large-enough audience in a well-defined manner to allow it to gain traction. The way an idea is conveyed is just as important as the idea itself. The techniques of propaganda films are extremely effective tools in the forwarding of a specific agenda. It's important to bring attention to them so audiences can recognize the real idea behind a story line. What you take for granted as an innocent form of entertainment may have an underlying message and agenda. In some films, the propagandist message can be very obvious and easily discernable. However, some of the most significant films ever made have been propaganda films, and they have wielded an enormous impact on people who did not recognize the manipulative aspect of the film used to covey a particular message.

Religion

Religion has not escaped the impact of propaganda as a tool to influence. The ultimate purpose of religious propaganda is to increase membership in a specific religious organization and oftentimes occurs in a vacuum in which other competing religions are unable to participate. The National Day of Prayer, established in 1952, is a congressionally mandated observance that occurs on the first Thursday of each May. In 2010, a federal court judge ruled it to be unconstitutional on grounds that it violated the First Amendment prohibition of government endorsement of religion. It was later deemed constitutional through an appeal process in the Federal Court of Appeals. This may not be the last time we see a challenge utilizing a different argument. It was originally meant to be an interfaith observance. But it has increasingly become a day of observance for fundamentalist Christians. The First Amendment requires a separation of church and state. By participating in and speaking about the importance of faith at an annual prayer event, the government is stretching this principle. Using this same line of reasoning, participation by the president and members of the Senate and House also reinforces a government religious connection.

Opponents also argue that although a few leaders from religions such as Judaism and Islam are present, the meeting undeniably has a Christian resonance and focal point. The focus on Christianity opens a conversation concerning an argument that the breakfast is an unconstitutional endorsement of a particular religious field. This is not the best way to promote better interfaith relations. Participation outside the Judeo-Christian tradition is discouraged. They are openly honest with respect to their agenda. In naming this event the "National Day of Prayer" and doing so by law seems to be in itself a misnomer. However, in its defense, religions with members suffering from persecution, oppression, and mistreatment all around the world are prayerfully recognized. The prayer march organized in September 2020 is another example of a wonderful idea that should have been extended to other faiths besides Christianity. The prevailing thread was that "our nation is in trouble." Therefore, a day of prayer should be extended to other faiths as well. Interreligious is more important than ever before. There is a strong need for interfaith partnerships to increase both hope and solidarity.

The Constitution in the first part of the First Amendment states, "Congress shall make no law respecting an establishment of religion, or prohibiting the free exercise thereof." A National Prayer Day that limits inclusion seems contrary to this amendment. We really need to get back to the true spirit of the Constitution today and eliminate laws that couple government and religion. Globally, 84 percent of people affiliate with a religion, and it is predicted that it will increase to more than 90 percent in the next few decades. If we really want to understand the world around us, we need to be able to not only respect our beliefs but to understand and respect the beliefs of others as well.

When considering the effect of propagandist activities with respect to religion, successful campaigns have been waged by the major religions of Christianity, Buddhism, and Islam. Although each has used different strategies to achieve their goals, they have all put their trust in the use of mesmerizing leaders, religious symbolism, a moral philosophy, and an understanding of their audience's weaknesses and hopes. Religion finds a way to replace the existing religious beliefs of people and win over both their minds and hearts. The propagandist aspects of religions are subject to change and variation over time depending on the social and political factors that are currently in play. For example, the humane practices of proselytizing by the early Christians were followed up with the brutal and often inhumane techniques of the sixteenth-century Spanish Inquisition. To this day, there is a wide discrepancy in the use of propaganda with respect to different religious denominations.

In the case of Islam, several interpretations exist concerning the strict application of religious law with respect to both various Islamic countries and various sects within countries over the centuries. Today, we are witnessing a renewed effort by fundamentalist Muslims to employ Islam as a means of fostering the cultural and political goal of uniting all Arabic nations under one religious rule and interpretation. A devoutly strict and oppressive religious interpretation is being unjustly forced on others. Muslim fundamentalists seek strict adherence and politicization to the religious laws of Islam as being the only way to counteract satanic materialistic Western beliefs. Religions have been used very effectively as propaganda vehicles for wider social and political motivations. The use of religion continues to be a very important ingredient in modern propaganda practices.

White supremacists, militia extremists, and violent antiabortion adherents have used religious concepts and scripture to justify threats, criminal activity, and violence. Religious extremism should not be confused with someone being extremely religious. It should not be seen as an assault on Christianity, but rather it signifies the blatant exploitation of Christianity to justify violent right-wing fanaticism. The exploitation of Christianity and other religions are utilized as a recruitment tool to attract American fundamentalists and to radicalize and mobilize them utilizing a violent ideology.

The "war on terror" is a phrase that has been portrayed by US policymakers and military commanders as a battle against radical Islam. Few, however, acknowledge or understand how American right-wing extremists have also used slogans with respect to religious concepts and scripture to recruit, radicalize, and mobilize their adherents toward hate and violence. Right-wing extremists use their interpretations of religious concepts and scripture to lash out and kill in

God's name. Many past confrontations such as holy wars, crusades, and the conquests of other peoples have been instigated or carried out in the name of religion. For example, Pope Urban II called the first crusade a "war against Muslims" using the slogan *Deus vult*," or "God wills it."

Throughout history, violent clashes between nations, religions, and civilizations have as a cause a difference in religious beliefs, interpretations, or practices. Both religious principles and written scripture are subject to propaganda in their human interpretation. Religious viewpoints have been used as a means of strengthening religious communities but have also been used as an exploitation device to justify threatening others, criminal acts, and violence against non-believers. They view their opposition as representatives of evil. They see their religion of violence as being part of a divine plan mandated as a mission from their God. Extremists run the gamut from right-wing extremist groups to the fanatical beliefs of terrorist organizations in other countries. They have in common an agenda to promote religious supremacy and generally do not respect the equality of other religions.

In summary, every piece of religious propaganda must claim an authority which justifies the veracity of its message and describes other religions and ideas in highly disparaging and even racist terms. The propaganda demands that you abandon false religion and adopt what is herein claimed to be the one true religion via their established methodology. The propaganda always casts their religion in an especially good light by casting other religions in an extremely bad light. The propagandist arguments presented against the other religions are dubious at best and bigoted at worst. We cannot overlook how propaganda in religion has been used throughout history to influence minds, control behavior and attitudes, and enforce social and cultural adhesion.

Education

Education is a process of receiving or giving specific instruction through the dissemination of information, especially at a school or university. Propaganda, on the other hand, deals with the dissemination of information; but it is of a biased or misleading nature and is used to promote a cultural, social, or political point of view or cause. Socialization takes place, in varying degrees, at all academic levels from K-12. But education seems to be a matter of socialization up to and including the end of high school. The emphasis is on helping students develop a moral sensitivity and a value system intended to serve them well moving forward to the future. But with the pursuit of higher education, there is some change in course. College environments for the most part nudge students a little more to the left. There is more freedom of thought in this atmosphere, and students are introduced on a more consistent level to the need for social and political reform. Students become more concerned about both social and political justice. They become somewhat distracted from an original focus to become part of a well-paying profession. Students are in an environment that encourages more freedom of thought. The socializing and value-instilling process of earlier education just does not work as much or very well at this level. A good portion of thought processes turns toward the question of fairness. The perceived repressive and alienating forces within society take on more scrutiny. Conventional wisdom and reasoning are placed under a microscope of skepticism. There is a movement away from socialization toward individualization. And this is where propaganda places a heavy hand.

As an example, let's use the field of history. Student understanding with regards to history is undergoing change as well. It is a fact that this is an area of study that is most certainly, to some extent, open to interpretation. The major function of teaching history is to preserve national identity, as well as foster patriotism. But at the present moment, within college environments, there is a focus on presenting history through the lens of critical enlightenment. This is where long-held political and social beliefs are presented with a different perspective and interpretation. History that was once taught without much critical contemplation has now been replaced with an agenda that places critical refection as the centerpiece in teaching history. Is this a bad thing? To answer this, one has to scrutinize the purpose behind the shift. I find it most troubling if the reason is that teaching history in a traditional manner is harmful and ignorant of the changing times. Getting students to think about their history and to foster independent research is a positive thing *but* not when it is done with the purpose of being politically profitable for the wrong people in charge of doing what could be the right thing. The quality of history education must be responsive to the experiences of the students involved. The social purpose of preparing students for life in our democratic society is a challenging endeavor. It must be conducted by those who do not carry with them into the classroom a specific agenda. Teachers will need to get creative about how to ensure students are thoughtful and intelligent about the information they consume, and teachers must remain neutral with respect to interpretations that add to the increasing polarization we are currently experiencing in our nation.

There's been a lot of discussion among educators about the importance of teaching students to critically analyze information. The public is slowly gaining awareness of the destructibility of educational manipulation. Most adults can't accurately judge the truth or falseness of historical interpretations, because they assume that content which aligns with their existing beliefs is automatically true. Many choices are available to students as consumers of historically manipulated interpretations, and it seems as if they have adopted a problematic post-truth attitude. If it's entertaining or coincides with their own views, who really cares if it's true? This makes it easy for creators of historical bias to manipulate student thought processes. Some college teachers manipulate historical information in such a way as to foster their personal political beliefs by presenting them with their perspective and interpretation. When historical content includes emotionally inflamed rhetoric or intense images, they spread quickly and reach a larger collegiate audience. Not only are we seeing more emotionally manipulative historical content being taught in the classroom, but it is also more challenging to find and validate the source of the data being consumed.

Students need to be taught to make a distinction between evidence-based and inaccurate historical interpretations. Teachers must take up the cause and help students analyze and evaluate the information they receive. The health of our democracy may depend on it. Most educators have an increasing interest in teaching students how to critically analyze media. The teaching of media literacy or practices that allow people to access, evaluate, and create media helps in developing a skill set that extends to all forms of communication even outside the classroom setting. A major goal of education should be to discourage students from taking in information without analysis and evaluation as to content, source, and source agenda. Especially with ideologically based information, students should be taught to check a variety of sources. Who is initiating this information? What is the purpose behind it? Is it being used to inform or misinform? Is it being used to reinforce a political power base or social power base? Or is it being presented because the teacher is truly passionate about the issue?

For too many American students, propaganda is often associated with activities involving the historical past of the twentieth century. As a result of purposeful bias and omissions in instructional content, some college students incorrectly see propaganda as only something that occurred in the past. In reality, it is everywhere, and it is now presented through new digital media and media platforms that muddle the lines between entertainment, information, and persuasion techniques. It is by no means solely negative. But the intent and purpose here are to reflect on the propaganda that is.

To truly become media literate, it is essential that students are made aware of how and why they choose to accept some information as truthful and other information as false. Making judgments about the potential benefits and harm of educational propaganda gives students an opportunity to become skillful at interpreting and evaluating content. Maintaining an integrity of curriculum is a challenging concern for both educators and students.

Finance

Money is the gas that runs economies, and the world of *finance* is the engine that keeps it structured and firmly moving along. Our economic system basically runs on one important aspect—confidence. The relationship between psychology and confidence, as well as politics and confidence, cannot be overstated. In politics, an economy with low demand and weak employment wreaks havoc on the party in power. Our capitalist economy depends heavily on encouraging and sustaining confidence. Smart politics, with respect to the economy, travels down a yellow brick road singing "Happy Days Are Here Again." This is what essentially occurred after the 2016 election.

Essential to all monetary manipulation is the fact that it often distorts markets and causes economic upswings followed by punitive busts. Misinformation in economic science has caused more harm than the prominent role of money and credit in economic booms and busts. The public disposition for lower interest rates, which reinforce consumer and business credit expansion, creates an irresistible temptation for the fed, politicians, and economists to concur with and use as an economic stimulator.

An important example of Wall Street's propaganda machine at work is its unwillingness to call attention to recessionary signals. The inverted yield curve is a good example. A case in point is the November 2006 story printed by Market Watch. The story was in print exactly one year before the 2007 recession responsible for wreaking exceptional havoc on the housing market. The stock market started its decline of more than half, and the global economy began to collapse at that time. The inverted yield curve was described at the time as being attributed to a move toward and appetite for worldwide consumer and business saving which was the catalyst for an increased demand for treasuries and bonds.

The major economists at the time took the position that the demand for treasuries and bonds was inconsistent with a threat of a recessionary possibility. In spite of past history consistently proving that an inverted yield curve was a precursor to a recession, the economic powers that be dismissed the curve inversion as not being the case in this instance. Some people may label this analysis as simply misinformation, but given the history of yield curve inversions as being harbingers of a recession, I am not so sure this was not disinformation. As matter of fact, despite its predictive ability with respect to foreseeing recessions, the fed claimed that it was not as accurate a measure in the current economy as it was in the past. So at the time, the inverted yield curve was seen as being caused by a global increase in savings and had nothing to do with economic slowdown.

Fast-forward to 2019, and we were hearing the same dismissal of the inverted yield curve, the reason being all is well in economic circles and the yield curve is not a good indicator this time around since inflation is not a major concern. However, the inverted curve has always been a sign of a slowing global economy. The inversion causes credit to evaporate. When a banks cost to borrow funds and the income from those assets both decrease to near zero, the incentive to lend money and increase credit decreases due to a fear of loan defaults and a low margin of returns. At the writing of this book, the yield curve has been inverted for a good part of the last half of 2019. A recession has always occurred within two years of an initial yield curve inversion. Now with the added health crisis of COVID-19, there is even more reason to believe movement toward a recession is inevitable. Time will tell how long it will last and how deep it will become.

Another area where there appears to be a disconnect from reality is the topic of inflation. It appears that the divide between the stated rate of inflation and bar code reality is not synchronized. To me, bar codes and pricing are the epitome of actual price information. It seems that whenever the government defines rate of inflation, the reality of real-world inflation is in shops and supermarkets, and government price information on inflation seems to be out of kilter. There appears to be a price-data manipulation geared to give the impression that inflation is lower than it actually is. Anyone who is charged with the task of buying food, paying rent, paying energy bills, or paying property taxes or car and home insurance knows that prices have been increasing, more so in some areas of the country than others. It's hard to understand how our country continues to utilize an average rate of inflation when location plays an important factor. With respect to food goods, we have all experienced the reduction in content with respect to food packaging. For example, at one time, coffee was sold by the pound and ice cream by the half gallon. With time, sizing on a broad spectrum has gotten smaller. Don't raise the price; just lower content. See, prices are remaining the same.

When we look at how the printing of money has gotten out of hand in the name of fiscal or quantitative easing (QE), the future for a substantial increase in inflation seems to almost be guaranteed. Sooner or later, the question of national debt will have to be addressed. The powers that be will have to deal with the debt-generated economy that has been created and is healthily chugging along. The national debt increases much more rapidly during an economic crisis, the stimulation of economic growth through social programs, or an increased spending for military purposes. The addition of a health crisis can recently be added to this list.

On a positive note, excessive debt has not stopped America from being the largest economic superpower of the world. The result of such monetary policy has led to vibrant capital markets. Up until the 2020 COVID-19 pandemic, the Dow Jones was at record-high levels and will most likely reach those levels again, but how soon is difficult to assess. The bull market in America was active and well up to the pandemic.

The US government has been paying historically low rates on its debt, largely because of the Federal Reserve's efforts to keep interest rates low during and after the 2008 recession. One may conclude that such low rates would stifle investment, but US government debt is considered to carry very little risk, and historically, demand for it has remained strong. However, if investor demand for treasuries softens, the government and ultimately the taxpayers will end up having to pay higher interest rates. In summary, since 2008, countries around the world have adopted practices such as currency manipulation and quantitative easing to maintain a healthy economy. The short-term benefits of this kind of currency manipulation have not been without its critics.

Health

Health education disseminates information on wellness and health by informing us of the best lifestyle habits to prevent illness and disease. An important part of our health information comes to us through the labeling on food packaging. At no point in time has food labeling been so extensive as it currently is. The packaging is an attempt to help consumers to become more aware of the nutrition they are ingesting in order to maintain a healthy lifestyle. It is also an incentive to get consumers to purchase products. For many consumers, the purchase of a product is dependent on the label. But the packaging does not address the whole story concerning wellness. For example, watching your food intake with regards to saturated and unsaturated fats is a really good way to prevent coronary heart disease (CHD). But in reality, many of the attempts to increase healthier lifestyles through food choice by consumers have not worked very well. There is very little hard evidence to support the idea that food labeling has resulted in a decrease in CHD. There has been much more success with the strategy of identifying individuals who are at high risk and then correct the adverse conditions through lifestyle change and medications.

What is seldom discussed is that dietary intervention plays a bigger role on health moving forward but does little to alter past damage. One cannot expect a big change in CHD after a few years of intervention with respect to a middle age or older adult with a lifelong past history of making poor lifestyle choices. Depending on the diagnosis, the enthusiasm and push through media emphasizing dietary change as an obscure panacea for health concerns is not as effective as the medical identification, intervention, and prevention with respect to health problems. Even so, food labeling has reached an all-time high in proclaiming nutrition and health benefits which approach a level of disinformation or misinformation at best. Labeling can be misleading. The most important consideration is to read the Nutrition Facts Panel. The panel contains a basic list and quantity for the main nutrients in a product. In 1990, Congress authorized the allowance of scientifically and substantially tested health claims on packaging and, in 1994, authorized the allowance of information regarding how the food product can be beneficial to various stated parts of the body. Most prominent is the American Heart Association symbol indicating "heart healthy" food products. The abundance of health claims for health benefits has exponentially increased.

So the question is, Do they actually produce the health benefit they claim? People tend to read the health claims on the front of packaging and ignore the Nutrition Facts Panel. The fact is that very few of the health claims on the front of packaging can be verified. The claim that a food contains antioxidants and can bolster immune systems is in most cases dubious. Most times, there is a lack of clinical trials and authentication of claims due to the expense involved in such testing. The product may, indeed, contain antioxidants, but at what percentage and quality? The fact is that the less processed a food is, the more nutrients it contains, and so-called healthier processed foods are not necessarily healthier. Sugar and salt content, with the exception of sugar-free and low-sodium products, is seldom discussed on front packaging labels. When a product is labeled 30 percent less salt, you have to ask yourself, 30 percent of what original amount? You have to find that information in the food panel. The propaganda of food packaging is actually a serious health concern. Companies are more interested in selling their products than the educational purpose of regulated labeling.

When it comes to vitamin and mineral supplements, the misinformation and disinformation are equally remarkable. More than four out of five American adults take vitamins. Most people can get the vitamins and minerals necessary for good health through a balanced diet. Having said that, lifestyles preclude that as being a simple achievement or goal. So people turn to supplements as an insurance policy. The intent here is not to review every vitamin and mineral out there. However, the purpose is to get the readers to involve themselves in research. Many medical field experts discount supplements as being a benefit at all. Stating that vitamin supplementation is a waste of money and time and dangerous across the entire spectrum of supplementation is just not true. Most people do not eat a balanced diet. And this is where supplementation can be very beneficial. There is compelling evidence as well that vitamin supplementation can preserve and restore good health. But it is important to research the literature.

Using vitamins and supplements touted as miracle cures for ailments without knowing anything about the product is not the way to go. It is my hope that this topic reinforces you to become more aware of available information before deciding on a supplement. They have to have scientific evidence to back up their claims, as well as be proven safe. It is important to understand that there are labels out there with the sole purpose of misleading the public. The simplest way to bring a health concern to the forefront of conversation is through constant repetition in the media. The more times you are exposed to a specific point of view, the more likely you are to believe it. Repetitive exposure to a particular piece of information makes it easier to process and easier to believe. For example, the hysteria surrounding vaping has been hard to ignore. Because of the media outlet push labeling vaping as a major health concern, laws are currently being changed that increase the age limit to purchase this product. I have seen very little in the media comparing the health ramifications of vaping compared to smoking. The deadly risk associated with smoking has been clearly identified.

If vaping is banned, what percentage of vapors will return to the use of cigarettes, which we know to be a less favorable alternative? With cigarettes, there is a strong connection between smoking and heart disease, chronic obstructive pulmonary disorder, strokes, and cancer. These risks are well established. Because of this fact, vaping at the present time, given the facts that we know, is a safer alternative to smoking. In summary, health propaganda is in plentiful supply. The most powerful promoter of good health resides within us and the behaviors we choose to adopt.

Fashion

The use of propaganda in *fashion* has a multilevel impact. Fashion advertising is geared to entice women to dress a certain way and to use the most current makeup to send that very important signal that they are in style. Advertising impacts the way men, women, and children dress. Clothing can be a sign of personality. To be in vogue means going with the latest trend, and those trends are constantly changing. In order to keep up with the times, you have to buy the latest fashion. The average person buys over eighty pieces of clothing a year. Purchasing new clothes and discarding older clothing keep the fashion industry humming. The United States discards more than eleven million pounds of textiles and clothing a year. This does not include donations to various charitable organizations, which is a much higher number. It is estimated that the average person discards in one way or the other about eighty-two pounds of clothing each year. Clothing is produced overseas because of the lower cost of manufacturing. The low wages paid for clothing production is explained as a positive, if at all, by the clothing industry because, regardless of low wages, they are providing work to people who otherwise would have no alternative. The function of this propagandist message is to portray the clothing industry in a positive light. Many workers are treated very poorly and basically function in economic servitude. The industry is a major producer of pollution. For example, the pesticide used in producing cotton.

Fashion is a social and economic phenomenon. The clothing and makeup you wear, choose, discard, and consume play a very important role in showing the world what kind of person you are. Fashion has become a multidynamic system. Not only is style important, but the label attached to the fashion item sends a message as well. That label has two purposes: it sends a status message to the viewer, and labels act as a propaganda instrument. The fashion you wear can be a sign of social status. It sends a message of how you relate to the world around you. It is an expression of the identity you wish to convey to others. There is a symbiotic relationship between what you choose to wear and the external message you want that choice to cultivate. What you wear enhances self-image, and self-image dictates what you choose to wear. However, self-image may be an unrecognizable part of one's true self. Therefore, fashion dictates can be in itself a propagandist activity. Self-expression through clothing and accessories is a central part of fashion. Emotional engagement plays an important role in consumption as well. It is a central motivating force behind fashion choice. The "rapid change" mentality of the fashion industry is to make the purchase of clothing as inexpensive as possible to induce discarding older choices for newer purchases and increase consumption.

Fashion products are becoming a major essence of society. It purposefully and constantly changes and is always incomplete. There is endless room for something new and something more. The propaganda lies in the industry psychology that fashion consumption is a necessary aspect of self-image, your relationship with society, and modern life. It constantly remains in flux. The industry objective is to have fashion-style change constantly and always remain as an incomplete aspect of life. It is meant to tie in perfectly with the pace and rhythm of an ever-changing world. Given this situation and the level of anxiety it produces, the redeeming value of compulsive buying will always remain a factor. Fashion seduces the consumer to always purchase something new which they know will entail a planned obsolescence at some point. "Out with the old, in with the new." It is the method used by the fashion industry to increase consumer spending through the introduction of constantly changing style.

As a result, overconsumption and habitual buying have become the norm. The consumer is exposed to a constant barrage of powerful and persuasive advertising pressure. The industry goal is to move the consumption of fashion from a need to a compulsion or addiction. This explanation is in no way intended to be a value judgment but rather an explanation of fashion strategy that dismisses any other alternatives. The pursuit of self-esteem is one of the most significant motivational factors in its overconsumption. As a relief valve for stress, anxiety, depression, and low esteem, it has become a medicine for the mind. The propaganda lies in the exploitation of the above situation. A specific emotional condition or state of mind reinforces hypermaterialism, when consumer buying habits, and especially overconsumption, are elevated to a consumer purchasing rationale.

Fashion choice has turned out to be an excellent personality predictor as well. Choices made through digital purchasing have been used as a determining factor in identifying right- and left-wing political adherence. As mentioned earlier, self-esteem and self-expression are high on the list of motivational factors when it comes to fashion choice. For example, the brands you choose to "like" or "dislike" on Facebook helps to magnify your interests. Your choices send a message about your character and psychological political leaning. This information has been used to target consumer audiences with political propaganda. You may feel that hitting "likes" and "dislikes" is a harmless activity, but by doing so, you are providing the powers that be information about your psychological framework. It has been found that the brand of clothing you like is a roadmap of your personality traits and an indicator of what targeted political messages may be most effective on you.

Without a doubt, men's fashion holds a level of importance in American culture, but that importance loses significance when compared to women's fashion, which changes more often and more radically than men's clothing. The overwhelming preponderance of advertising goes toward the women's fashion industry. It has taken on many forms and many meanings and has been received with mixed feelings by their contemporaries. It has been used as a tool to mold and conform the consumers' cultural tastes and has also been instrumental in challenging and breaking fashion rules which has resulted in a fashion history that still continues to change and will continue to do so as long as fashion remains a fundamental extension of self-confidence and self-esteem.

Legal System

The *legal system* is based on the premise that its purpose is to defend equality in all matters related to law. One of the major topics in the media as a result of the 2016 election and the inauguration of a new president is corruption. It can broadly be described as an abuse of office or position by a public official, a private citizen, a political, or a public or private organization. The abuse stems from the fact that the offending party is either not performing the duties required by his position or performing those duties in an improper manner to the detriment of an individual or an entire group. The reason or purpose of corruption is to attain a personal advantage or private gain. Permeating this definition is the presumption of the existence of a legally injured person or group. The injured group could be an entire nation depending on the scope of corruption. It can include, for example, such offenses as illegal political manipulation, money laundering, mail fraud, and drug trafficking. In broader terms, it is a common thread found in varying degrees in most political and business transactions. We have heard many of the abuses on media—extortion, bribery, and manipulation of those involved in the political arena. There has been a moral collapse in the American legal system. Legal organizations such as the FBI, CIA, and the federal court system have all been dealt a black eye in the media. Judicial law has now been relegated to an unprecedented level of interpretation. The American people have been witnesses to an extraordinary amount of investigation and prosecution.

My contention is that in most of these instances we have yet to hear the "whole" story. There appears to be a level of fear when it comes to unfolding the entire truth involved in a corruption case. The legal system is at a point, and has been for many years, where judges are appointed to federal positions not so much for their knowledge and experience but rather for their political ideology. This practice is present at all levels of government including, as we have seen, the Supreme Court. Bias is defined as prejudice in favor or against a thing, person, or group compared to another. The phrase "Justice is blind" means that justice is impartial and objective. The allusion that justice wears a blindfold is meant to infer equality before the law. But when you bring an ideology with you to the bench, are you still easily capable of wearing that blindfold?

We can actually forward the premise that the American legal system is functioning just as it was designed to do. The formula in its creation was to create a blind justice, but even though justice is considered blind, there is nothing wrong with its hearing. Justice is open to listening to the various biases of the world. From the lower courts to the Supreme Court, bias plays a role in the decision-making process. The legal system is not broken. The design is beautifully constructed. The problem lies in the fact that it is not always doing what it was designed to do. The problem is not the system but rather the people in charge of it and involved in its utilization. The propaganda lies in the continued belief that every person or subject matter taken on by the judicial system is entitled to a "fair" hearing. Our understanding and definition of fairness can be developed into an infallible construct. But the real failure lies with the powerful interests, politicians, and lawyers who have a specific agenda and "skin" in the game. When it comes to legal reasoning and legal decision making, there is almost always someone with their finger on the scale. The main purpose of the legal system, and the penal system as well, is to preserve wealth, property, and safety. Decision making leans to the benefit of the ruling class. Even the words we use for the legal bureaucracy such as "justice department," the criminal justice system (for some of us), and law enforcement (but not all laws) do not fully live up to their names and are propagandists by definition.

Celebrated legal decisions revolving around segregation have not truly remedied the problem. This system of oppression is not going to be eradicated by a legal decision. The catalyst for originally addressing the problem did not come from the legal system but rather from the "power of the people." The loudest voice gets the most attention. This has also been the case in other landmark decisions such as same-sex marriage. For forty years, the issue fell on deaf ears. It was the ground swell of people (who also happen to vote) who exerted both influence and pressure that changed the way we think about same-sex marriage. All of the most meaningful changes occur when a groundswell of support makes it uncomfortable and politically unpopular to hold back the tidal wave of demand in its support. What we need to understand is that change will necessitate the development of a social movement that alters the way we think about the judicial system. Until a national cry in support of remedying the problem is developed and until we all become part of that movement, I do not believe that the system will fundamentally improve. Until then, the values of true equality, fairness, and justice will continue to be tainted by the power of bias and the propaganda to support it.

Race and Racism

Race and *racism* are relentlessly used by both politicians and the media as weapons of national destruction to systematically explain the decision-making process of our national leaders. When it comes to propaganda, the continuous repetition of an allegation can catapult a falsehood to a heightened level of believability and acceptance. After the 2016 election, the race card was used to forward the unsubstantiated smear that the newly elected president and his supporters were racists. There are many who have heard this oft-repetitive message and have firmly placed it within their "fact bubble." Has racism been eradicated in the United States? Absolutely not. But the kind of systemic institutional oppression that existed one hundred years ago has been eradicated.

With the adoption of laws, policies, and cultural progress, citizens of color have made remarkable strides in both society and culture. But make no mistake. We are all well aware that the poison of racism still exists in our ever-struggling imperfect world. But the present-day attacks by both media and politics are propaganda scare tactics designed to further the already existing divisions within our country. For example, a White supremacist rally is magnified to the point that gives the audience the impression that this behavior is a norm rather than an exception. Why is this taking place in the media? One main reason is to ensure that a healthy divide remains between liberal and conservative ideologies and political identity. The purpose is to promote political captivity.

Our nation is one of cultural diversity. We are a nation of both native-born Americans and legal immigrants. In the name of both safety and law, enforcing border security to protect American citizens is not an act of racism or bigotry. Rather, it is an act of concern, responsibility, and, yes, common sense. Lax immigration policies are a precursor to increased crime and competition among the minority citizens of our country and illegal aliens who unfairly and illegally compete for jobs in our labor market.

Interestingly enough, racial accusations promoting cultural and political division come not only from within our country but from outside of it as well. The media coverage of outside political interference in our election has been repetitively driven home by the various news outlets and digital platforms. Russian protagonists are responsible for the creation of hundreds of messages and ads that promote racial division within the United States. They are using the well-known cliché "divide and conquer" to foster unrest. These tactics can only be described as propagandist in nature. While some of their posts attacked the Black Lives Matter Group, other posts attacked White nationalism in America. The purpose was to influence public opinion on racial issues. America's cataclysmic history of racial violence and segregation was used by Russian sources to further hammer the wedge of division within our country. The long game is to destabilize American democracy by inflaming our nation's inner turmoil mostly through the use of phony Facebook accounts. The strategy is nothing new. It originated in the 1920s and increased in sophistication at the height of the cold war. An additional purpose was to deflect criticism of the Soviet Union for its own human rights violations at this time. In psychology, this is known as *projection*.

Russian attempts to utilize social media to compromise the Black Lives Matter movement emphasize the danger faced by all domestic social justice movements. As they have been in the past, they find themselves under government scrutiny and surveillance and are used as scapegoats by conservative political ideologies. To make matters worse, they are exploited by media users whose agenda includes starting arguments and upsetting the media audience (trolls) seeking to undermine American democracy. The propaganda from Russia accentuates the notion that racial discrimination continues to plague American democracy. The objective is to proliferate discord. They will continue to exploit racial tensions well beyond Russia's social media and misinformation efforts tied to the 2016 election. The Mueller Report detailed how Russian trolls deliberately incited racial tensions by spreading false and explosive stories to African Americans via social media. One objective was to suppress Black turnout in the 2016 US election. They constantly push and incite propaganda efforts to stir up negative opinions about both the United States and Europe.

The Internet has become a weapon of choice to influence and reinforce divisiveness in America through propagandist techniques. Race polarity is reinforced through blogs, news commentary websites, forums, and chat rooms. The media focus on hate crimes, racism, anti-Semitism, White nationalism rallies, and discrimination against immigrants helps to foster the division our country is currently experiencing. Americans have a past deeply rooted in fear, hate, and violence. And while these stories have shaped our country, it is also important to look at the reactions to hate and intolerance. When the stories are not viewed as singular incidents but rather as proof of a dangerous political ideology, then propaganda has done its job. We have truly become a disconnected country.

There are many ways to explain the polarized politics of a nation. You can stand back and look for broad patterns like electoral results or policy debates we experience each and every day. You can view the vicious rhetoric and accusations on media platforms—in the press, newspapers, and television—and ask yourself, Just what is the agenda that is currently in place and fueling this behavior? But before answering that question, ask yourself what part you play in all of this. As far as social media is concerned, whenever you leave a comment about a polarizing subject, there is a chance you are opening the wound of polarity even further. And to be sure, there are online actors in place whose job is to do exactly that. As we have witnessed in the media, for example the tearing up of the presidential State of the Union speech by the House speaker on national TV, there are many people who have issues with both anger management and emotional control. So we have the people who do not think through the consequences of their actions, and we have those actors with a deliberate propagandist agenda to inflame divisiveness within our nation.

Immigration

Bias toward *immigration* is nothing new. Throughout our nation's history, there has been quite a bit of pushback with respect to immigration. Sentiment opposing Irish, German, and Italian immigration, as far back as the late 1800s, grew more and more popular with the continued influx of new immigrants. There was a continued growth in anti-Catholic, anti-immigrant sentiment. Chinese immigration fell in such disfavor that Congress passed a law putting an end to it. The Chinese Exclusion Act of 1882 curtailed Chinese immigration as well as the attainment of Chinese citizenship, and it was not officially repealed until 1943. The immigration act of 1924 placed limitations on allowable immigration from Southern and Eastern Europe, as well as a complete ban on Asian immigration, and quotas were in place until 1965. The propaganda at the time was quite robust. "Immigration causes economic problems," "The American way of life is being threatened," "They will never adapt to our customs," and "They are taking away American jobs" were part of the conversation of the day. A good part of the rhetoric included a healthy dose of propaganda.

We now fast-forward to the present, and we find a harsh anti-immigrant sentiment in place coinciding with the 2016 presidential election. A hardline approach to immigration has become the new standard. And just as in the past, propaganda freely flows. The current policy undermines human rights, expands the use of detention facilities, limits access to asylum, and has enhanced enforcement along the border. One would think American leadership is purely evil and without a heart.

But as with most problems, there are two sides of the story. The United States, since the 2016 election, has been attempting to adopt an immigration policy that serves the national interest. Things like rule of law, border security, unlawful immigrant entry, and protecting American workers are just a few. There are those who feel illegal immigration is an attempt to build a larger future voter base for the ideologically liberal party in our country. Can this be considered a national interest?

Much of the rhetoric can be summed up by the following statements: There is an anti-immigrant and anti-refugee policy in the country. Life is now substantially more difficult for immigrants. We hear an awful lot about the harshness of the conservative political agenda spearheaded by the president. The United States has reneged on its promise of opportunity and safety for all immigrants. They are not treated fairly, equally, and with dignity. These feelings are some of the many out there.

To be able to have a meaningful conversation about the above and add some clarity to the problem, other statements deserve consideration: There are anti-*illegal*-immigrant and anti-*illegal*-refugee policies in the country. The current situation is substantially more difficult for *illegal* immigrants. The United States continues to support a program of opportunity and safety for all legal immigrants. They are treated fairly, equally, and with dignity. Illegal immigration is a concern for a large number of Americans. The deportation of *illegal* immigrants is required by law and reinforces the current fair consideration of legal immigrant rights. Illegal immigrants put themselves and their children in harm's way by the process of illegally entering our country. Seventy five percent of illegal immigrants skip deportation hearings.

The political will to solve the immigration crises has been non-existent for decades. Laws are needed that will clarify a legal pathway for immigration. Immigrants can be an important part of the American labor force, but a documentation pathway has to be in place. Many immigrants constitute a hardworking portion of the labor force. A vast majority find employment because they are willing to work for less money. They work in areas that are either physically demanding such as construction or commonplace positions in the service industry as maids and cleaning personnel. It is estimated that illegal immigrants make up about 5 percent of the American workforce. The fact that national laws having any real consequences for violation have not been enforced as a method to curtail the hiring of undocumented workers reinforces their importance in the workforce. An adequate workforce is the backbone of every economy.

On conservative TV and media platforms, the argument is constantly forwarded that illegal immigration is one of the main causes of crime in the United States. We are fed by the media's constant examples of the connection between undocumented immigrants and increased violence. In fairness, examples of crime caused by illegal aliens within our country cannot be extrapolated into an argument that large numbers of illegals are the cause for higher rates of violence and property crime. But the argument can be made that this group is certainly one of many contributing factors. It is unfair and propagandist to point to incidents and use those incidents to castigate the entire illegal immigrant population. We certainly do not do that with any other ethnic population. Nor should it be done in this instance. Having said this, studies show that illegal immigrants have a higher likelihood of being convicted of a crime than legal immigrants but a lower likelihood of being convicted of a crime than native-born Americans. Statistics such as this are manipulated in ways that open up a lot of possibilities for the propagandist.

Conservative media pushes the notion that illegal immigrants bring in and spread disease in the United States. Again, there are examples of this being the case, but the overwhelming majority enter the United States tired and dehydrated. There are cases of illnesses but rarely from a communicable disease. Other propagandist attacks include assertions that Spanish-speaking illegals do not assimilate into our culture as well as past immigrants did. A quick study of the immigration of the late 1800s and early 1900s will show that contact and interaction with other nationalities was at the time quite problematic and more so than what is experienced with Mexican immigration. Another argument is that illegal immigrants are taking advantage of America's financial resources. Conservative media platforms are quick to forward this argument. But it is important to have a better understanding of the entire economic framework involved. Almost three million undocumented immigrants pay taxes. Immigrants and their employers contribute roughly $9 billion to the economy. Immigrants do so even though they are not eligible for Social Security benefits upon retirement. They use false Social Security numbers or an Individual Taxpayer Identification Number. They hope that paying taxes will help them avoid extradition and one day help them to become a citizen. Illegal immigrants are not eligible to enroll in Medicare, Medicaid, or Obamacare. But they can go to community health centers for primary care. Around $2 billion a year in emergency Medicaid funds go to hospitals who must care for anyone who shows up at the emergency room. Hospitals report that most of them are undocumented immigrants. This partial explanation will hopefully add some balance to the discussion. But none of these arguments change the fact that illegal immigration is a violation of the rule of law. Labeling them as undocumented does nothing to solve the issue. As previously mentioned, we are a country of laws. And it must remain that no one becomes above the law, lest we become even more a nation of liberty and justice for some of us.

Freedom

The concept of *freedom* fosters a belief and ides that we can become whatever we "choose" to be. Many would argue that the existing inequality in our nation serves as a proof of choice. However, class, education, and financial status dramatically impact the opportunities available to people; and by definition, the underprivileged are inevitably less free. But freedom and opportunity are not one and the same thing. And the illusion of choice may actually be an indicator of just how "free less" we really are. The definition of *freedom* must overlap the definition of *choice*. *Freedom* incorporates the ability to choose. The greater your choices, the greater your freedom. Then again, maybe not. One can become so involved in the process of making choices that it becomes detrimental to being really free. Where is the freedom in being obligated to spend a good portion of your time involved in a decision-making process?

A capitalistic democratic society is considered the best of the worst as an environment to achieve freedom. We are constantly told we can choose our own destiny, as well as enjoy creative autonomy and individual self-development. Again, this really sounds great. But actually, is it a propagandist idea developed by the wealthy and powerful? Choice comes with multiple restrictions. One restriction comes from the fact that we are divided into economic classes. For the most part, there is little interconnection between them. The greater one's economic and social privilege, the more numerous their choices. Those who work for a wage are generally much more limited when it comes to options. Society promotes the propagandist belief that all of us are able to make unlimited decisions and choices concerning self-development and destiny. But for many people, what they really have is the illusion of choice and, therefore, the illusion of freedom.

Freedom is a broad term for what is actually an elusive construct. Yet it is something everyone in this country values. It is often suggested that we compare our freedom to the quantity of freedom in other countries which are lacking with respect to the autonomy enjoyed here. The question is, Are we really as free as we are being told we are? With respect to law and government, we actually only have two viable choices. The choice between liberal and conservative ideologies is actually a restriction of choice. And those involved in our government actually have limits on their choices due to lobbyist funding. The purpose of a lobbyist is to buy and pay for politicians which they monopolize when it comes to making decisions. Where is the freedom in that? Choice is relegated to the decision of choosing one corporate puppet over another.

Media platforms do a wonderful job of selling the idea that voting equates with democracy and freedom. But media corporations are beholding to the same institutions and companies that influence politicians, so the messages distributed by media are messages controlled by corporations with an agenda. I forward the idea that our day-to-day existence is controlled more so by political lobbyists rather than politicians.

We are constantly being conditioned to believe that we actually act out of "free" will. But the outside influences around us are the true authors of our decisions. For example, a decision about vaccinations is slowly being taken out of our realm of choice and is slowly becoming a mandate of the government in the name of ensuring the "common good." In order to attain an education, maintain a job, enter a hospital or clinic, shop or travel, or function on any practical level within society, you may be required to catch up on mandated vaccines because the government says so. Need to renew a license? Show your vaccination record.

Not only are individuals losing their freedom of ability to choose but states as well. Whenever states accept federal funding and subsidies, there are certain requirements and requests that go hand and hand with that funding. Both people and states are gradually losing the right to make decisions for themselves. There is a pattern of compliance that has taken hold with respect to reactions toward this assault on our freedoms. Without the ability to choose, there is a lack of freedom. The highest form of free thought occurs when it is free from outward control. It is not free when there are penalties and retribution involved in the expression of a different opinion or belief. Freedom of thought is certainly influenced by media presentation. There is a perversion of evidence when an argument is extended in which one side of the controversy is presented in a continuous fashion and in a very favorable light while opposing arguments actually require the audience to do their own research. The most effective way to control thought processes is to present information in an uncontested manner so the audience fails to see the entire picture. With the presentation of a one-sided argument, there is certainly less to consider. But the illusion of choice is seldom overtly impacted.

People do not regularly realize that they have little choice in a one-sided presentation. To increase the level of truth in discourse, all sides of an argument must be heard and all relevant facts presented. We have to learn how to control personal bias and to keep an open mind. Choosing on the basis of selecting the option that most fits into the realm of your preconceived standpoint can only be productive if it is a properly informed choice. Unfortunately, many of our most important choices seem to be made on the basis of more or less deliberate misinformation. Misinformed choices are sometimes themselves defended in the name of freedom. But choice can only be free if the decision made is a properly informed one based on adequate understanding.

We live in a society that is essentially free, but media platforms conduct their presentation of information so as to limit choice. The media partisanship associated with ideological pressure systematically works to reduce choice. The freedom to make truly meaningful decisions is increasingly compromised. Choice is not a consumer product that you can just simply buy. It is hard to achieve, and in many cases, information is presented so as to lead to a "fixed" choice outcome. Freedom to choose based on the presentation of all relevant facts is an indispensable component of a free and healthy society.

History

George Orwell once declared that *history* stopped in 1936. After that, there was only propaganda. In the name of restoring calmness, truth became the first victim of the Great Depression. Deception revolving around the Depression was considered a necessary route to take due to the seriousness of the situation. Even the word used, *depression*, is a more emotionally neutral term than what was actually occurring, which in fact was a financial crisis and an ensuing financial panic. During World 1 and more so during World War 2, history is replete with example after example of propaganda used to corrode civilian morale. Even Hitler, determined to find a scapegoat for Germany's problems, focused on slogans attacking Jewish communities and appealing to already existing sentiment among the people. The Depression was used as a tool to promote the acceptance and support of his ideology. The Nazi party came to fruition to serve as a vehicle to disseminate both his political ideology and emotionally charged propaganda. It was the beginning of the destruction of a national culture and the rise of a new one. Under the rule of Stalin, the axiom of the day was "If it is true, don't say or mention it." Within a background of turmoil and stress, the reality of one's senses was usurped by falsehoods about the people, the Soviet Union, and the entire world. A campaign of lies and propaganda became the focus of the Marxist regime. The information of the time confused the world as to what was actually a true analysis built on knowledge and understanding or ingenuous propaganda designed to brainwash the entire world.

In today's reality, school history textbooks are written by authors who genuinely believe they have the only correct information. A great deal of these texts make a valiant effort to convey the most accurate and factual information, but sometimes personal bias is included as well. The fact is that with the abundant amount of analysis and evaluation on the Internet, it is easy to see how small historical facts can be misinterpreted. Every author of a new history textbook is strongly tempted to insert personal opinion within the subject matter. And they sometimes include their opinions in what they write. Whether it is intentional or not, the author's beliefs can oftentimes be found between the lines, and human error will always come into play where textbooks are involved. Bias can greatly alter the composition of the text. When it comes to an American history book, the author could either be extremely patriotic or portray the past the way they see it. They could view the great westward expansion in terms of our great manifest destiny while someone else may stress it as the genocide of the American Indian nation. Both human error and opinion cannot be avoided in texts. Textbooks have become all-encompassing with respect to the information they provide and coupled with the instructor's lecture on the subject may actually paint an entirely different viewpoint on the subject.

History books are filled with a generous amount of what can be described as a stretched truth or the promotion of myths that are far from accurate in the sense that they do not tell the entire story involved in an event. As one example, Paul Revere was not alone in his famous ride that warned of the British approach. Paul had quite a bit of help in sounding the alarm. He was just one of a large group of patriots who all had the same responsibility and equally did their part. The ensuing mobilization was, indeed, a collaborative effort. Another and more profound example of the distortion of fact is the focus on Thomas Jefferson as one of the architects of the Declaration of Independence without a mention of the political climate at play. Independence was a main topic of conversation and resulted in the creation of ninety previous documents that were produced on either state or local levels. So here we have just two examples where history magnifies the reputation of a historical actor by playing down the entire reality at the time. So some folks might conclude that the omissions of the entire factual framework are no big deal. But in a way it is. It downplays the role that collaboration had at the time. The presentation of history as an individual achievement, when in fact it was not, diminished the concerted effort and role played by the entire population. The story gives little credit to the collaborative effort that existed at the time.

To sum up, when it comes to historical textbooks, there is quite a bit of room for improvement. The idea that unity and cooperation are fundamental aspects of any endeavor is not reinforced. The reasoning behind the masking of stories to emphasize individual heroism over teamwork and cooperation is to promote a sense of nationalism and pride. History actually suffers when its explanation is diluted or clouded in textbooks. We are in an age now where the history of the past is being rewritten and reevaluated through the lens of a more unflattering and different point of view. To truly understand history, empathy, perspective-taking skills, and impartiality are all necessary requirements. History is a resource that shapes national identity. There is more focus now than any other time in finding those truths in history that fit a political, social, or ideological agenda. Propaganda lies in the advancement of a given interpretation of history and uses the current cultural perspective as the basis of analysis. It is often presented in the guise of a revised point of view to foster acceptability. To make this history more acceptable, a measure of credibility is added to the historical record. But the viewing of history through the lens of our current social and political culture gives us very little help in understanding the political and social culture of the historical context in which the history took place.

War and Peace

Media and information control related to war and peace utilizing widespread political propaganda can either enhance or diminish public sentiment and attitude. When propaganda is used as a means to an end to rally a nation behind a cause through exaggeration, misrepresentation, or outright lies, it usually comes at an enormous cost. Should such behavior carry a criminal penalty? At the very least, the use of a well-orchestrated propaganda campaign as a determinative for war deserves legal scrutiny. It is manipulation with an objective plain and simple. It can be found everywhere. By simply using selective stories or partial facts, opinions can be easily swayed. But it becomes serious business when used to shape attitude and opinion toward a world conflict.

Using carefully selected experts to provide insights concerning a situation through a narrow presentation of reason and motivation is another method of controlling conversation and information. The demonization of a nation, a group, or an individual by the method of supplying just one perspective does not serve the interests of the audience. A narrow focus only serves the interests of the propagandist. At times of world conflict, the rationale to take action often comes with messages of fear and hate and at the same time is combined with emotions of honor and righteousness. This use of interplay provides a powerful propaganda for a cause. It has often been repeated that truth is the first casualty of war. Another reality is that in war, there are no winners or losers, only survivors. War should be the very last resort taken. It must never be considered inevitable. Yet most war propaganda in the past had as its objective to pull nations closer to war. It has two main outcomes: it kills people, and it makes other people rich.

During a state of war, the enemy is constantly portrayed in a negative light, and this occurs on both ends of the battlefield. Both sides bolster their cause, with each nation involved, in promoting the notion that what is being done will have a positive and beneficial outcome. The opposing nations try to demonize each other in the eyes of their people and reinforce the claim that what has been undertaken is based on a morally responsible decision. Propaganda is used to place blame for the conflict on the other side. The causes of escalation leading to violence and war are always explained with a one-sided focus, and media coverage reinforces this approach to the conflict. Rather than withhold the other sides point of view, a more productive and morally responsible approach would be to expose the truths backed by fact and with the perspectives of both sides of the conflict.

War always begins with a mounting concern. As an example, Iraq was accused of having a stockpile of WMDs (weapons of mass destruction). Public opinion was manipulated, and the country was informed that a dangerous situation exists and must be addressed. When conflict does ensue, coverage of the intervention is controlled. In the case of Iraq, justification certainly involved either misinformation or disinformation. Saddam Hussein was constantly demonized by the press, and examples of heinous and atrocious acts were presented through the media—all with the purpose of justifying the action that would take place. We must accept the fact that media coverage is not always flawlessly true and presented with guaranteed objectivity. The problem lies in determining what to believe and what not to believe. Media tactics play just as important a role, if not more so, than the military tactics involved in a confrontation. Media drives the military agenda, placing our cause in a positive light, reinforcing existing concepts with respect to the cause, and using repetitious emotional phrases to emphasize success. But when the rationale for the conflict becomes fuzzy or doubt about the righteousness of the conflict comes into play, the media dissipates the memory of the role it played and acts just as wounded as everyone else.

The military is in a position to control the media platforms. It is the disseminator of information and, therefore, orchestrates media direction. It actually becomes a battleground unto itself-information warfare. In order to maintain public support, it is important that information is carefully managed. When this occurs, propaganda is often the result. The idea behind Military Information Operations (IO) is media control. When needed, the use of military deception or psychological manipulation is not out of the question. These methods are used to disinfect information which is detrimental to the cause. Tactics such as putting a spin on information released or even withholding information are in this playbook. During the 2003 Iraqi invasion, journalists were assigned and immersed into various coalition forces. In the name of cooperation and ensuring a flow of information, journalists had to think twice about reporting unfavorable news concerning forces they were placed with. This tactic allowed the military more control over media message. Journalists were placed in a mostly controllable position. To be sure, this is not a one-sided situation. Both sides of a conflict are involved in an emotion war when it comes to the release of information to the public. History is, indeed, a cemetery filled with troublesome emotions.

A powerful tool utilized by the propagandist is the art of supposition. The propagandist forwards an idea or belief that they accept as truth even though there is no proof that it is true. It is basically planting the seed of analysis about an issue based on nothing more than unproven theory. It is the use of assumptions to fuel dissent. The lack of censorship is the greatest friend of supposition. The use of name-calling to characterize and label an opponent is a favored tactic used in propaganda. Making generalizations from a single example of behavior is another. Another is the use of fear tactics or what I call the "what could happen" technique to arouse people's concerns and get them to feed into opinions and actions.

A focus on words can also be a tool of propaganda. Repeating the words of a government official without additional comment may foster a claim of journalistic neutrality. Or does it? It depends on the comment made. When what was said contains emotional content and is repeated over and over, without analysis, explanation, criticism, or defense, it is not a neutral stance. Concentrating and reporting on the official line without offering a wider set of perspectives can actually impact people's opinions. When a country reports and comments on the negative behavior of another country without describing the reason for the viewpoint, stand, or action, the report actually manipulates the audience to feel that the country reported on is the only culprit involved in the incident. This message repeated tirelessly and often enough eventually gets through to the audience and functions as an important method to foster propaganda through factual reporting which contains important omissions.

The Lottery

Americans spend over $70 billion a year on lotteries. The government takes a protectionist approach to many negative activities in society. "Don't drink and drive," "Don't do drugs," "You must use seat belts," and "Smoking is unhealthy" are just a few of the warnings for negative behavior. The government is very proactive when it comes to establishing laws to curtail behavior that is not in the best interest of the American people. Negative behavior is defined as antisocial behavior not acceptable by society in general or which can cause harm to the well-being of individuals. But when it comes to the lottery, everything changes. This form of gambling is encouraged, and over $1 billion a year goes toward advertising this addictive behavior. The argument most often heard in defense of lotteries is that the money raised goes toward education. Supporting this good cause is a primary message used to justify this particular gambling habit.

It is true that profits from lottery sales go toward education. But it is also true that tax dollars which were earmarked for educational purposes are redirected to other priorities and spent in areas other than education. In essence, school funding breaks even when all is said and done with lottery profits taking the place of earmarked but diverted tax dollars. Lottery funding for education goes hand in hand with the reduction of tax-supported funding. Expenditures for education are not increased, and school budgets, for the most part, remain pretty much the same. Lotteries act as tax-funding substitutes. Most lottery players come from the low-income, low-education portion of society. Lottery profits do not come from expendable cash in entertainment budgets. Most lottery gambling is supported by spending less money on nongambling items such as food, clothing, and shelter. Advertising reinforces the notion that winning is easy. They never advertise that losing is easier. There is clearly a great demand for this type of gambling, and it has become a national fixture that will never disappear. Public-relations tactics and advertising propaganda designed to boost lottery sales will continue. Lotteries are, in essence, a hidden tax for anyone who buys a ticket. They reduce spending that would otherwise go to local businesses. At the bottom of the economic ladder, the lottery inflicts the most harm on those who can least afford it. In general, the lottery diverts billions from the economy.

One of the biggest objections to the lottery should be families spending money that they are in no position to be losing. It winds up destroying the potential for more positive economic possibilities. We all understand that the odds of winning a lottery are astronomical. So why has the lottery enjoyed the success that it has? If winning the lottery is unlikely to occur and drawing after drawing you wind up with losing tickets, why march forward on an economic road to nowhere? The psychology and propaganda used to draw people to plunk down their hard-earned cash is easy to identify. First, there is the siren call of almost winning, have some or most of the winning numbers but just not all of them. When this occurs, you are self-encouraged that there is hope in getting all the winning numbers. But in reality, your chances moving forward are not affected by how many of the winning numbers you have on your ticket. The only positive is that most times you collect a nominal prize. Another false premise is that when you buy a ticket, you have the same chance as everyone else who purchases a ticket. However true, the odds of having that winning ticket still remain at multimillions to one. Most people play the lottery without really fully comprehending the reality of the odds of winning.

When a big win occurs with a lottery, it makes the news. The emphasis is on the randomness of how the ticket was purchased. The message is that anyone has a chance to win. The message is true, but what is neglected is the message concerning the people who have been playing consistently for years and years, and there are millions of them and are never part of any story. This propaganda technique, focusing on part of the story, makes players feel they to have a good chance to win, that winning is possible. However, as we all know, losing is definitely even more possible. But lottery ads never ever dwell on that negative. All lotteries afford the player an ability to choose their own numbers. Players feel this gives them more control over the game. It also affords players the opportunity to pick their "lucky" numbers. The lottery is a totally random process, and as such, the use of strategy and choice in the selection of numbers is fruitless. However, the illusion that a player can have control is powerful enough to influence how someone thinks and sustain their irrational behavior. So when the lottery managers ply their propaganda and suggest you play your lucky numbers, they are really trying to make sure you become a steady participant in the game.

Another motivating factor in consistent lottery play is the feeling that you have already invested so much, so you persevere in the hopes of making up for past losses. In reality, money spent cannot be recovered. If you plan a vacation and get sick prior to leaving, the impulse is to go on vacation even if you do not feel well. The point is that no matter if you go or not, the money has been spent. Because you already paid for the vacation, it can never be recovered. The fact that you visit a casino and lose five hundred dollars the first day and win five hundred dollars the next day does not negate the fact that you lost money on the first day. In reality, the experience of the first day and the experience of the second day are in no way related. They are simply separate experiences. There are those among us who play the lotto as an entertainment venue. They do not play for the sole purpose of gaining a financial windfall. They treat the lottery in the same manner as people treat going out for dinner—an entertaining pastime. Usually, people who fall into this category have the necessary means to support their entertaining activity. The excitement of having a chance to win is the motivating factor for their behavior. Our world is filled with all kinds of seemingly irrational behavior.

War on Drugs

The United States is currently involved in a *war on drugs*, but from what can be observed, the war is based somewhat on the scientific assessment of the risks involved in the use of only some of the drugs available. The risks involved with a drug are used to emphasize importance. Risk is currently centered on drugs that cause immediate death by overdose. Let's begin with a premise and then explain the rationale behind it. The premise is that our country will never ever win this so-called war. The use of the term *war* is actually meaningless. A better terminology may be to label it as a *conflict*. A war indicates that there exists between enemies the outcome that one of them can possibly be defeated or victorious or an amicable resolution can be found. With the drug problem, none of these outcomes are possible. It is one thing to win a skirmish; it's another to win a war.

We can agree that the drug issue mostly targets specific groups that may not be as consequential to society as other groups. From the opium laws of the 1800s to the cocaine and heroin laws of the 1900s, there was one common denominator. The laws mostly targeted those at the lower end of the social economic ladder. It has also been used, in the past, to discredit those who protested government policy. In the 1960s, drug usage became synonymous with those who protested government actions which became very prevalent on college campuses. Students were holding the government accountable for what they felt to be an unjust war in Vietnam. What better way to discredit protestors than to point out their connection to drug use?

In the '80s and '90s, incarceration for drug offenses became very prevalent. But you cannot incarcerate your way into solving this problem. Again, mostly targeting those considered insignificant to society. And currently, we seem to be in an era that favors "sensible" drug reform, as well as social and health-based recommendations. An idea gaining popularity is the decriminalization of all drug use. The door to this idea was further opened through the legitimization of marijuana in certain states and will most likely push forward.

In 2001, Portugal decriminalized all drugs, and the results are defined by the interpolation of the statistics used. Some statistics point to positive trends, while others, not so much. I believe, in summary, it would be fair to state that there was no real significant change when statistically discussing their entire population. It would be fair to say there was progress with some demographics and setbacks in others. Therefore, we can see that decriminalization does little to solve the problem, nor does it exacerbate it. The only real winner is the tax man. To me, this is not a phenomenal solution. If it were, a lot more countries would be jumping on this bandwagon.

With the drug problem, both decriminalization and criminalization may not be the best avenues of approach. So what's left? I believe we have to stop looking at this as a war but rather an issue where success can only be measured one addict at a time. The door to drug use is opened wider by both the use of alcohol and tobacco, which impacts about 20 percent of our population. The outcome of tobacco abuse results in a loss of health. The consequences of alcohol abuse are a loss of health and economic productivity and an increase in violence. Alcohol is the leading drug that is responsible for causing harm to others. Their legality is the reason for their becoming a major health threat, as well as a catalyst for the use of other drugs. And this may never substantially be addressed.

The only other option that comes into focus is the most difficult. It is rehabilitation and addiction treatment, and by this, I do not mean maintenance therapy. This is a conflict and strategy that should be emphasized. Address one addict at a time both medically and psychologically with each individual's success becoming the goal. The stumbling blocks to this approach are long-term commitment and funding. The spirit is willing, but the wallet, not so much. So we will continue stumbling down the road we have been traveling for years with results that have been less than exemplary. And we will continue to call this conflict a war—in reality, a struggle with no real victors. And propaganda certainly will continue to come into play. It lies in giving the impression that the "war on drugs" will eventually be successful in eradicating most if not all drug abuse.

Science

Science can have a propagandist element when it comes to scientific conclusions. A basic problem lies in the interpretation of facts gleaned from scientific inquiry. Science can also be adversely affected by political ideology. So an important question to ask is, What is the ideological background of those giving their support to scientific conclusions and interpretations? Given a scientific fact, a number of conclusions can be implied. The conclusions are usually discussed separately from the facts, and clarification of the facts is separated from the context of the conclusions. When looking at scientific fact, there are a number of criteria that need to be identified. The first thing to ascertain is how the research was funded. Was it a scientific group or company with a specific political ideology or a lobbyist group who would achieve a personal gain from the research findings? How unbiased were the scientific study and the techniques utilized? Have there been other studies that corroborate the results?

A bona fide empirical study must outline the exact methodology and research blueprint. The methodology used has to be based on expert knowledge and design. For this reason, top research journals publish only about 10 percent of the research studies that come across their desks. Everyone has the ability to decide how much they trust findings of individual studies and if propaganda played a role or if it is an empirically sound work. There is ample reason academic journals that are experienced in research assessment require all technical details and a peer review. Researchers have a tremendous responsibility to avoid any prejudicial feelings in interpreting the results of their scientific work and their significance to the general public. Propaganda has its uses and abuses. Failing to give the public all the results obtained from a research endeavor to persuade the audience to think a certain way is certainly an abuse of the facts. The purpose of all propaganda is to influence the thinking and behavior of an audience. Slanted research that spreads information promoting a political or moral viewpoint is a disservice to us all. Science concerns itself with issues of strong impact on our thinking, emotions, and development of beliefs.

The issues of global warming, pollution, environmental disasters, and depletion of natural resources name just a few. All presented to the American people with accompanying varieties of propaganda. At one point, activity such as the fluoridation of water supplies and the use of mercury fillings to repair tooth decay and assorted vaccinations were all accepted without pause backed by the somewhat questionable science in existence at that time. Lobbyists were very proficient and persuasive when it came to convincing scientifically naïve politicians to accept their arguments. In this world, there are two kinds of science—one whose sole interest is monetary profit and one whose sole interest is altruistic and concerned with human advancement. Now which of these two kinds of science do you suppose would be weighed down with a healthy dose of propaganda? The science controlled by profit-seeking corporations must be approached with extreme caution. Ethical principles are often replaced by the ethics of business. The pharmaceutical industry is another perfect example of profit-seeking science at the cost of an unsuspecting public. Many times, their drugs and vaccines are not completely safe and often come at a tremendous financial cost which burdens the families and systems that pay for them. Pharmaceutical companies that fund, design, and manage research; keep a rigid control over the data from that research; and, if necessary, slant statistics to achieve FDA approval for a research product are not uncommon.

When billions of profit dollars are at stake, ethical regulation is put on the back burner.

Another example of where propaganda is employed is in the development and advancement of weapons of mass destruction which bring with it a huge corporate profit. There is an untold relationship that currently exists between universities and the weapons industry. Universities across the country receive millions and in some cases billions of dollars to support nuclear weapons development. Both universities and private companies are directly involved in the operation and management of nuclear weapons laboratories. Agreements with these labs and related production sites have resulted in the development of research partnerships with nuclear weapons scientists, as well as provision of human resources for these facilities brought about partially by a current high-retirement level in this government sector.

When it comes to science and food, scientific studies often present conflicting results with the passage of time. What is deemed healthy one year is put on the taboo list during the following years. Eggs, wine, coffee, meat, salt, sugar, and chocolate have enjoyed both positive and negative feedback over the years, being considered as either a poor or a positive health choice. The problem stems from the research studies themselves as well as the entities either paying for or conducting the research. At one point in time, research actually was published which downplayed the effects of both sugar and saturated fat on heart health. The research was funded by the sugar industry. Again, government lobbying plays an important role in both the activities and information we receive as consumers. Because of lobbying and the agricultural industry, the production of high-fructose corn syrup from excess corn production is alive and well.

The medical field is another area where quite a bit of ambivalence exists. Doctors are not infallible. They can be misinformed, prejudiced, or extremely inflexible. It is very important as a patient to ask questions and do the research when your doctor recommends medications, surgery, or treatment. You alone are your own best advocate. The pharmaceutical industry reinforces doctors who prescribe the drugs developed by their companies. Then there is the issue of faulty reasoning. Errors in cause-and-effect deductions have led to many erroneous conclusions on the part of the scientific community. Correlation does not prove cause. Yet exaggerations and misjudgments are constantly fed to the American consumer. The rallying call for these types of research findings is "Better safe than sorry." Oftentimes, the research behind correlation studies leaves a lot to be desired.

Love and Hate

Both *love and hate* involve conscious, subconscious, and intellectual manipulation. In modern society, there is no shortage of each emotion. The definitions for *love* are more variable than the definitions of *hate*. In actuality, both love and hate can be the catalyst for the same emotional responses of anger or happiness. One can hate someone and learn to love them or love someone, only to find it turn to hate. And to confuse matters more, one can love and hate someone at the same time. Love is considered a positive emotion, hate a negative emotion. But from my standpoint, both can result in negative or positive consequences. It is said that love is the basis of all positive actions, and hate is the basis of all negative actions. However, I would not want to defend this statement in a debate.

Lately, hate seems to be the fuel of politics. Discourse on media platforms are filled with hate. One-half of the country does not see eye to eye with the other half, and feelings are made known at every opportunity. During holiday get-togethers, many families cannot enjoy a festive meal without a disruptive political discussion. "Please pass the turkey platter, and I'll take a little hate with that." Hate gives us the illusion of being right in all things no matter what. We understand our hate, and by golly, we have good reasons for it (in our own minds). It has become so common that we are becoming numb to it. Most times, hate is answered with even more hate and as a result escalates even further. Hate, especially in politics, has become the status quo. Its origins go way back. History is filled with hateful actions and is devoid of compassion, empathy, and the all-important quality of perspective taking (looking at something from another person's perspective). As a result, it continues to grow in the world while love is in a downhill slide. So where does propaganda fit into this discussion?

Hate has become the rhetoric of both liberal and conservative media platforms. It is the prime motivation for the most horrible and destructive political attacks taking place on media. This depiction of the political landscape by the media does not focus on the real nature and motivation of both right-wing and left-wing platforms, which is to increase ratings and profits; and they do everything they can to prevent us from recognizing how empathy, compassion, and perspective taking could be a solution to improving harmony between the ideologies. The current reality of a hateful political divide is troubling. The propaganda arises from the slant taken in the interpretive opinions associated with a news event. The point is that, first and foremost, the audience loves their own media platform ideology which employs propaganda to fuel hatred for any opposing ideology. Both sides are acting out of concern not for country, not for the average citizen but for the ideological banner they wave day in and day out. When anger and hatred are used to defend a political movement, the claim they are motivated by concern is disqualified.

The effects of hate on values and culture can be observed every day in the media. It is responsible for the radicalization we see at both ends of the political ideological spectrum. As with the political spectrum, hate has a spectrum of its own. There are the supporters near the middle who are basically partisan toward an ideology. Moving outward along the spectrum, you find actual members of an ideological group. They strongly identify themselves with an ideology. At the end of the spectrum, we have the hardcore audience. They identify most strongly with an ideology and are sometimes willing to protest and commit illegal, violent, or criminal acts to support their beliefs. Media platforms make it easier to influence audiences to embrace one ideology over another. Their role in adding to the divisiveness we are witnessing within our country cannot be overstated. The habitual content of the various media platforms act with a brainwashing effect. The younger generation is more obsessed with their image on social media and is losing their ability to think on their own. There is more concentrated concern with the virtual world than the real world, which is fostering less social contact and cohesion. This adds to building solidarity among the viewers. A consistent and constant dose of media ideology strengthens the beliefs and resolve of the audience. The selective exposure to a media platform content leads the audience of that platform to believe in the prevalence of their ideology. The world becomes definitive and simplistic with respect to social, cultural, and moral issues. There is right. There is wrong. And that's all there is. And if you don't believe in my ideology, you are labeled an archenemy. To establish the superiority of one ideology, the opposing ideology is labeled as inferior and dehumanizing. Young people are especially vulnerable to the mechanism described above because many are looking for groups or causes that will give them a sense of identity. However, when a media platform becomes the basis for how you view the world, you have become immersed in what is actually a hostile environment that eliminates all compassion, empathy, and perspective taking.

Those audiences that allow hatred to become a part of their inner "fact bubble" manifest and project their thoughts and feelings to the outside. It is our thoughts and feelings that create our reality. Be more aware of your reactions to media content. Most times, you will assess the emotion felt as anger or disappointment. You seldom experience feelings of well-being and positive emotions. Agreeing with negative rhetoric is certainly not a generator of inner happiness. The media may not sow the seeds of our beliefs, but they are the fertilizer that gives them life.

Media propaganda surrounding love is pervasive. Sometimes, we believe what we want to believe. It doesn't matter if it is a fictional account; we simply want to believe it. Media ideas of love are based on fiction. The ideas we garner remain with us long after the stories are forgotten. The concept of love is depicted in a way that just does not easily exist in reality. Seventy five percent of Americans believe their soul mate is out there waiting to be discovered. However, about 50 percent of marriages end in divorce. The media message is that our true love is out there and when we find him or her, we will live happily ever after. Statistics prove there is a disconnect between media propaganda and reality when it comes to love. Couples do not remain exactly the same during a lifetime of marriage. Long-term relationships take work, compromise, patience, and understanding. Unlike media depictions, the rose of "Happily Ever After" comes with some thorns.

Contrary to media fiction, love has a pattern. It is not random. People date within the same area of financial status, education, and attractiveness. There are exceptions to the rule, but they are just that—exceptions. The concept of "love at first sight" is media propaganda at its worst. It takes time to determine if someone can possibly be a long-term partner. And it takes more than the eyes. It involves getting to "really" know the other person's heart and mind. Those who profess their relationship started as love at first sight remain the exception and not the rule. Romantic comedies always finish with a happy ending. Unfortunately, real life does not always end the same way as it does for the characters in a movie.

Journalism

Journalism has undergone many changes over time. The focus of this book has been awareness, and it is my hope that we all become a more questioning audience. In the name of being analytical, news stories are presented with increased opinion and not just the fact part of a story. They are now presented with more analysis, with more interpretation. We are now enjoying the pleasure of having our news stories explained to us. Isn't that just dandy? We no longer have to think about what we are viewing. Someone else is doing the thinking for us. The question is, Are the folks doing the thinking for us being truly objective?

Most media and printed platforms derive their news from news agencies. The objective is to report news to all subscribers. They do not attach a conservative or liberal slant to the stories they report. They simply report the story. Their reputation relies on impartiality and remaining nonjudgmental. They report with a high degree of neutrality and avoid input of personal values. They remain detached from the information. The business of news agencies such as Associated Press is to communicate fact with utmost precision.

But when stories are reported again on media and printed platforms, something else is added. That something else is a slant on news stories, misinformation, disinformation, and the use of propaganda. This added feature became very obvious in the 1960s and 1970s. Today, the notion of objectivity in the media is nearly impossible to attain. There are those who argue that objectivity leads to a passive acceptance of news information. The audience today requires critique and analysis. My question remains: Whose critique and whose analysis? There are those who believe that objectivity reflects a shallow understanding of news being reported. Perhaps a more appropriate standard for media should be fairness and accuracy.

The days of Walter Cronkite are long gone. I believe objectivity has received its last rites quite a while ago. It's just that somebody failed to bury the concept. Media platforms should all provide a clear disclaimer. That what you are about to see and hear may be subjective and, yes, perhaps a little biased. We are obligated to be the investors of our media platform. The audience should be made very aware that what they are reading, seeing, or hearing is point-of-view journalism. While it is true there is a sharp increase in reporting both disinformation and misinformation and an obvious increase in partisanship reporting, most audiences watching media platforms fail to consciously surmise the problems associated with news slant and sloppy reporting. The pre-Second World War gatekeepers that ensured a high level of objectivity in the dissemination of information have been replaced by the pursuit of personal influence; financial profit; and cultural, social, and political squabbling. One of the consequences is the ever-growing political polarization that is negatively impacting social trust and erodes the influence of those in the media who claim to be a voice of reason and balance. Where there is no trust, unification becomes an impossibility. Where there is no trust, the concept of "common good" becomes a mute issue. Without trust, the very identity, power, and prestige that our country enjoys are at stake.

Let's be real. We live in a world of bias. Everyone brings both their conscious and subconscious experiences and feelings in discerning and evaluating the information they receive. We just can't avoid doing that. As a result, much of the media we choose to watch is influenced by both our conscious and subconscious predilections. If you want to reinforce your "fact bubble," just remain on the current path you are on. The media platforms have your biases covered, and you know dam well which channel to select. Perhaps a better alternative to reach a level of "fair and balanced" would be to view a variety of news sources across the spectrum. And this is a second-class alternative at best without the addition of self-analysis and info scrutiny.

There are those that argue objective news would be boring and dull in the current world. My question is, How is what we have now working out for us? On one side, you may have dull and boring; but on the other side you have slant, division, and partisanship. Would we be a more informed society if given a story with color or given a story with objective fact? I believe there is a very important place for investigative journalism in the world where you start from a biased starting point and research the veracity of that starting point. But investigative journalism and objective news are two different entities. Objective news should allow the audience to determine meaning. The conclusions arrived at using this process will be stronger because they are yours. You created them. You own them. Doing this takes practice, and skill will improve over time. We expect objectivity from doctors, lawyers, police personnel, and judges. Why not the media as well?

COVID-19

With the *COVID-19* pandemic, information and misinformation spread very quickly due to the technology we now enjoy. There was a prevalence of accurate reporting, but misinformation and disinformation were interlaced with the data. The widespread presence of detailed reporting went a long way to keeping us safer. Along with the steady stream of information, there were growing concerns leading to worry and anxiety. Americans had to deal with both fear and confusion. The disruption in economic activity and the curtailment of personal freedom were bitter pills to swallow in the efforts to make America well again. With the overabundance of information, through the media and daily briefings, there were substantial changes in what was considered to be the best available evidence at the time in how to best deal with the virus. What at first was thought to be reliable intelligence changed in accuracy as we moved forward. This can be labeled crisis misinformation and is a common occurrence in times of catastrophe. It had little effect on the trust people demonstrated with respect to guidelines being implemented.

We were also subjected to disinformation. The purposeful telling of untruths mostly originated from outside our country—China, Russia, and Iran. Misinformation, on the other hand, which is the spread of information that is truly believed to be accurate, was more of a homegrown affair. The stories either were unvetted and premature or came from poor sources but, nonetheless, were genuinely felt to be true at the time. A century has gone by since experiencing a health crisis of major proportion, so dealing with the pandemic was actually a work in progress. The more we suffered through it, the more we learned. Even information from very authoritative and knowledgeable sources changed over time. The media did a pretty good job with correcting misinformation and disinformation before most of the misleading stories became set in stone. The goal was to present the most accurate data at the moment which was modified as we learned more. In this case, social media really stepped up to debunk most false information and rumors very expeditiously. The daily government briefings also had a lot to do with keeping misinformation to a minimum and correcting it when further findings became available.

The origin of the virus became a subject of contention and led to the formation of conspiracy theories which did nothing to calm concern and did more to raise doubts. This was a time where trust and cooperation were badly needed and most Americans came through with flying colors. Citizens handled this health crisis with the same strength and fortitude displayed with 9/11. When it comes to pulling together, we all grab onto the rope and work as a unit of hope, compassion, and strength. When it comes to a crisis, we deserve five stars. There is an air of uncertainty in how the pandemic will affect both economic and health concerns in the long term. As we move forward, the effects of this pathogen on both will become clearer. It is important that the long-term effects of the infection, if any, on bodily organs be examined closely. Ten years after the World Trade Center terrorist attack, it became clear that over thirty-five thousand workers have health problems related to working at the site. Days after the attack, the Environmental Protection Agency (EPA) announced that the air was safe to breathe. A better evaluation has to be done with respect to the pandemic. Victims of COVID-19 deserve to be made aware of any possible long-term health effects from exposure to the virus.

As time moves on, and as the virus is contained, the blame game will be one centerpiece of discussion. Propaganda machinery will be put into motion both globally and domestically. Conspiratorial narratives will become the focus, as well as discussions of what we "could, would, and should" have done. And this, my friends, will bring us back and very deeply into the political realm, which will again be used to move us from a state of interconnectedness to the normal proclivity of being a disconnected society. Please pardon my cynicism that any event will ever produce a lasting positive change in how we behave and treat one another.

What Will the Future Be Like?

Let me state that my guess is as good as yours. So here are some thoughts on what I know and what I think I know and some pontification on what I don't know at all. Let's start with some facts we may be able to agree on.

- Our democracy is either in a crisis or a state of evolutionary metamorphosis.
- An evolving media landscape has complicated the way we process information.
- Our politics has evolved into a battlefield of accusations, belligerence, intolerance, and partisanship.
- Technology is changing the world.
- Justice and the rule of law are being challenged continuously.

- The responsibility for the future lies in the hands of our citizens.
- America is a nation of growing cultural diversification, with expanding divergent ideals, values, and principles of representative democracy.
- America's past is not without its critics: the injustices toward Native Americans, slavery, segregation, political injustice toward women, a civil war between our states, internment of Japanese families during World War 2, first to use the atomic bomb, and the Iraqi war based on disinformation, to name a few.
- There is a disconnect between American prosperity and the working class.
- There are times in the past when we were in worst situations than now: World War 1, the 1929 Depression, and World War 2.
- Those progressive Americans looking for a utopia—good luck with that.
- Evil is a constant. You can never destroy what was never created.
- In order to build, you have to destroy.
- Artificial intelligence (AI) will seriously impact economics, society, and culture.

So now let's discuss some observations where fact and so-called alternative fact are alive and well. Two basic concepts have existed in America that insured a system of checks and balances and was actually something that was part of our political landscape. It was a system best described as separate with mutual aspirations for the American people. The compelling rationale was that competing parties viewed each other as competitors in the game called Power. But the concept of mutual tolerance has and continues to rapidly erode, and the future of democracy in America is at stake. Let's be clear. The history of the United States is wrought with examples of disorder, struggle, violence, authoritarian digression, antiliberalism, and anticonservatism that compare with the current conditions in the political arena. To be sure, our country travelled on a road filled with violent pit stops. Try finding democracy in the South until antisegregation movements took hold. Our early history was not one of a united democracy, and to this day, it remains imperfect. But the two factors that played an essential part along with every pitfall in our country's journey have been hope and resolve.

We need to realize that the strands of liberal-leaning democracy have been with us long before 2016. The very architecture of American politics has been predominantly liberal and has become a very vocal force with the election of an extremely conservative-oriented president. And as well, conservative strands have long been with us, but in 2016, those strands were very much tapped into. With 2016, there was a deviation from a more peaceful, liberal, democratic system. Violations of liberal democracy often work their way through courts, Congress, and government bureaucracies. There is a changing of the guard as we have seen with the appointment of both supreme court and federal judges. It is the friction of progress and the challenge to an otherwise unchallenged status quo that has scared Americans about the state of our country. The disorder that comes as things change is more visible than the order that often is observed when they don't.

We are currently in a turbulent period in our politics. We find ourselves in an unprecedented moment of pervasive anxiety. A new political ideology has become overwhelmingly dominant and has taken center stage. Today, no ideology in America feels comfortably dominant. Each ideological group feels attacked and pitted against one another not just for power but for the right to define the nation's identity. With these conditions, democracy devolves into a very competitive competition. Dominant groups do not give up power easily. The current political climate can distract from what is actually good news. A country where no political group is secure in their dominance over political power is also a country where fewer groups are continuously being oppressed, where more groups can fight for increased equality. But this situation carries a social cost which is that the sense of security created by pre-2016 stability from political ideological dominance is gone. Is the instability we experience now a by-product of ideological change or an unrepairable fracture?

The instability argument is a factor in how American politics feels particularly to those at the ideological spectrum extremes. It can be argued that too much discord can shake the fundamental consensus American politics requires to operate, and the result could be disastrous. A good percentage of the public is losing faith in liberal democracy altogether. Antidemocratic attitudes have increased but not on the large-scale basis purported by the media. For example, the percentage of Americans who say they have a favorable opinion of more traditional political leaders rather than a strong-minded leader is on the rise.

I don't pretend to know what is truly in the heart of the American voter. I feel I am solely an information warrior and perception analyst. The nearness of the undemocratic past of the south in the early and midtwentieth century is proof of the possibility of an undemocratic future. There is nothing in our nature that guarantees liberalism or conservatism, and that ensures progress. The American dilemma is how a political system, that does more to amplify conflict than calm it, will govern a country that is slowly becoming the first truly multiethnic liberal democracy in world history. So far, we are navigating this course without the level of violence and social, cultural, and political repression that was part of America's recent past. Groups in the past that were excluded from exercising influence are now having their concerns and interests heard by those in power. Most people believe we live in a good country and have faith in the resilience of our democratic systems.

The ideology of socialism has surfaced as a viable threat to our democracy. Some people say there is no past, present, and future—just the present with the past being repeated over and over again. The socialist idea that is in vogue within the radical left is not new. What is new is its use to discredit an entire political faction. It is serving a political purpose just as McCarthyism served a purpose in the early 1950s. That was a campaign against alleged communists both in the US government and other institutions and initiated under Senator Joseph McCarthy. Many of the accused, including Hollywood personalities, were blacklisted or lost their jobs, even though most of those accused did not belong to the Communist Party.

President Lyndon Johnson drew on this tactic by accusing war protestors and those involved in rioting as having communist ties. Medicare, the food stamp program, and the Affordable Care Act found resistance with the use of the socialism label. What is different now is it is being used to define an entire political party because of the actions of a single minoritized group, and that is what is problematic.

Throughout politics, the word *socialism* has been used as an attack mechanism for both national and foreign ideas on how to solve an issue. Some of the best kinds of political, cultural, and social improvements have been generated through political grassroots movements—the civil rights movement and the feminist movement, just to name a few. The 2016 election can be considered a grass-roots movement as well. However, many are of the opinion it has not moved us in a progressive direction. Many believe that movement destroyed many fundamental elements of American political institutions. That it has put the constitutional balance of power in jeopardy. Others see it as a victory for the Constitution, as a victory for American pride. So the question can be asked: What is the future democracy of our country going to metamorphosize into, or is it going to change at all? Is democracy going to be reminiscent of the fall of communism at the end of the previous century? Your guess is as good as mine. Anything is possible. No one could have predicted the breakup of the Soviet Union in the 1980s. And I do not believe anyone can predict with certainty the future of our democracy.

The one thing we can do is explore some of the most probable possibilities. Currently, our country is in the deep trenches of partisan polarization. There are serious disagreements on many, many issues all fueled by divergent political values. These disagreements only continue to grow in size and scope. With the 2016 election, the dialogue of politicians certainly has changed. Politics is more like a high school sports locker. Inhibitions have gone out the window. The rhetoric has gotten quite salty. Both sides of the aisle for the most part view their counterpart as enemies. With this reality, progress on important key issues affecting our country has been inhibited.

The neutrality of the intelligence departments, the courts, and ethics committees has been attacked and, in doing so, weakened. There are attacks being made on voter rights rules, the redrawing of voting districts, and our electoral rules. All of this is being done in the name of maintaining or gaining a power foothold. It is my belief that this series of events were not orchestrated by outside influences. American politicians are the authors of this drama. Our somewhat chaotic two-party system, virulent partisanship, and out-of-touch politicians are to blame for the chronic failures of governance. Members of both the Congress and the Senate are viewed as puppets to corporations, wealthy donors, and special interests. In other words, they are seen as "bought and paid for." The money involved in election campaigns is, indeed, eye-opening. The politicians took a sledgehammer to the code of dialogue and ethics surrounding democratic discourse. Yet it is a time in which America's diplomatic power and influence have been somewhat uplifted mainly due to economic and military stability and strength.

It is of utmost importance that the American people become informed. And that does not mean only watching your favorite media platform that happens to coincide with your personal "fact bubble." Develop your own opinion, not that of a news commentator. Reinforce your capacity to think and judge by questioning what you hear on media platforms. Become informed through personal introspection and inspection of news context. It is very difficult to raise your personal bar once it has been lowered. The current political and media platform state of mind has done irreparable harm. Bringing back a copartisan frame of mind in Congress and the Senate will not be an easy task. There is a deep cataclysm of trust and confidence that has to be overcome. The current state of radical partisanship affects US citizens and all those around the world who hold up the US democratic system as an example worthy of emulation.

We are constantly being discouraged in attempts to find out the truth. Avoiding propaganda is hard work. It takes time and effort to discover the truth. To disprove propaganda is more difficult than its production. All information to some degree is infected with propaganda or misinformation. If you question propaganda, be prepared to be chastised. To openly criticize leads to alienation by those who accept the propaganda as gospel truth. For most people, it is more convenient to remain neutral on the subject.

Totalitarian governments utilize effective, comprehensive, and institutionalized systems of propaganda and censorship. Censorship actually expedites and supplements the spread of propaganda in society. In the twentieth century, during the heavy use of propaganda, authoritarian governments were able to implement strong, single-minded national views by propagating political messages in the media while censoring those views that conflicted with the government's line of thought. With the advent of the digital age, a propaganda strategy has developed to combat the newfound power of the average Internet user, who shares information with the click of a mouse. It has completely reformed the way in which media users approach disseminating and controlling information. While the basics of propagandistic strategy continue to persist, fundamental changes have occurred as a response to this shift in information sharing and seeking. It has completely reformed the way in which media users approach disseminating and controlling information.

Disinformation and propaganda interfere with democracy, dominating and distorting the public's understanding of an issue, thus manipulating any decision-making process. The emergence of social media was the beginning of a new user-friendly communication interface that allowed for the presentation of content without economic or educational barriers. This has allowed for the creation of innovative techniques utilized to support business interests and political opportunists. The culture of knowledge has been replaced by a culture of opinion and disinformation through which fear, anger, and anxiety are created and reinforced. Besides manipulated information, data protection, privacy, human dignity, and our personal autonomy are at issue as well. Open public discourse is one of the basic precursors of democracy. This is how citizens can discuss their common concerns; form political, cultural, and social opinions; and ultimately reach a rational conclusion based on introspection and fact.

In our current media environment, the abundance of thoughts, opinions, and ideas is staggering. This overwhelming amount of information makes the research and access to trustworthy information a difficult task. Without regulatory intervention, technology developers will take the exploitation of their audiences, psychological manipulation, and digital engineering to new levels. Regulations must be enacted to establish a level of control but by no means through censorship. No easy task.

In summary, we are a freedom-of-speech nation. Along with the right of free speech comes the problem of propaganda. Accountability in free speech is sorely lacking. Propaganda, as we have already discussed, is a method of coercion and control. In a democracy, there is no control by force, but rather control is dependent on law. In a society where there is no control through brute force, laws are the answer as well as control of how we think. How we think is being manipulated by the propaganda we are exposed to in the media, on TV, and in print. In a democratic society, journalism also acts as a critic of those in power who decide every day what is best for us.

The purpose of law can be summed up as rules for the common good. Propaganda is often used to soften the masses into a better frame of acceptance for what is decided upon as being for the common good. We are often reminded that we live in the greatest country on earth. We are also reminded that there are forces at work whose sole objective is to destroy the greatness that we enjoy. These reminders play on our fears and generate concern and worry within the population. The reminders appear as truthful, logical, and factual interpretations of the events that happen around us. The rationale behind these reminders is usually that we have to remain vigilant against threats to our democracy and our "way of life." The interpretations that go hand in hand with the communication of the news are narrow and focused and usually coincide with the ideology of the media platform presenting the information.

Media platforms have a dual purpose of reinforcing the ideas of an already captive audience and enlarging that captive audience through their interpretive presentation of news events. In the name of ideology, news interpretation can become somewhat distorted to fit a specific narrative. Interpretive news can take on a life of its own. Everyone has a fact bubble. If the interpretation of a news story fits well with an individual's heartfelt beliefs, research involving proof will not be investigated. The media is very astute when it comes to driving their own agenda. We must really ask ourselves two questions: What is the ideology a media platform has circled their wagons around? What is the reason behind my attachment to a particular media platform?

The impact of media platforms cannot be understated. They can sell a product, and just as easily, they can sell an idea. They contributed to the avoidable casualties of the Iraq War simply by taking a prowar stance. They were a major factor in selling the war to the American people. And just as easily, they are promoting certain political policies and ideologies. The media platform agendas are no longer hidden. They wear their ideology on their sleeves. It has become their brand-name. The investigation of the sources of news has taken a back burner. Both misinformation and disinformation have become quite common—all in the name of reinforcing the acceptance of an ideology. And then they chastise the nation on the current diversity that has become more exemplified and reinforced by their actions.

There no longer is very much that can be called pure and unadulterated truth. Truth now comes mixed with a healthy dose of opinion, meaning, and intent. And we accept this cocktail most times without holding our noses and drink it right down. And this is the problem. It is us. It is our blanket acceptance of what we hear on mainstream media and especially when it fits into our all-important "fact bubble." To put it lightly, the news we are receiving is constantly being massaged with the oil of propaganda. One way to accomplish this is narrowing a stories range. Create a political discussion that remains in a very controlled and narrow range. The manipulation is both covert and effective. It is a pervasive and sophisticated system of control. An emotional discussion is a great mobilizer and puts into motion actionable responses. This all occurs within an atmosphere in which media puts on their Superman capes and portray themselves as the spokesmen and defenders of free speech. And the more educated you are, the more at a disadvantage you are. With respect to news, the educated simply read more, watch more, and, as a result, take in more propaganda in their information diet than a less educated audience.

Do not become complacent. Question what you see and hear. Over time, our eyes and ears have caused irreparable harm that could have been avoided. There are times our senses have caused a tremendous loss of life and incredible suffering. Question what you know, because what you know, you may not really know at all.

About the Author

Mr. Rizzi was born in Jersey City, New Jersey. He attended Rutgers University in New Jersey, University of Miami in Florida, Oakland University in Michigan, and Seton Hall University in New Jersey. In 1968, he received his BA degree in psychology followed with a MA and PhD equivalency in education.

His career centered around the education of students in an inner-city environment. He was involved in inner-city education for thirty-eight years. During that time, his focus was to help children develop the skills of listening, evaluation, and problem-solving. And through that process—and practice—he helped students develop ideas and strategies to improve their focusing skills. His premise was that without student focus and interaction, learning would be limited. He feels it extremely necessary to zero in on learning skills sometimes using material outside subject content. His strategy was to actively engage students by becoming involved with the subject at hand through outside research. He developed effective ways to check for understanding, ways that allowed all students to process and respond to the subject at hand. Every month, students were involved in a project requiring research. He used questioning as the main tool to maintain student interest and classroom momentum, questions that reflected the objectives of lesson content. More importantly, he strived to instill in students an ability to question and challenge what was being taught. He varied instructional activities that engaged students. There was an emphasis on responsibility and accountability. Instructional techniques were meaningful and hands-on. He instilled in students a need for empathy when responding to the ideas and responses of others. He strived to make the learning environment as comfortable as possible to allow all students to actively demonstrate their learning.

His interest in media, empathy, and propaganda grew out of his experiences in education and became more fueled by the changes in our culture after 9/11, as well as the increased focus on technology as an educational and political tool in the past two decades. More and more, he witnessed information presented through media that was more opinion than substantiated fact. "Fact-checking" in the media is an attempt to counter this phenomenon, but it occurs ever so rarely. He decided to write a book that points out the concerns related to acceptance of information without verification or backup research.

9 781638 143482